Y0-AAA-681

ANTHONY PLATT is an assistant professor at the School of Criminology, University of California at Berkeley. Author of *The Child Savers* and *The Politics of Riot Commissions,* he has published several articles in sociology and criminology. He has also worked in political campaigns supporting community control of the police.

LYNN B. COOPER is a graduate student at the School of Criminology, University of California at Berkeley. She is on the editorial staff of *Issues in Criminology* and has taught at the university. She is currently writing her dissertation on the police.

POLICING AMERICA

ANTHONY PLATT

LYNN COOPER

Withdrawn from UF. Surveyed to Internet Archive

Prentice-Hall, Inc. A SPECTRUM BOOK *Englewood Cliffs, New Jersey*

Library of Congress Cataloging in Publication Data

Platt, Anthony M

Policing America.

Includes bibliographical references.

1. Police—United States—Addresses, essays, lectures. I. Cooper, Lynn, joint author. II. Title.

HV8138.P57 363.2'0973 73–23026

ISBN 0-13-684910-5

ISBN 0-13-684902-4 (pbk.)

363.20973
P719p
c.2

Copyright © 1974 by Prentice-Hall, Inc., Englewood Cliffs, New Jersey, A SPECTRUM BOOK. All rights reserved. No part of this book may be reproduced in any form or by any means without permission in writing from the publisher. Printed in the U.S.A.

10 9 8 7 6 5 4 3 2 1

Prentice-Hall International, Inc. (*London*)
Prentice-Hall of Australia Pty., Ltd. (*Sydney*)
Prentice-Hall of Canada, Ltd. (*Toronto*)
Prentice-Hall of India Private Limited (*New Delhi*)
Prentice-Hall of Japan, Inc. (*Tokyo*)

Contents

Preface

The idea for this book developed while we were teaching a course on the police and found many problems with the existing literature. Through teaching, discussions with students, and involvement with community organizations, we were able to formulate both the contents and perspective of this anthology.

We are grateful to the following persons and organizations who helped us with ideas, criticisms, and production: Valentina Agpaoa, Karen Bailey, Rebecca Cohen, Elliott Currie, June Kress, North American Congress on Latin America, Linda Peachee, David Serber, Gregory Serber, and the Union of Radical Criminologists.

This book is an outgrowth of the research and practice of the Union of Radical Criminologists in Berkeley, California.

Contributors

Eldridge Cleaver
Joseph Goulden
Michael Klare
Knapp Commission
National Advisory Commission on Civil Disorders
Harold Nelson
North American Congress on Latin America
Vincent Pinto
David P. Riley
Jerome Skolnick
I. F. Stone
Joe Stork
Walker Report
Robert Wall
Lee Webb
Alan Wolfe

Introduction

The Whole World Is Watching

During the last ten years, the police have become a controversial public issue and the object of political investigations, exposés, and academic studies. The "discovery" of this issue by the mass media and academics resulted from the prominent role the police played during the 1960s in attempting to subdue political and racial conflict. The police, in addition to other sectors of the State apparatus, were called upon to combat ghetto rebellions, student protests, labor organizing, antiwar demonstrations, and other popular movements that challenged the legitimacy of existing political, economic, and social arrangements.

Characteristically involved in "low visibility" activity,[1] the police became visible and explicit, abandoning even the appearance of a "public service" role for counterinsurgency operations (including crowd control, informers, agents provocateurs, extralegal violence, etc.) in order to maintain the existing order and political stability in the face of widespread dissent. "The whole world is watching," chanted the crowd in Chicago at the 1968 National Democratic convention, as the police cleared the streets with clubs and tear gas, and television cameras recorded the event. Although the use of excessive force by the police, especially against the white sons and daughters of the respectable middle classes, caused considerable public indignation and outrage, the mood of surprise quickly gave way to resignation and cynicism. Police brutality, like the war in Vietnam, became a routine spectacle on the evening news.

Studying the Police

The amount of recent literature on the police is overwhelming, including everything from the serious and dry President's Commission on Law

[1] Joseph Goldstein, "Police Discretion Not to Invoke the Legal Process: Low Visibility Decisions in the Administration of Justice," *Yale Law Journal* 69 (1960): 543–94.

Enforcement and Administration of Justice (1967) to Joseph Wambaugh's best-selling, autobiographical novel, *The New Centurions.* The majority of serious investigations have been written by either academics or government commissions. The academic literature ranges from narrowly oriented administrative studies to more analytical organizational and comparative studies.[2] Due to the proliferation of commissions during the last few years, the police have been extensively investigated by a variety of local and national bodies, including the McCone Commission (1965), the Kerner Commission (1968), the Cox Commission (1968), the National Commission on the Causes and Prevention of Violence (1969), and the President's Commission on Campus Unrest (1970).[3]

This collection is not, for the most part, drawn from the conventional literature on the police because we find several limitations in its perspective and analysis, limitations that serve to mystify or obscure the political role of the police and rationalize their resistance to change. We find three major problems in the established literature.

First, the failure to understand the police historically has created considerable confusion and misunderstanding. The domination of criminological theory by pragmatic and social engineering approaches has led to a narrowing of scientific interest, to a parochial concern for solving immediate, short-run problems, and to a neglect of more fundamental and enduring issues. The history of the police in the United States is for the most part unwritten, with the exception of "house" histories and a few microscopic case studies. Consequently, many critiques of the police assume that brutality, overreaction, corruption, etc., are somehow new or unique. But even the most superficial historical perspective suggests that police were also repressive in the late nineteenth century in controlling the urban poor and "dangerous classes," in the "red scare" of the 1920s, during the first fifty years of efforts to organize labor unions, and against Third World and progressive political organizations at various times during this century. Similarly, critiques of the police are not new and can be traced back to at least New York's Lexow Commission (1894), the Wickersham Commission (1930), and LaFollette's Congressional Committee (1939).

Secondly, the ahistoricism of the conventional police literature is generally accompanied by a technocratic perspective that separates the police from their political underpinnings and emphasizes the internal dynamics

2 See, for example, Michael Banton, *The Policeman in the Community* (London: Tavistock, 1964); Jerome H. Skolnick, *Justice Without Trial* (New York: Wiley, 1966); Arthur Niederhoffer, *Behind the Shield* (New York: Doubleday, 1967); David J. Bordua, ed., *The Police* (New York: Wiley, 1967); James Q. Wilson, *Varieties of Police Behavior* (Cambridge, Mass.: Harvard University, 1968); and Arthur Niederhoffer and Abraham S. Blumberg, eds., *The Ambivalent Force* (Waltham, Mass.: Xerox College, 1970).

3 For an analysis of commissions, see Anthony Platt, *The Politics of Riot Commissions, 1917–1970* (New York: Macmillan, 1971).

of police bureaucracies, the relationship between administrative and legal rules, and different styles of policing. This level of analysis, while important for understanding day-to-day routines and procedures, obscures or ignores the relationship of the police to other sectors of the criminal justice system and the dependency of the whole system on larger political and economic forces. Most critical discussions of the police focus on lower- and middle-level agents of social control, debunking the police for their crudeness, ignorance and lack of professionalism, while the ruling institutions and powerful class who control and benefit from the police are ignored or legitimized.[4]

Thirdly, conventional studies of the police are guided by a liberal and reformist perspective on social change. What distinguishes liberal reformism from more fundamental anticapitalist criticisms of American society is the belief that it is possible to create a well-regulated, stable and humanitarian police system under the present economic and political arrangements. While criminologists and other social scientists are often critical of the police—for inefficiency, mismanagement, corruption, brutality, etc.—the absence of a historical and class analysis inevitably sets the stage for nihilism or a wishy-washy relativism, and their reform proposals are typically designed to shape new adjustments to corporate capitalism.

Liberal reformism supports the extension of the welfare state and gradualist programs of amelioration, while rejecting more fundamental forms of change. This is usually accompanied by a reliance on the development of technical solutions and a belief that progress will occur through enlightening managers and policy-makers rather than organizing the oppressed.[5] Liberals do not envision ordinary working people as the motive force in history but regard themselves as enlightened experts fighting a difficult battle against an ignorant public and corrupt government.[6] They fail to point out, however, that the experts have played an important role in constructing the existing criminal justice system. As the American Friends Service Committee has observed, "the legacy of a century of reform effort is an increasingly repressive penal system and overcrowded courts dispensing asssembly-line justice." [7]

The dominant emphasis in the conventional police literature—lack of

[4] Alvin W. Gouldner, "The Sociologist as Partisan: Sociology and the Welfare State," *American Sociologist* 3 (May, 1968): 103–16; Alexander Liazos, "The Poverty of the Sociology of Deviance: Nuts, Sluts and Perverts," *Social Problems* 20, no. 1 (Summer, 1972): 103–20.

[5] See, generally, Irving Louis Horowitz, ed., *The Rise and Fall of Project Camelot* (Boston: M.I.T. Press, 1967).

[6] For an example of this kind of paternalism, see Jerome H. Skolnick, "Perspectives on Law and Order," unpublished lecture delivered at the Interamerican Congress of the American Society of Criminology in Caracas, Venezuela (November, 1972).

[7] American Friends Service Committee, *Struggle for Justice* (New York: Hill & Wang, 1971), p. 9.

a historical perspective, pragmatism, and concern for short-range solutions—reveals an attitude of cynicism and defeatism about human potentiality. This approach serves to exclude or underestimate the possibility of a radically different society in which cooperation replaces competition, human values take precedence over property values, exploitation is eliminated, and basic human needs are fulfilled.

Towards a Radical Analysis of the Police

Most of the materials for this anthology are drawn from unconventional sources—political journals, radical publications, pamphlets, magazines, etc. The selection of articles, even from these kinds of publications, was difficult because left-wing and other progressive critiques of the police are characterized by a low level of analysis[8] and a tendency to indulge in horror stories.[9] Nevertheless, we have managed to select essays that are analytical as well as descriptive, and that keep in mind that the police are a part of the state apparatus and an instrument of political policies that they do not initiate.

The selections in this book do not focus on routine police practices, or on the biases of police officers, or on their psychological and organizational problems. The writers are more concerned with understanding the police as a political institution—its relationship to the state, its role in maintaining imperialism abroad and colonialism at home, its ties to various industries that profit from police equipment and materiel, its programs and ideology of counterinsurgency, and its general functions in capitalist society.

Although the perspective of this book suggests that the police have become a dangerous and pervasive institution, it should not be concluded that their power is self-contained or invincible. Their position in society derives from historical conditions which are *socially* created and therefore subject to change. There is nothing inherently sacred or fixed about present social arrangements. All around the world—in Latin America, Africa, Indochina and the Middle East, for example—systems of unjust power are being resisted, confronted and challenged by revolutionary movements.

Popular control of the police, however, can not be undertaken without a strategic understanding of the ruling interests which they serve and protect. Although the police practice discrimination and brutality against the poor and disenfranchised, they are also themselves exploited not only by miserable working conditions and social isolation but also as instruments of laws and policies over which they have little control and from

8 See, for example, the Weatherman's analysis of the police in Hal Jacobs, ed., *Weatherman* (California: Ramparts, 1970), especially pp. 84–87.

9 See, for example, Ross Firestone, ed., *Getting Busted* (New York: Douglas, 1970).

which they derive no benefit. The police protect private property but do not own it; as guardians of the peace, the police defend government policies of imperialism and racism but do not profit from them; and in their repression of popular movements, the police legitimize a political order which they did not create. Transformation of the police, therefore, must take into account their dual role as victimizers and victims. For as Felix Greene has observed, "if I were being clubbed or beaten by them I would call them pigs too, no doubt, or epithets much worse. Yet, in spite of our outrage, I feel it is important for us to remember that those who are using the clubs against us are the victims of imperialism as well as its agents, and that under other conditions they would be on our side." [10]

This anthology attempts to describe and analyze the dialectics of police power, its larger political functions in society and its relationship to those ruling interests which are "beyond incrimination"—that is, condoned or ignored by the state.[11] The limitations of this book reflect the general absence of rigorous and critical scholarship, uncontaminated by managerial or liberal perspectives. There is an urgent need for historical research, for analysis of contradictions and grievances *within* the police establishment, and for evaluation of different reform strategies. There are no simple or quick panaceas for controlling the police and solutions can not be found without understanding and challenging the political economy of capitalism. The radical transformation of the police must be analytically and strategically connected to long-range political struggles. For the present, we need to discover and implement structural reforms that limit arbitrary power, expose the political functions of the police, create new centers of popular control, and create the conditions in which the power of the people is realized, tested and put into practice.[12]

[10] Felix Greene, *The Enemy: What Every American Should Know About Imperialism* (New York: Vintage, 1971), p. 378.

[11] Mark C. Kennedy, "Beyond Incrimination," *Catalyst* (Summer, 1970): pp. 1–37.

[12] For a more extensive discussion on reform strategies, see André Gorz, *Socialism and Revolution* (New York: Anchor, 1973), especially pp. 134–177.

I

SERVANTS OF THE STATE

The political structure of the police and their relationship to other sectors of the state apparatus have generally been neglected. This is due partly to the narrow focus by social scientists on the organization and occupation of policing[1] and partly to the more general lack of theoretical work on the state.[2] The articles in this section are selected in order to locate the police within the larger framework of social control (Wolfe), to understand the police as an instrument of domestic coercion analogous to the role of the military in international relations (Cleaver), and to evaluate the economic resources and political underpinnings of the police, especially their role as a customer of private industry (Goulden).

The police as a political institution do not operate in isolation nor as an autonomous unit. At the local level, they are dependent on mayors, boards of supervisors, city councils, and city managers for their budgets, personnel policies, and various ordinances; similarly, at the state and federal levels, the police rely for their political and economic support on legislatures, commissions, and special agencies. They are also an integral part of the criminal justice system, thus having administrative and other forms of reciprocal relationships with courts, district attorneys, jails, and prisons. By virtue of their role as "servants of the state," they operate under similar political and ideological conditions as teachers, social workers, probation officers, public defenders, etc.

Alan Wolfe's essay, while not specifically about the police, presents a framework for considering how the police are one of several devices used to maintain inequality. The police, according to this analysis, neither initiate nor benefit from the policies that they implement. Rather they are called upon to perform preventive or reactive repression, depending on the strength of popular opposition and/or the adequacy of other non-

[1] See, for example, Arthur Niederhoffer, *Beneath the Shield: The Police in Urban Society* (New York: Doubleday, 1967) and Jerome H. Skolnick, *Justice Without Trial* (New York: Wiley, 1967).

[2] For a more general discussion of this point, see Ralph Miliband, *The State in Capitalist Society* (New York: Basic Books, 1969), pp. 1–22.

violent strategies of control (education, political negotiation, mass media, etc.). In this sense, the police operate both as victimizers of mass movements and as victims of those who benefit from what the police do.

Contrasted with Wolfe's analytical formalism, Eldridge Cleaver's essay seems somewhat raw and rhetorical—a reflection of the different classes and racial backgrounds of the authors. The importance of Cleaver's essay should not be underestimated. Written in a California prison in the early 1960s while under the strong influence of Malcolm X, *Soul on Ice* had a profound impact on the theory and practice of many people, including Angela Davis, George Jackson, and Bobby Seale.[3] Although Cleaver sometimes appears to be making obvious points or overstating them, his emphatic approach was dictated by the tendency of contemporary academics to mystify the central issues or ignore them altogether.[4]

Cleaver's analysis is dialectical and unsentimental. For him, the police are an instrument of policy that they do not make. "The real problem is a trigger-happy social order." The police should not be the main objects of criticism and opposition, for "behind police brutality there is social brutality, economic brutality, and political brutality." Like Wolfe, Cleaver suggests that the use of massive force to smash popular opposition is a last resort of those in power, not only because it creates bad publicity for the United States internationally, but also because it releases new sources of opposition and solidarity. "Violence may breed counterviolence, leading to instability," notes Wolfe. Cleaver puts it more vividly: "Those corpses (in Watts) spoke eloquently of potential allies and alliances. A community of interest began to emerge, dripping with blood, out of the ashes of Watts. The blacks in Watts and all over America could now see the Viet Cong's point: both were on the receiving end of what the armed forces were dishing out."

Although the modern police in the United States have always been an instrument of repressive policies against popular movements, their effectiveness has often been undermined by inefficiency, poor organization, and lack of discipline. This deficiency has been noted by the police themselves and various commissions throughout this century.[5] Since the passage of the Omnibus Crime Control and Safe Streets Act in 1968, there have been renewed efforts to make the police more centralized, more technologically proficient, and better prepared for "riot" situations. Jo-

[3] See Maxwell Geismar's introduction to Eldridge Cleaver, *Soul on Ice* (New York: McGraw-Hill, 1968), pp. xi–xv.

[4] For a critique along similar lines of Skolnick's *Justice Without Trial,* see William Cook, "Policemen in Society: Whose Side Are They On?," *Berkeley Journal of Sociology* 12 (Summer, 1967): 117–29.

[5] See, for example, the work of police theorists like Raymond Fosdick, Arthur Woods and August Vollmer, as well as the National (Wickersham) Commission on Law Observance and Enforcement (1930), the President's Commission on Law Enforcement and Administration of Justice (1967), and the National (Kerner) Advisory Commission on Civil Disorders (1968).

seph Goulden documents the legislative and political history of this act, examining its sources of support, and concluding that it provides the police with a "repressive capacity unparalleled in history." Goulden describes in detail the congruence of interest between the police, Department of Justice, Ford Foundation, and private industry, thus demonstrating how the police get their support from corporate and political leaders.

Goulden's catalogue of new technological devices and strategies of counterinsurgency creates an impression of indestructible strength and viciousness. For Wolfe and Cleaver, however, this massive apparatus of repression is an indication of desperation and weakness, of a ruling class that, according to Wolfe, "is so unsure of its rule that it seeks the protection that only troops and police can provide. . . ." Repression is a paradoxical strategy, exposing the illegitimacy of those in power and making it vulnerable to political attacks. As Cleaver puts it, there is nothing sacred about the present system; the more force that is required to protect it, the more people realize that "new deeds can be drawn up" and "a mood sets in, spreads across America . . ."

Suggested Reading

Gerth, Jeff. "The Americanization of 1984," *Sun Dance,* April–May, 1972, pp. 58–65.

Gramsci, Antonio. *Prison Notebooks.* New York: International Publishers, 1971.

Lenin, V. I. *The State and Revolution.* Peking: Foreign Languages Press, 1970.

Miliband, Ralph. *The State in Capitalist Society.* New York: Basic Books, 1969.

Silver, Alan. "The Demand for Order in Civil Society," in David Bordua, ed., *The Police,* pp. 1–24. New York: Wiley, 1967.

"The Police." *North American Congress on Latin America Research Methodology Guide* (1970). This and other NACLA publications are available from NACLA, P.O. Box 57, Cathedral Park Station, New York, 10025 or P.O. Box 226, Berkeley, California, 94701.

Turner, William. *The Police Establishment.* New York: G. P. Putnam, 1968.

Wolfe, Alan. *The Seamy Side of Democracy: Repression in America.* New York: McKay, 1973.

ALAN WOLFE

Political Repression and the Liberal Democratic State

Repression in a bourgeois-democratic society is not as clearcut a phenomenon as it is under, say, a police dictatorship of a fascist order. The state seems to operate in contradictory fashion, smashing certain groups while ignoring others, the reason for the distinction not always being clear. At other times a political trial is proof of repression, while a verdict of innocence is taken as a sign that the state really is not so repressive after all. In short, the dynamics of how repression works in the liberal state are little understood, even by those who are repressed.

A full understanding of political repression would be obtained if a comprehensive theory of the state existed, because repression is a form of rule, a method of preserving capitalism.

That theory, however, does not yet exist; the political dimension of Marxism is one of the most poorly worked out.[1] Thus, for the present, we shall not be able to understand completely the nature of political repression in democratic societies. But we can, at the very least, address ourselves to conceptions, shared to some extent by both liberals and radicals, which are very likely incorrect. In that spirit, I offer the following seven propositions.

(1) *Repression is one of a number of reproductive mechanisms which capitalism requires in order to maintain itself as a system.* One of the most powerful notions in all of Marxist theory is the concept of reproductive mechanisms, those aspects of capitalism which tend to perpetuate traditional forms of institutions and behavior, as well as stabilizing new ones. Consumerism is a good example. The economic system requires that a goodly amount of products be manufactured. The very existence of such quantity creates a justification for quantity. To the extent that con-

From the Monthly Review *23, no. 7 (December, 1971), pp. 18–38. Reprinted with permission of the author and publisher.*

1 The most interesting attempt to work on this problem is Nicos Poulantzas, *Pouvoir Politique et Classes Sociales* (Paris: François Maspero, 1968). See also Ralph Miliband, *The State in Capitalist Society* (New York: Basic Books, 1969).

sumers come to depend on the existence of a certain number and kind of products, to that extent has capitalism created a mechanism for its own reproduction.

Matters cannot be left to the economy alone, however. One of the functions of a government is to create the conditions under which the system will be successfully reproduced. At certain points, there are more important ways to reproduce a society than by the ruling class acting alone in furtherance of its economic control over the society. At those times (some of which will be discussed shortly), the state is asked to play a major role in preserving the capitalist order. In doing this, the state can act in a number of ways, all of which are repressive in the sense that they are designed to stymie those forces which work for revolutionary change, but only one of which is generally called repression, i.e., the physical use of force or the threat of force by those in power to meet challenges to their legitimacy. In order that this discussion be generally understood, I will accept this distinction between repression and other reproductive mechanisms, so long as it is understood that all these tactics are dedicated to the same end—the maintenance of the order.

Repression can be understood by comparing it to these other non-terroristic reproductive mechanisms. One of them is clearly co-option, the blunting of a revolutionary challenge by partially accepting either some of its premises or some of its leaders, in the hopes of absorbing the threat. Similarly, political reform is a reproductive mechanism. There are times when sections of the ruling class become sponsors of reform in order to rationalize the system and make it work better. Each of these strategies has advantages and disadvantages to both the state and the revolutionary movement, but it is not my intention to go into them here. The point is that both of them are seen by rulers as conscious alternatives to repression, alternatives in the sense that they may obtain the same end at less cost.

The most important reproductive mechanism which does not involve the use of state violence is consciousness-manipulation. The liberal state has an enormous amount of violence at its disposal, but it is often reluctant to use it. Violence may breed counter-violence, leading to instability. It may be far better to manipulate consciousness to such an extent that most people would never think of engaging in the kinds of action which could be repressed. The most perfectly repressive (though not violently so) capitalist system, in other words, would not be a police state, but the complete opposite, one in which there were no police because there was nothing to police, everyone having accepted the legitimacy of that society and all its daily consequences.

Democratic societies, in general, stress consciousness-manipulation over violent repression to a greater degree than do other political forms of capitalism, though this may be changing at the moment, at least in the United States. This means that within liberal society a series of institutions—ranging from the family through schools, the media, the churches, athletics, etc.—will have a political function that sometimes meshes with and sometimes contradicts their other functions, be they child rearing, product-selling, knowledge-accumulating, or rest and relaxation. Those operating within these institutions often perceive the contradictions, as students did when they first began their critique of their university. In other words, there are times when attempts to manipulate consciousness fail because the contradictory nature of the institution reveals a hypocrisy which creates as many activists as it does passivists.

This discrepancy between the professed goals of a nongovernmental institution and its actual reproductive consequences does not exist when the state itself becomes involved. The goal of a state propaganda apparatus is to coerce mentally, and little attempt is made to suggest anything else. The origins of a state propaganda machine in the United States can be traced back to George Creel's Committee on Public Information (CPI), designed to win support for the First World War (and the capitalist system) among the two groups whose support was least likely to be spontaneous: labor union members and immigrants. The CPI worked among Swedes, Danes, Norwegians, Finns, Italians, Czechs, Poles, Hungarians, Germans, Russians—twenty-four ethnic groups in all—utilizing secretly financed members of those groups and a variety of other covert practices. CPI functionaries sent material to all 745 foreign-language newspapers in the United States, attended conventions, published leaflets, and gave lectures.[2] Reviewing these efforts, Creel noted the systematic nature of this type of activity:

> The loyalty of "our aliens," however splendid as it was, had in it nothing of the spontaneous or the accidental. Results were obtained only by hard, driving work. The bitterness bred by years of neglect and injustice were not to be dissipated by any mere war-call, but had to be burned away by a continuous educational campaign.[3]

That campaign was continued, especially after the New Deal and the Second World War. The Harness Committee of the House of Representatives found in 1947 that the federal government spent $74,829,467 on publicity alone, while the 1950 Hoover Commission put the figure at $105 million.[4] It is impossible to estimate the current rate, but that it is much

[2] James R. Mock and Cedric Larson, *Words That Won the War: The Story of the Committee on Public Information 1917–19* (Princeton: Princeton University Press, 1939), p. 219. George Creel, *How We Advertised America* (New York: Harper, 1920), pp. 192–194.

[3] Creel, p. 184.

[4] Final Report of the Subcommittee on Publicity and Propaganda (Harness Committee), *Twenty-Third Intermediate Report of the Committee on Expenditures in the Executive Departments* (Washington: Government Printing Office, 1949). 80th Congress, Second Session. House Report No. 2474. The figure cited is from a summary of the Report, *Congressional Record,* vol. 96, part 17, p. A6861. 81st Congress, Second Session.

higher is indicated by the fact that the printing budget of the Army Department alone in 1970 was $43 million.[5] State-directed propaganda is now a permanent feature of the liberal democratic state.

Permanent conscious-manipulation is only one reproductive mechanism. In spite of being heavily propagated, the ideology of capitalism is not always well received. When the mechanisms of consciousness-manipulation break down and threats to the stability of the system are real, then chances are that a new reproductive mechanism will be used: state violence, commonly called repression. This does not mean that all uses of state violence indicate that the other mechanisms have failed. Repression might be used because it is cheaper, because the spirit of a group has been broken and the state wishes to wipe it out, or for essentially irrational reasons having no apparent, coherent motivation. But in most cases, the existence of political repression testifies to a struggle taking place between those in control of the system and those trying to change the system's nature. The dynamics of that relationship is what much of the rest of this essay is about.

(2) *Repression is an essential aspect of liberal rule, not something alien to it.* The theory of liberal democracy, from Locke through Mill to the corporate liberalism of the twentieth century, is a series of agreements on how repression is to be practiced. Assume for the moment that liberalism's goals could actually be reached. The result would be something like the following: (a) access to the means of repression, open only to a few, would be egalitarian; anyone would have as likely a chance as anyone else to obtain the requisite positions; (b) the practice of repression would always be done according to certain well-defined rules and would never be arbitrary; and (c) any group would be as likely as any other group to be repressed, the distribution being without regard to class. That would be the case for an ideal liberal society, but none has so far existed. Instead, access to the means of repression is closed to most of the population, due process is rarely followed when it is against the interests of the state, and a ruling class exists which benefits from repression at the expense of those who challenge their rule. But phrased in this way, it is clear that much liberal criticism of repression covers only the failure to reach the ideal. What must be understood is that the ideal itself is a rationale for repression.

There is a reason for that. By its very nature, capitalism benefits a few at the expense of the many; if it did not, as Lenin once remarked, it would not be capitalism.[6] The maldistribution of rewards in the eco-

For a summary of the Hoover Commission, see *Congressional Record, ibid.* For a discussion of the whole problem, see Francis E. Rourke, *Secrecy and Publicity* (Baltimore: Johns Hopkins Press, 1961), p. 187.

5 Appendix, *The Budget of the United States (Fiscal Year 1971)* (Washington: Government Printing Office, 1970), p. 274.

6 V. I. Lenin, *Imperialism* (New York: International Publishers, 1939), p. 63.

nomic sector means that the political system is faced with an enormous task, which is to convince people that something which is not in their best interest *is* in their best interest. Liberal democracy, because it includes a political sphere in which access is slightly more egalitarian than it is in the corporate order, is an ideal answer. And if the historical conditions are right, it is possible for a liberal democratic society to undertake its task under conditions of relative peace, relying on non-terroristic reproductive means to make its case. But class struggle is never muted for good. The more unequal the distribution of the economic rewards of the society, the greater will be the chance that challenges will arise, which means that the use of state violence will be that much more frequent. Hence the repressive nature of capitalism and the built-in repressive quality of that liberal theory (and practice) which has been designed to serve as its ideology.

Radicals do not always act on these premises; there is a tendency to think of one's own repression as unique. In his account of his own experience with the liberal state, for example, Tom Hayden noted:

> [The Chicago] trial . . . symbolized the beginning of full-scale repression in the United States. . . . Future histories will locate the sixties as the time when America's famous democratic pragmatism began hardening into an inflexible fascist core. . . . The pursuit of imperialism created a necessity for repression, even fascism, to stabilize the home front.[7]

Hayden is wrong. While any historical event is unique, there was nothing startlingly new about the Chicago trial. Judge Hoffman was no more notoriously idiosyncratic than the man who tried the IWW in 1919 (also in Chicago and also on a conspiracy charge), Judge (later Baseball Commissioner) Kenesaw Mountain Landis.[8] Nor was he more severe; sentences for the IWW defendants were much higher. Nor was the reaction of the defendants all that different. Some fled the country (just as some of those prosecuted in the Smith Act cases did, after their experience with another egocentrically repressive judge, Harold Medina), while others went on to further radical activity. If repression is basic to the society, certain methods, once found to work, will be repeatedly used. The Chicago trial was such a method. Far from being a unique event, it was part of a show which has had a long run.

(3) *The history of repression does not necessarily reveal a linear development.* There are two positions here which need examination. One held by liberals like Milton Konvitz is that the civil liberties of Americans have been continually on the rise, implying that state repression has continually decreased. The other position, generally associated with radicals like the late Bertrand Russell, is that the United States has increas-

[7] Tom Hayden, *Trial* (New York: Holt, Rinehart, and Winston, 1970), pp. 4, 9, 11.

[8] For details, see Philip Taft, "The Federal Trials of the IWW," *Labor History* (Winter 1962), p. 60.

ingly become a repressive society, to the point where it may emerge into fascism.[9] Neither view is necessarily correct, though Russell comes closer to the truth than Konvitz.

One should avoid being abstract here, talking about repression as if it materialized out of thin air. It is not the amount of repression over time which is important, but the forms that repression takes. In fact, the amount of repression is probably a function of governmental output, i.e., the more the state is called upon to do, the more repression there will be, because that is one of the things it does. A discussion of the changing nature of repression, then, invariably implies a discussion of the changing nature of the capitalist state, of the shift from essentially private to essentially public activities.

In the latter part of the nineteenth century, while capitalism was still basically private, repression tended to be left in private hands. Corporations had their own police forces (or hired agencies like the Pinkertons) for purposes of breaking strikes. Even the non-terroristic reproductive mechanisms were private. In the town of Pullman, this was an exaggerated development in which the corporation controlled all information and nearly all private activities, including religion, a model which reveals in its clearest form the general case. However, as the entire corporate order became professionalized, with the state intervening to benefit the corporate class as a whole, the means of repression came to be centralized in the state. The crucial period, as James Weinstein has shown, was 1912–1920, when a new capitalist order emerged in which the state was to play a crucial role.[10]

In other words, it was liberalism which led to the modern repressive state and it was liberals who brought it into existence. In the search for ways of expanding state power in order to protect an emerging ruling class, it was a short step for progressive thinkers of the time to expand the repressive role of the state as well as its other aspects, especially when the force would be used against "unruly," "ill-behaved," "uncivil" elements who did not understand that politics required delicate balances among gentlemen. Only this paradox faced by liberals explains why the man who trained a whole generation of progressives to aid the state in extending its welfare privileges, Felix Frankfurter, could also be credited, as Melvyn Dubofsky so credits him, with developing the means for the destruction, through violent repression, of the Industrial Workers of the World.[11]

The modern repressive state was formed at the same time that the modern corporate state was formed—in the years of Woodrow Wilson. Con-

[9] The argument between Konvitz and Russell is summarized in Milton Konvitz, *Expanding Liberties* (New York: The Viking Press, 1967), p. xiii.

[10] James Weinstein, *The Corporate Ideal in the Liberal State* (Boston: Beacon Press, 1968).

[11] Melvyn Dubofsky, *We Shall Be All* (Chicago: Quadrangle, 1967), p. 916.

sider some of the unique "firsts" of the Wilson administration. Besides the appointment of George Creel to head the first important state propaganda machine in the United States, Wilson's second administration also saw the following, more directly repressive, developments: the appointment of J. Edgar Hoover to head the Radical Division of the Justice Department;[12] the first extensive use of deportation as a political weapon;[13] the first use of systematic, nationally planned raids on the offices of local political groups;[14] the first use of a selective service system (and the first arrests, like that of Eugene Debs, for interference with its functioning);[15] the first important racial pogroms of the twentieth century (Omaha and Chicago), and the first co-ordinated eflort by police to develop a strategy for controlling them, including coordinated police work and the publication of riot-control manuals;[16] the first intervention into the affairs of another country for purposes of containing an explicitly socialist revolution (because it was the first country to have an explicitly socialist revolution);[17] the first attempt by the government to take over the hiring of undercover agents to report on "subversive activity" (such as Francis Morrow, who became the agent who revealed the location of the Communist Party's Bridgman, Michigan meeting, leading to one of the largest political raids in American history);[18] the first extensive recruiting of labor leaders by the state to work directly in repressing their own memberships;[19] the creation of a Militia Bureau to centralize somewhat the use of state and federal troops (the Militia Bureau later became the National Guard);[20] and the first ruling by the Supreme Court interpreting the First Amendment in such a way as to provide a justification for governmental repression.[21] In addition, the same period also saw the federal trials of the IWW and the first general strike in American history.

Clearly, elements of all these things existed before 1919. And that year,

[12] On Hoover's appointment (from a favorable point of view), see Don Whitehead, *The FBI Story* (New York: Random House, 1956).

[13] William Preston, Jr., *Aliens and Dissenters* (New York: Harper Torchbooks, 1966), p. 83.

[14] Robert Murray, *Red Scare* (Minneapolis: University of Minnesota Press, 1955).

[15] On the use of the Selective Service Act as a political weapon, plus material on the Debs case, see H. C. Peterson and Gilbert C. Fite, *Opponents of War, 1917–18* (Seattle: University of Washington Press, 1968).

[16] William M. Tuttle, Jr., *Race Riot* (New York: Atheneum, 1970). Arthur Waskow, *From Race Riot to Sit-In* (Garden City: Doubleday Anchor, 1967).

[17] William Appleman Williams, *American-Russian Relations, 1781–1947* (New York: Rinehart, 1952).

[18] The story is contained in Theodore Draper, *The Roots of American Communism* (New York: Viking Press, 1957), pp. 366–375.

[19] Ronald Radosh, *American Labor and United States Foreign Policy* (New York: Random House, 1970).

[20] Martha Derthick, *The National Guard in Politics* (Cambridge: Harvard University Press, 1965).

[21] *Schenck v. United States*, 249 U.S. 47 (1919).

which novelists like Dos Passos saw as a turning point in the development of America, represented a culmination of all these trends. It is therefore hardly good history to date the emergence of the modern repressive state to that time.[22] The story of state repression since 1919 has been one of refinement, one which has seen the emphasis shift from one reproductive mechanism to another. But it has not differed in any fundamental degree from what emerged during the Wilson administration.

Since that time, the amount of state violence actually used has varied up and down, though the repressive potential of the state has always been large. For example, use of the National Guard for explicitly political purposes—a good indication of violent repression—has varied tremendously. In the decade of the 1920s, the Guard was used 78 times, while from 1940 to 1949 it was used only 22 times. By comparison, the Guard was called out 25 times in 1967 alone and 101 times in 1968.[23] Such figures suggest that the use of violent repression is a cyclical phenomenon, high in some periods, low in others. A hypothesis might be that while there is almost always some violent repression (the Wilson administration, criminal syndicalism laws in the 1920s, strike-breaking in the 1930s, "relocation camps" in the 1940s, McCarthyism in the 1950s, what we just saw so much of, in the 1960s), it will decrease when there is little active struggle taking place and increase as other reproductive mechanisms break down. The important point is that such a hypothesis is not a commentary on the role of the state, which is by its nature repressive, but a comment on the role of a dissenting consciousness.

(4) *Repression is not a policy question; conventional thinking is confused as to who supports what kinds.* No administration, whether Democratic or Republican, can ever end repression. This point needs emphasis because—even if radicals understand it intellectually—there is still the unconscious feeling that a political leader like Nixon is "worse" than someone like Kennedy on the repression "issue." This is a variation on the theme of liberals like Richard Harris, who argue that John Mitchell inaugurated a new era of repression, turning his back on the liberal tolerance of Ramsey Clark.[24] Yet it was Clark himself who began the current wave of political trials through his indictment of Spock, Coffin, and their co-defendants.[25] In other words, no matter what their

22 John Dos Passos, *1919* (New York: Harcourt, Brace, 1932). Waskow, *From Race Riot to Sit-In,* p. 1, also attaches a great deal of importance to this year.

23 These figures were compiled from a variety of sources, including: *Annual Report of the Chief of the Militia Bureau* (Washington: Government Printing Office, 1920–1932); *Annual Report of the Chief of the National Guard Bureau* (Washington: Government Printing Office, 1933–1969); *New York Times* (various issues, 1919–1969); and Philip Taft and Philip Ross, "American Labor Violence: Its Causes, Character, and Outcome," in Hugh Davis Graham and Ted Robert Gurr, *Violence in America* (New York: Signet Books, 1969), pp. 270–376.

24 Richard Harris, *Justice* (New York: Dutton, 1969).

25 See Jessica Mitford, *The Trial of Dr. Spock* (New York: Vintage, 1970).

attitude toward political dissent when out of office, liberals like Ramsey Clark will act repressively when in office or find the office taken away from them.

To this point one might wish to argue that while both Democrats and Republicans will be repressive, there is a real difference between them, and that—unless one wishes to follow the disastrous policy of supporting quasi-fascistic leaders in order to make things worse so that they might then get better—one should see this difference in degree as vitally important. Such an argument holds or implies that liberals will place more of their faith in consciousness-manipulation and long-term repressive strategies, while conservative Republicans are more likely to use the police and military in order to get their way. Since the latter policy involves greater threats to human life, while the former presents more contradictions which can be exploited, the Republican-type approach should be avoided if possible.

The conventional wisdom on this point is strong, but it falls apart on close examination. The presidents most inclined to use the instruments of state violence for purposes of repression in this century have been liberal Democrats, not Republicans. Why, to cite one rather typical yet good example, did Woodrow Wilson spend so much time sending Debs to jail, and why was it Harding who freed him? The usual answer sees the repressive character of the Wilson Administration as irrelevant to Wilson himself, as the fault of men like his Attorney General, A. Mitchell Palmer. Yet Wilson was quite aware of what his administration was doing. A more likely explanation is the one advanced above: liberals are much more likely to use the state as an instrument of corporate rule, playing a "progressive" role in helping the economy resolve, at least temporarily, some of its contradictions. As the state takes on a more positive role in the affairs of the citizenry, it is a small step to make the repressive role of the state more positive as well.

It follows that conservatives, who tend—at least in rhetoric, but also to some extent in practice—to rely on "individual initiative" rather than the state, will be reluctant to see the means of repression centralized in a federal bureaucracy in Washington. This has by and large been true. Eisenhower, for example, did not contribute as much to the growth of the FBI as Kennedy. And even though Eisenhower's attitude toward McCarthy was characterized by inconsistencies, who among the liberal Democrats at the time was an outspoken opponent of that form of repression? This general conservative reluctance to use the state as an instrument of repression has been discussed candidly by the man most responsible for repression in the Nixon Administration, Deputy Attorney-General Richard Kleindienst. Asked if he felt that the liberal government of Pierre Trudeau in Canada had overreacted to political kidnappings, Kleindienst replied:

> We conservatives would not have reacted that way. Cool-headed Wall Street types—like Nixon, Mitchell, and me—would never respond emotionally. We would be conservative in invoking extraordinary powers. You liberals, on the other hand, you don't anticipate crises; you worry about upsetting constituencies. When you finally do act, things have gotten so far out of hand that you have to overreact. That's why liberals are more likely to invoke emergency powers than conservatives.[26]

Granted that mere words do not a policy make, and that the Nixon Administration may be more repressive than Eisenhower, Harding, and Coolidge, nonetheless Kleindienst's point is worth considering.

(5) *The relationship between violent repression and the tactics of dissenting groups is probably the reverse of what is most often suggested.* In the world of the daily newspaper columnist and editorial writer, repression is "caused" by groups on the Left when they choose certain tactics. Such groups are urged not to engage in disruptive and militant activities because that will bring down the full power of the state against not only them but all right-thinking people as well. In one sense this argument is correct, for if there were no obvious and visible dissent, there would be no need for violent repression. But it is not an argument based on either the empirical evidence concerning the use of repression or the logic of the situation, as a few examples might make clear.

It has most often been the case that groups have been violently repressed, not when they have made their activities more militant and terroristic, but when they have softened their rhetoric and pursued mass-organizing techniques. The IWW, for example, was put on trial and raided just at the point when it stopped talking about armed self-defense and began to stress its non-violent aspects.[27] There is a logic to this. The continued escalation of rhetoric often comes about when a group has little mass support; revolutionary rhetoric then serves as a surrogate for the lack of anything else. Since little support exists, there is no real reason to repress because there is no real danger. In those periods, the role of the state is actually the opposite of trying to repress out of existence revolutionary rhetoric; in fact, through its undercover agents, the state seeks to encourage the group to engage in more terroristic words, not, as most people hold, in order to repress it later, but to isolate it from a mass base. If a group gets through that period and does begin to organize, then its rhetoric and tactics will become decidedly less militant and terroristic, as if almost by law. But it is at that point, when the state's policy of encouraging more militance breaks down, that the use of violence by the state is substituted as a form of repression, because that is when the group is most dangerous. It is interesting that the most severe

[26] Quoted in Alan Dershowitz, "'Stretch Points' of Liberty," *The Nation* (March 15, 1971), vol. 212, p. 329.

[27] For documentation of this point, see Dubofsky, *We Shall Be All.*

repression of the Black Panther Party came, not after it carried guns into the California legislature, but after it instituted a program of free breakfasts.

It should also be pointed out that there are times when the tactics of dissenting groups have nothing to do with repression. Because of its ties to the Soviet Union, the U.S. Communist Party was continually under siege by the government of the United States. After the Second World War the government moved to destroy it, and it was irrelevant whether the CP adopted a popular front line or an ultra-leftist line. Thus even in situations like this, the point holds that the state's decision to use repression is not determined by a dissenting group's choice of tactics but by the state itself.

(6) *Repressive forces are not omnipresent and impenetrable.* It is fairly easy to overestimate the potential danger of repression, if the number of people who do so is any indication. At times, for example, Herbert Marcuse can be read in such a way that there is almost no hope for those struggling to create a non-repressive society.[28] The means of repression are so subtle, so internalized, so changed from basically political phenomena to basically psychic ones, that even a struggle for liberation can actually be part of a repressive strategy. In contrast, I would argue that the strength of repression is about as great as the strength of the capitalist system it is designed to support. And since the system is rendered unstable and ultimately self-destructive by its internal contradictions, so the repressive apparatus is replete with paradoxes which, while not rendering it impotent, at least make it vulnerable to some forms of attack.

For example, there are times in the development of the liberal state when the very means of consciousness-manipulation create the basis for radicalization. In most urban high schools at the moment, students are either on drugs (in the case of heroin, clearly a form of repression) or are enemies of those who run the schools and, in that sense, also of the state. Originally designed to foster obedience and teach traditions, American public secondary schools currently do neither: they are vast breeding grounds for discontent, even though there are ruling-class spokesmen (like Charles Silberman) who realize this and periodically make eloquent pleas to reform the schools.[29] Perhaps this is because the schools simply cannot do what the society asks of them in the face of enormous political and cultural change. The same is true of many other institutions. It is the nuclear family which is responsible for the commune and the collective, the media which created the underground newspapers, religion which breeds agnosticism or the search for new spiritualism, work which creates alienation and discontent. The new society is being born of the old, and the at-

[28] Herbert Marcuse, *One-Dimensional Man* (Boston: Beacon Press, 1964). However, Marcuse seems to have moderated his view in *Essay on Liberation* (Beacon Press, 1969) and *Five Lectures* (Beacon Press, 1970).

[29] Charles Silberman, *Crisis in the Classroom* (New York: Random House, 1970).

tempts by the old to reinforce patterns which have become illegitimate in the eyes of many simply create further illegitimacy.

Increased use of the means of state violence—repression—is a response to those breakdowns. Often, in a short-term sense, this violence may be effective. Repression of the Black Panther Party seems to have destroyed the viability of that organization. The McCarthy period clearly stifled political discussion for a long time. Yet even in spite of that effectiveness, such repression creates its own problems. Out of the experience of the Panthers black groupings have arisen in parts of the country which are consciously trying to avoid the pattern into which the Panthers fell. And the McCarthy period, effective for a while, may just have postponed a confrontation with virulent anti-communism until the present time. But the best example of the paradoxical nature of such repression is the Chicago Eight trial. Whatever the motive of the government in prosecuting, that event contributed to massive feelings of illegitimacy toward the state on the part of young people throughout the country. It confirmed for many the idea that something is fundamentally wrong with America, for the obvious reason—but one that it is essential to continually remember—that something *is* fundamentally wrong with America. It was not "we" who thought up that trial but "they"; they acted as we expected them to act, which is all we could have asked of them.

There may well be times when repressive policies force political groups into dilemmas from which there is no easy way out. But there are also times when the rulers of the democratic state face impossible situations as well. Should Lt. Calley be found guilty? If the answer is no, then an indictment of the entire army is the result. If the answer is yes, then troops will be encouraged not to shoot in Vietnam. What made this dilemma (for them) real was the massive opposition to the war on the part of most Americans and many soldiers. That consciousness forced the Army into a position from which it could not extricate itself simply. For a moment in history, it was the army, not the antiwar movement, which was up against the wall.

The state's use of repression is also hindered, particularly in liberal democracies, by a rhetorical commitment to due process. Originally an aspect of liberal thought, because it afforded protection to businessmen to accumulate capital undisturbed, due process of law has increasingly been interpreted by the courts to apply to civil liberty cases. This does not mean an end to repression; it means that repression should not be arbitrary. For example, after the May Day events of 1971 in Washington, the American Civil Liberties Union ran a full-page ad critical of the Nixon Administration's handling of the arrests, suggesting that the same goal—keeping the government functioning—could have been obtained by means more in keeping with the Bill of Rights. There are, then, people who are interested in procedure to the point where ends are irrelevant, and often their voices are eloquent, sometimes even influential.

The development of a concern with civil liberty does complicate matters for the repressors. They are not free to switch back and forth in a search for the best repressive policy. Traditions and procedures do play a role, and it is perfectly natural that dissenting groups, when being repressed, will exploit these contradictions and use procedures and traditions to protect themselves whenever possible. It is also clear that to the extent that the tradition of civil liberty is near extinction, the threat comes from those who wield state power, not from those who challenge them.

(7) *It follows from this that the use of violent repression by the state could easily be a sign of its weakness, not its strength.* The ruling class is armed and dangerous; of that there is no doubt. It possesses an enormous amount of destructive weaponry, and—as the case of Fred Hampton indicates—it is not afraid to use it. It is clearly an error to take a Pollyannaish view of such a violent potential. But though tigers they may be, there is some truth in Mao's dictum that the tigers may be made of paper, and the reasons for that should be stated.

Violent repression exists because there is struggle; without a political movement, there need not be any repression. Instead of reacting with hurt surprise at the existence of such repression, and instead of simply calling for civil liberty—which means acting in a civil fashion—that repression should be understood as an opportunity to teach something about the nature of the liberal state. When a repressive society acts repressively, it is, in other words, doing what it is supposed to do. If it acted in any other way—say, by appointing members of the Black Panther Party to commissions instead of raiding their offices—it would not be what it is. This is a simple point, but it has taken a while for it to sink home. The defendants in the Spock trial, from this perspective, acted wrongly in restricting themselves to an insistence on procedure and fairness. They were found guilty anyway. On the other hand, the defendants in the Chicago trial had a remarkably sophisticated understanding of what repression meant. They used the trial in a political way, proper because it was a political trial. By their response, they put the government on trial for trying them, and they even won some sympathy from the jury in doing that. (This, plus the astounding support from the jury received by the Panther Thirteen, where an alliance was created between defendants and jury against the credibility of the state, indicates that such a strategy need not mean an automatic jail sentence.) Both groups used their trials to expand the political movement which brought them to trial, and they undoubtedly had an important effect upon the consciousness of, in the one case, young people and, in the other, black people.

Since non-terroristic reproductive mechanisms are generally preferred by the rulers of the bourgeois-democratic state, when state violence is used it is most likely an indication that affairs have not been running smoothly. In that sense, it indicates a crisis for the state, a period in which the ruling class is so unsure of its rule that it seeks the protection that only troops and police can provide, which turns out to be ambiguous protection at best. It follows that those periods which see an increase in violent repression are the same periods in which dissenting groups are most successfully building their movement. The present moment is such a time. The extraordinary number of political trials (Chicago Eight, Harlem Five, Panther Thirteen, Spock, draft resistance cases, drug frame-ups, indictments of May Day organizers, etc.), the return to raids and evidence-seizures, the drastic increase in the use of National Guard troops, and the revelations of the use of infiltrators and informers do not necessarily mean that the democratic state is turning into a fascistic-type police state, as some on the Left feel. That can only take place when there is no important progressive movement. On the contrary, the increase in violent repression is a response to a progressive movement (and its potential) and is being determined by that movement itself. If the movement went away, so would violent repression. In other words, it is not the tactics of any one group which affects repression, but the state of the movement as a whole.

If the reactionaries are paper tigers, it is because time is not on their side. Those who see fascism as inevitably coming out of the repressive potential of the democratic state give more time to the rulers of that state than they actually have; they give them more credit than they deserve. It is true that there is a fascist potential in liberal-democratic societies, but it is just as true that socialist movements—in the United States and abroad—have the potential to prevent that from materializing. Why assume that one side will win and not the other? Those who are disillusioned by the amount of state violence in the United States are those who had illusions about the democratic state in the first place. If we understand that repression is used out of desperation, we are one step closer to understanding how a non-repressive society can be built.

Domestic Law and International Order

The police department and the armed forces are the two arms of the power structure, the muscles of control and enforcement. They have deadly weapons with which to inflict pain on the human body. They know how to bring about horrible deaths. They have clubs with which to beat the body and the head. They have bullets and guns with which to tear holes in the flesh, to smash bones, to disable and kill. They use force, to make you do what the deciders have decided you must do.

Every country on earth has these agencies of force. The people everywhere fear this terror and force. To them it is like a snarling wild beast which can put an end to one's dreams. They punish. They have cells and prisons to lock you up in. They pass out sentences. They won't let you go when you want to. You have to stay put until they give the word. If your mother is dying, you can't go to her bedside to say goodbye or to her graveside to see her lowered into the earth, to see her, for the last time, swallowed up by that black hole.

The techniques of the enforcers are many: firing squads, gas chambers, electric chairs, torture chambers, the garrote, the guillotine, the tightening rope around your throat. It has been found that the death penalty is necessary to back up the law, to make it easier to enforce, to deter transgressions against the penal code. That everybody doesn't believe in the same laws is beside the point.

Which laws get enforced depends on who is in power. If the capitalists are in power, they enforce laws designed to protect their system, their way of life. They have a particular abhorrence for crimes against property, but are prepared to be liberal and show a modicum of compassion for crimes against the person—unless, of course, an instance of the latter is combined with an instance of the former. In such cases, nothing can stop them from throwing the whole book at the offender. For instance, armed robbery with violence, to a capitalist, is the very epitome of evil. Ask any banker what he thinks of it.

From Soul on Ice *(New York: McGraw-Hill, 1968), pp. 128–37. Reprinted with permission of the author and publisher.*

If Communists are in power, they enforce laws designed to protect their system, their way of life. To them, the horror of horrors is the speculator, that man of magic who has mastered the art of getting something with nothing and who in America would be a member in good standing of his local Chamber of Commerce.

"The people," however, are nowhere consulted, although everywhere everything is done always in their name and ostensibly for their betterment, while their real-life problems go unsolved. "The people" are a rubber stamp for the crafty and sly. And no problem can be solved without taking the police department and the armed forces into account. Both kings and bookies understand this, as do first ladies and common prostitutes.

The police do on the domestic level what the armed forces do on the international level: protect the way of life of those in power. The police patrol the city, cordon off communities, blockade neighborhoods, invade homes, search for that which is hidden. The armed forces patrol the world, invade countries and continents, cordon off nations, blockade islands and whole peoples; they will also overrun villages, neighborhoods, enter homes, huts, caves, searching for that which is hidden. The policeman and the soldier will violate your person, smoke you out with various gases. Each will shoot you, beat your head and body with sticks and clubs, with rifle butts, run you through with bayonets, shoot holes in your flesh, kill you. They each have unlimited firepower. They will use all that is necessary to bring you to your knees. They won't take no for an answer. If you resist their sticks, they draw their guns. If you resist their guns, they call for reinforcements with bigger guns. Eventually they will come in tanks, in jets, in ships. They will not rest until you surrender or are killed. The policeman and the soldier will have the last word.

Both police and the armed forces follow orders. Orders. Orders flow from the top down. Up there, behind closed doors, in antechambers, in conference rooms, gavels bang on the tables, the tinkling of silver decanters can be heard as icewater is poured by well-fed, conservatively dressed men in hornrimmed glasses, fashionably dressed American widows with rejuvenated faces and tinted hair, the air permeated with the square humor of Bob Hope jokes. Here all the talking is done, all the thinking, all the deciding. Gray rabbits of men scurry forth from the conference room to spread the decisions throughout the city, as News. Carrying out orders is a job, a way of meeting the payments on the house, a way of providing for one's kiddies. In the armed forces it is also a duty, patriotism. Not to do so is treason.

Every city has its police department. No city would be complete without one. It would be sheer madness to try operating an American city without the heat, the fuzz, the man. Americans are too far gone, or else they haven't arrived yet; the center does not exist, only the extremes. Take away the cops and Americans would have a coast-to-coast free-for-all.

There are, of course, a few citizens who carry their own private cops around with them, built into their souls. But there is robbery in the land, and larceny, murder, rape, burglary, theft, swindles, all brands of crime, profit, rent, interest—and these blasé descendants of Pilgrims are at each other's throats. To complicate matters, there are also rich people and poor people in America. There are Negroes and whites, Indians, Puerto Ricans, Mexicans, Jews, Chinese, Arabs, Japanese—all with equal rights but unequal possessions. Some are haves and some are have-nots. All have been taught to worship at the shrine of General Motors. The whites are on top in America and they want to stay there, up there. They are also on top in the world, on the international level, and they want to stay up there, too. Everywhere there are those who want to smash this precious toy clock of a system, they want ever so much to change it, to rearrange things, to pull the whites down off their high horse and make them equal. Everywhere the whites are fighting to prolong their status, to retard the erosion of their position. In America, when everything else fails, they call out the police. On the international level, when everything else fails, they call out the armed forces.

A strange thing happened in Watts, in 1965, August. The blacks, who in this land of private property have all private and no property, got excited into an uproar because they noticed a cop before he had a chance to wash the blood off his hands. Usually the police department can handle such flare-ups. But this time it was different. Things got out of hand. The blacks were running amok, burning, shooting, breaking. The police department was powerless to control them; the chief called for reinforcements. Out came the National Guard, that ambiguous hybrid from the twilight zone where the domestic army merges with the international; that hypocritical force poised within America and capable of action on either level, capable of backing up either the police or the armed forces. Unleashing their formidable firepower, they crushed the blacks. But things will never be the same again. Too many people saw that those who turned the other cheek in Watts got their whole head blown off. At the same time, heads were being blown off in Vietnam. America was embarrassed, not by the quality of her deeds but by the surplus of publicity focused upon her negative selling points, and a little frightened because of what all those dead bodies, on two fronts, implied. Those corpses spoke eloquently of potential allies and alliances. A community of interest began to emerge, dripping with blood, out of the ashes of Watts. The blacks in Watts and all over America could now see the Viet Cong's point: both were on the receiving end of what the armed forces were dishing out.

So now the blacks, stung by the new knowledge they have unearthed, cry out: *"POLICE BRUTALITY!"* From one end of the country to the other, the new war cry is raised. The youth, those nodes of compulsive energy who are all fuel and muscle, race their motors, itch to do something. The Uncle Toms, no longer willing to get down on their knees to lick boots, do so from a squatting position. The black bourgeoisie call for Citizens' Review Boards, to assert civilian control over the activity of the police. In back rooms, in dark stinking corners of the ghettos, self-conscious black men curse their own cowardice and stare at their rifles and pistols and shotguns laid out on tables before them, trembling as they wish for a manly impulse to course through their bodies and send them screaming mad into the streets shooting from the hip. Black women look at their men as if they are bugs, curious growths of flesh playing an inscrutable waiting game. Violence becomes a homing pigeon floating through the ghettos seeking a black brain in which to roost for a season.

In their rage against the police, against police brutality, the blacks lose sight of the fundamental reality: that the police are only an instrument for the implementation of the policies of those who make the decisions. Police brutality is only one facet of the crystal of terror and oppression. Behind police brutality there is social brutality, economic brutality, and political brutality. From the perspective of the ghetto, this is not easy to discern: the TV newscaster and the radio announcer and the editorialists of the newspapers are wizards of the smoke screen and the snow job.

What is true on the international level is true also at home; except that the ace up the sleeve is easier to detect in the international arena. Who would maintain that American soldiers are in Vietnam on their own motion? They were conscripted into the armed forces and taught the wisdom of obeying orders. They were sent to Vietnam by orders of the generals in the Pentagon, who receive them from the Secretary of Defense, who receives them from the President, who is shrouded in mystery. The soldier in the field in Vietnam, the man who lies in the grass and squeezes the trigger when a little half-starved, trembling Vietnamese peasant crosses his sights, is only following orders, carrying out a policy and a plan. He hardly knows what it is all about. They have him wired-up tight with the slogans of TV and the World Series. All he knows is that he has been assigned to carry out a certain ritual of duties. He is well trained and does the best he can. He does a good job. He may want to please those above him with the quality of his performance. He may want to make sergeant, or better. This man is from some hicky farm in Shit Creek, Georgia. He only knew whom to kill after passing through boot camp. He could just as well come out ready to kill Swedes. He will kill a Swede dead, if he is ordered to do so.

Same for the policeman in Watts. He is not there on his own. They have all been assigned. They have been told what to do and what not to do. They have also been told what they better not do. So when they continually do something, in every filthy ghetto in this shitty land, it means only that they are following orders.

It's no secret that in America the blacks are in total rebellion against the System. They want to get their nuts out of the sand. They don't like the way America is run, from top to bottom. In America, everything is owned. Everything is held as private property. Someone has a brand on everything. There is nothing left over. Until recently, the blacks themselves were counted as part of somebody's private property, along with the chickens and goats. The blacks have not forgotten this, principally because they are still treated as if they are part of someone's inventory of assets—or perhaps, in this day of rage against the costs of welfare, blacks are listed among the nation's liabilities. On any account, however, blacks are in no position to respect or help maintain the institution of private property. What they want is to figure out a way to get some of that property for themselves, to divert it to their own needs. This is what it is all about, and this is the real brutality involved. This is the source of all brutality.

The police are the armed guardians of the social order. The blacks are the chief domestic victims of the American social order. A conflict of interest exists, therefore, between the blacks and the police. It is not solely a matter of trigger-happy cops, of brutal cops who love to crack black heads. Mostly it's a job to them. It pays good. And there are numerous fringe benefits. The real problem is a trigger-happy social order.

The Utopians speak of a day when there will be no police. There will be nothing for them to do. Every man will do his duty, will respect the rights of his neighbor, will not disturb the peace. The needs of all will be taken care of. Everyone will have sympathy for his fellow man. There will be no such thing as crime. There will be, of course, no prisons. No electric chairs, no gas chambers. The hangman's rope will be the thing of the past. The entire earth will be a land of plenty. There will be no crimes against property, no speculation.

It is easy to see that we are not on the verge of entering Utopia: there are cops everywhere. North and South, the Negroes are the have-nots. They see property all around them, property that is owned by whites. In this regard, the black bourgeoisie has become nothing but a ridiculous nuisance. Having waged a battle for entrance into the American mainstream continually for fifty years, all of the black bourgeoisie's defenses are directed outward, against the whites. They have no defenses against the blacks and no time to erect any. The black masses can handle them any time they choose with one mighty blow. But the white bourgeoisie presents a bigger problem, those whites who own everything. With many shackled by unemployment, hatred in black hearts for this system of private property increases daily. The sanctity surrounding property is being called into question. The mystique of the deed of ownership is melting away. In other parts of the world, peasants rise up and expropriate the land from the former owners. Blacks in America see that the deed is not eternal, that it is not signed by God, and that new deeds, making blacks the owners, can be drawn up.

The Black Muslims raised the cry, *"WE MUST HAVE SOME LAND!"*

"SOME LAND OF OUR OWN OR ELSE!" Blacks in America shrink from the colossus of General Motors. They can't see how to wade through that thicket of common stocks, preferred stocks, bonds and debentures. They only know that General Motors is huge, that it has billions of dollars under its control, that it owns land, that its subsidiaries are legion, that it is a repository of vast powers. The blacks want to crack the nut of General Motors. They are meditating on it. Meanwhile, they must learn that the police take orders from General Motors. And that the Bank of America has something to do with them even though they don't have a righteous penny in the bank. They have no bank accounts, only bills to pay. The only way they know of making withdrawals from the bank is at the point of a gun. The shiny fronts of skyscrapers intimidate them. They do not own them. They feel alienated from the very sidewalks on which they walk. This white man's country, this white man's world. Overflowing with men of color. An economy consecrated to the succor of the whites. Blacks are incidental. The war on poverty, that monstrous insult to the rippling muscles in a black man's arms, is an index of how men actually sit down and plot each other's deaths, actually sit down with slide rules and calculate how to hide bread from the hungry. And the black bourgeoisie greedily sopping up what crumbs are tossed into their dark corner.

There are 20,000,000 of these blacks in America, probably more. Today they repeat, in awe, this magic number to themselves: there are 20,000,000 of us! They shout this to each other in humiliated astonishment. No one need tell them that there is vast power latent in their mass. They know that 20,000,000 of anything is enough to get some recognition and consideration. They know also that they must harness their number and hone it into a sword with a sharp cutting edge. White General Motors also knows that the unity of these 20,000,000 ragamuffins will spell the death of the system of its being. At all costs, then, they will seek to keep these blacks from uniting, from becoming bold and revolutionary. These white property owners know that they must keep the blacks cowardly and intimidated. By a complex communications system of hints and signals, certain orders are given to the chief of police and the sheriff, who pass them on to their men, the footsoldiers in the trenches of the ghetto.

We experience this system of control as madness. So that Leonard Deadwyler, one of these 20,000,000 blacks, is rushing his pregnant wife to the hospital and is shot dead by a policeman. An accident. That the sun rises in the east and sets in the west is also an accident, by design. The blacks are up in arms. From one end of America to the other, blacks are outraged at this accident, this latest evidence of what an accident-prone people they are, of the cruelty and pain of their lives, these blacks at the mercy of trigger-happy Yankees and Rebs in coalition against their skin. They want the policeman's blood as a sign that the Viet Cong is not the only answer. A sign to save them from the deaths they must die, and inflict. The power structure, without so much as blinking an eye, wouldn't mind tossing Bova to the mob, to restore law and order, but it knows in the vaults of its strength that at all cost the blacks must be kept at bay, that it must uphold the police department, its Guardian. Nothing must be allowed to threaten the set-up. Justice is secondary. Security is the byword.

Meanwhile, blacks are looking on and asking tactical questions. They are asked to die for the System in Vietnam. In Watts they are killed by it. Now—*NOW!*—they are asking each other, in dead earnest: Why not die right here in Babylon fighting for a better life, like the Viet Cong? If those little cats can do it, what's wrong with big studs like us?

A mood sets in, spreads across America, across the face of Babylon, jells in black hearts everywhere.

JOSEPH C. GOULDEN

The Cops Hit the Jackpot

Its original good intentions notwithstanding, the federal government has taken the first dangerous steps toward transforming the *United States into a society whose police agencies have a repressive capacity unparalleled in history.*

The responsible organization, by default as much as by design, is the Law Enforcement Assistance Administration (LEAA), a little-known but fast-growing division of the Justice Department created by the Omnibus Crime Control and Safe Streets Act* of 1968. LEAA's purpose, when conceived by Atty. Gen. Ramsey Clark, was to improve America's chaotic criminal justice system at all levels—arrest, trial, incarceration and release. The Safe Streets Act, Clark told a Senate committee, "is the one appropriate way the federal government can make a major difference. It is based on the demonstrated need for more resources, better applied, to improve the state of criminal justice in America."

In fact, however, the LEAA has become a pork barrel whose chief beneficiaries are the uniformed police. A vast amount of money is involved. LEAA's annual budget has soared in three years from $63 million to $480 million and the Senate recently *authorized $1.15 billion and $1.75 billion for fiscal 1972 and 1973;* House authorizations are $1 billion and $1.5 billion respectively. Whatever the final appropriation, therefore, LEAA is to be a $1 billion agency next year. Judging by procedures thus far, the bulk of it will flow directly to the police. *In 1969, 59.3 cents of every LEAA action-grant dollar went for police functions;* in 1970, 51 cents. Courts, corrections, juvenile delinquency, received minute dabs of cash.

LEAA disburses most of its funds in the form of block grants to the states, which spend the money as they wish, within wondrously broad guidelines. And the ways they are spending federal dollars—with federal

From The Nation, *November 23, 1970, pp. 520–33. Reprinted in edited form with permission of the author and publisher.*

* For convenience, the title will hereafter be abbreviated to Safe Streets Act.

blessing—raise serious questions about the future of criminal justice in the United States.

In the name of "law and order," LEAA is providing local police with sophisticated "crime prevention" hardware and with techniques developed by many of the same specialists who put men on the moon. The purpose is to curb robberies, burglaries and violent street crimes. The result, however, enables police to keep citizens—the innocent and the guilty alike—under electronic and photographic surveillance while they are shopping, walking public streets, driving automobiles, and visiting both private and public buildings.

Using infrared cameras and zoom lenses, combined with video-tape recorders (the "instant replay" gadget of pro football), police can make instant photographic records of citizens' activities, even in total darkness. Clarence M. Coster, associate administrator of LEAA, looks forward to the day when police will make sound and photographic recordings of "mass protests" and rock festivals, as evidence for future prosecutions. *The sensor devices developed to detect guerilla movements in Indochina are being adapted for domestic law enforcement. LEAA is even giving the cops an air arm:* grants support helicopter patrols in Los Angeles, Washington, Atlanta and elsewhere, and short-takeoff-and-landing (STOL) aircraft are being tried out in Dade County, Florida.

In the name of "civil tranquillity," Washington is banding state and local police into compacts to cope not only with violent disorders but also with peaceful protests against defects in American education, foreign policy and racial equality. *With federal dollars, the police are constructing massive computerized "intelligence systems" intended to predict unrest—through inputs of information on where citizens travel, what they say, with whom they meet.*

The police are being armed to the teeth. *For $16,464, LEAA bought the tank that Louisiana police used on September 15 to storm a Black Panther headquarters in New Orleans;* the same tank had been used earlier against demonstrating black college students. Pick a state at random. Colorado: 165 riot helmets, 126 gas masks, 118 riot batons, seventy-six cases of Mace, 500 pairs of plastic handcuffs (cheaper than the metal variety, thus useful in mass arrests), thirteen shotguns, three pepper fog machines, with both smoke and gas mixes, four grenade launchers, ninety-four smoke and gas grenades, projectiles, launching cartridges and flares; thirty-three "riot shields," twenty pairs of riot coveralls and gloves. Asking for even more such stuff in 1970, Colorado complained that police lacked equipment in "countries and towns which have *college, migrant* or *minority populations. . . .*"

In the name of *"law enforcement professionalization"* LEAA is pouring millions of dollars into the hands of such blatantly racist police groups as the Mississippi Highway Patrol and the South Carolina State Law Enforcement Division (SLED)—agencies with blood on their hands from past confrontations with civil rights protesters and other "agitators." Washington's dollars go to such groups without the slightest attempt at racial integration.

LEAA is strengthening the police politically as well as physically, for "professionalism" gives the cops an aura of infallibility when they deal with lay politicians. Traditionally isolationist and elitist, the cop is using his new wealth to withdraw even further from the restraints of elective government.

In the name of President Nixon's "new federalism," Washington is yielding control of millions of federal tax dollars to *police-dominated "state planning agencies."* LEAA claims its *laissez-faire* attitude toward state activities is mandated in the Safe Streets Act. But Charles H. Rogovin, LEAA administrator from February 1969 until he quit in disgust in April 1970, disagrees. "LEAA shouldn't dictate, but it sure as hell must provide leadership, and LEAA hasn't done this."

Political influence, not actual need, frequently determines which agencies receive funds. Wesley Pomeroy, former LEAA associate administrator, now a private police consultant, reports: "In talks with [police] chiefs around the country, I detect a positive fear that if your Senator or Congressman makes trouble for Nixon on the war your chances of getting LEAA money are hurt." William Johnson, director of public safety in Gary, Ind., told me: "Several times we've submitted proposals [to the Indiana State Criminal Justice Planning Agency] that were identical to ones from South Bend. The agency, which is dominated by downstate Republicans, will approve South Bend, but table us." South Bend is Republican; Gary is Democratic (and run by a black mayor, Richard Hatcher).

Congress made Safe Streets a state-oriented program to avoid creating a vast new federal bureaucracy, but the result has been to create cumbersome, ill-directed state bureaucracies, more than half of which changed chief executive officers during their first eighteen months. A substructure of regional fiefdoms inside the states, many with paid staffs, further dilutes LEAA planning funds. For example, a California city that develops a program must get it past five review hurdles before it comes up for final approval or disapproval by the California Council on Criminal Justice. These administrative layers absorbed $21 million of LEAA's total budget of $268 million in fiscal 1970.

"Congress passed a 'Safe Streets' program. The states turned it into a 'Safe Pastures' program." This bitter comment comes from a middle-level LEAA official, a holdover from the Ramsey Clark days, who is now seeking work elsewhere. A blatant example of the LEAA pork barrel in action is to be found in Michigan. Grand Rapids, with a population of 200,000 and a police budget of $2.9 million, had through mid-1970 received one LEAA grant: $188 for a 75 per cent share of two Polaroid cameras and a fingerprint kit. Another Michigan town, of 7,500 population, got during the same period $1,650 for an infrared scanning device, $1,275 for a surveillance camera, and $2,400 for basic radio equipment. A National League of Cities survey of mayors found similar discrepancies in a number of other states.

Federal Funds and Local Justice

Peculiarly, these things are happening in an atmosphere of almost total silence. The big-city mayors and the municipal lobbyists—specifically, the U.S. Conference of Mayors, the National League of Cities and the Urban Coalition—complain about *who* is handling the money (governors, rather than mayors), but offer relatively little criticism about *how* it is being spent. The Urban Coalition has called for more nonpolice spending; however, the thrust of its reports on "Law and Disorder," its evaluations of LEAA, has been that Washington should deal with cities, not with states. But some of the more questionable schemes financed thus far were city proposals, and there is no evidence that mayors would put the LEAA money to wiser use than do the states. Says a high LEAA official: "The mayors are so worried about budgets that they'd use Safe Streets money for hardware, and nothing else. Their bind is such they can't bother with long-term pilot projects. . . ."

LEAA began in 1965 with a rather low-keyed attempt by President Johnson to give the federal government an enlarged role in crime fighting. At his urging, Congress created an Office of Law Enforcement Assistance (OLEA) in the Department of Justice to give grants-in-aid to cities as well as states, and to finance research in criminal justice. Congress gave OLEA less than half of the $42 million it requested in three years, but the fledgling agency did finance 330 projects aimed at helping local governments improve their overall criminal justice systems. The attorney general controlled the program.

Meanwhile, two Presidential commissions reached sobering conclusions on law and order. The President's Commission on Law Enforcement and Criminal Justice found that police were ill-trained and ill-equipped; about half had less than 12.4 years of education. The system was also fragmented, *with no one official or agency responsible for coordinating courts, police and prisons*. Cooperation between police departments was (and is) almost nonexistent, save for routine operational necessities. The National Advisory Commission on Civil Disorders (the Kerner commission) also criticized police, citing "hostility between police and ghetto communities as a primary cause of the disorders surveyed by the commission."

Further, cities suffering most of the crime had reached their financial limits. State, city and county governments together spend about $6 billion annually on criminal justice; a quarter of this figure is spent by the twelve largest cities, which have 12.5 per cent of the U.S. population, but 26 per cent of the reported serious crimes and more than half the reported robberies. The crime rate in cities larger than 250,000 is double the national rate.

To Attorney General Clark and other Johnson Administration officials involved in writing the Safe Streets Act the answer was to be greater federal expenditures—not for operations but to "strengthen the system and to encourage the kind of innovations needed to respond to the problems of crime in America," as the President told Congress in a special message on February 6, 1967.

The proposed expanded program would have continued the attorney general's authority to make grants, much as he had done under OLEA. These would have gone directly both to states and to local governments, the latter receiving them either individually or in combined units with a population of 50,000 or more. The population limit was imposed to reduce the number of direct federal-local contacts; to encourage consolidation of criminal justice functions, a key recommendation of the President's Crime Commission, and to concentrate spending on high crime areas. OLEA would have been expanded into LEAA as a part of the Justice Department on a par with the antitrust, civil rights and other divisions, and headed by an administrator of rank equivalent to assistant attorney general. Grant recipients would be required to increase anti-crime spending by 5 per cent annually, and to submit annual comprehensive plans to the attorney general, showing how their spending fit a master scheme for systems improvement.

Mauling the Program

Congress went to work on the bill with a mixture of wisdom, mischief and barely disguised malice for its primary spokesman, Ramsey Clark. There were three issues: the grant mechanism, the leadership of LEAA, and the respective roles of cities, states and the federal government.

"What Congress feared most about this bill was Ramsey Clark," states a man intimately involved in the legislation. "Ramsey had a soft-on-crime reputation, and the police and 'law-and-order' Congressmen didn't want him to control this program. What it comes down to, I suppose is that McClellan and Hruska just didn't like Ramsey."

The statement is an exaggeration, although it does much to explain why LEAA was so mauled by Congress. It is true that the Senators mentioned—John McClellan (D., Ark.) and Roman Hruska (R., Neb.)—had an abiding distaste for Clark. Equally intense, however, was their determination that LEAA not be empowered "to lord it over the states with all those administrative guidelines" as does the detested (by conservatives) Department of Health, Education and Welfare. Governors have been tell-ing one another for years that they can run programs better than can the federal government, and a few people—for the most part, those who haven't looked too closely—actually believe them. Added to these feelings was a general agreement that the federal government shouldn't be allowed to get too close to local police policy and operations.

McClellan's inclination was to spend Safe Streets funds in the form of block grants to the states, which would in turn pass the money down to local governments, rather than let Washington dole out cash directly to cities. . . . The state approach prevailed, thanks chiefly to the vigorous floor work of William T. Cahill, then a Representative, since 1969 the Governor of New Jersey. The Cahill amendments—supported by the McClellan/Hruska axis—produced a bill providing:

> Planning grants for state-level *law enforcement and criminal justice planning agencies* (SPAs, in LEAA parlance). The governors create and direct the SPAs, which receive a flat $100,000 plus a per capita share of whatever planning funds are left in the LEAA budget. (Amounts paid in fiscal 1970 ranged from $1.566 million for California to $121,000 for Alaska.) The SPAs must be "representative" of state and local government functional agencies. They are responsible for preparing a "comprehensive and innovative" statewide plan for criminal justice; for developing and coordinating projects, establishing priorities, and making grants to "general units of local government or combinations thereof." The SPAs must pass 40 per cent of their planning funds along to local governments.
>
> A requirement that, before receiving action funds, SPAs must file with LEAA an annual comprehensive plan describing the existing system, and what is proposed to improve it. The SPAs, in turn, receive local applications for action money, determine whether they are in accord with the state plan, and then disburse funds. At least 75 per cent of all action funds received from LEAA must be "passed through" to local governments.
>
> That 85 per cent of LEAA's annual appropriation for action funds must be allocated to the states. LEAA may spend the remaining 15 per cent as it sees fit, in the form of discretionary grants.
>
> That state and/or local governments must put up matching funds in order to receive federal aid. The Act set the maximum federal share as 90 per cent for planning; 60 per cent for action grants; 75 per cent for *organized crime, and for riots and civil disorders;* and 100 per cent for research, education, training and demonstration grants.
>
> A stipulation that LEAA officials may not exercise "any direction, supervision, or control over any police force or any other law enforcement agency" of any state or local government.

Senator McClellan wanted to remove LEAA from the Justice Department altogether. He failed, but did manage to put LEAA under *three* directors rather than one—an administrator and two associate administrators. No more than two members of the troika can be of the same party. The Act describes the three LEAA officials collectively as "the administration" and says it shall "exercise all of the functions, powers, and duties created and established" under the Act. The language is so vague that no one is sure what McClellan intended, and even troika advocates acknowledged the solution was not perfect. . . .

That is the basic framework of LEAA, a piece of experimental legislation, in that it departs sharply from the pattern of federal-state relations of the last three decades, and relies heavily upon the state governments as planners, administrators, coordinators and innovators. LEAA and its central and regional staffs must see that federal funds are properly and wisely spent, but without having recourse to the "conditions" upon which federal agencies can normally rely in grant programs. . . .

The Lame Ducks Go to Work

President Johnson signed LEAA's authorizing legislation on June 19, 1968; by mid-October the new agency had its first-year appropriation of $63 million, and was sufficiently staffed to open its doors. The first administrator was Patrick V. Murphy, who had briefly headed the OLEA before becoming director of public safety for the District of Columbia. One of the associate administrators was Wesley A. Pomeroy, a veteran California lawman with sufficient breadth of talent to direct security for both the 1964 Republican National Convention (the one that nominated Barry Goldwater) and the Woodstock festival.

"As we saw the mission of LEAA," Pomeroy recalled recently, "it was to develop a broad understanding of the provisions of the legislation and the program so that our clients—the police, the courts, etc.—would know how to use it. This was a strong principle. We wanted them to tell us what they wanted. It was to be a client-run program, but with a strong coordinating voice at the top, at LEAA in Washington." Pomeroy recruited some two dozen chiefs and sheriffs—officers whose rank brought them immediate respect among colleagues, "without any credibility problem"—put them through a brisk crash course in Washington, and sent them on the road to sell the LEAA message to local officers. . . .

Much of this gearing-up was done by lame ducks, for soon after his election Richard Nixon let it be known that he intended to choose his own LEAA administration. Murphy, Pomeroy and the other associate administrator, Dr. Ralph Siu—all interim appointees never approved by the Senate—decided to stay on as long as possible to keep things moving, on the assumption it would be unprofessional to abandon LEAA during the critical formative period. The states faced a May 1 deadline for the comprehensive plans, and "were having a devil of a time getting organized," in the words of an LEAA regional officer.

Soon after January 20, the lame ducks received their first, and only, directive from Attorney General Mitchell: henceforth, any *discretionary grants awarded by LEAA must be approved by Deputy Atty. Gen. Richard G. Kleindienst,* the Justice Department's chief political operative. . . .

The language of the Safe Streets Act suggests that Mitchell was on very thin ice in giving Kleindienst a veto over discretionary grants. Section 306 states that they shall be made "as the [LEAA] Administration determines." Further, Congress made clear that it intended the troika—and not the attorney general or his deputy—to run LEAA. . . .

To replace Murphy, Mr. Nixon picked Charles H. Rogovin, a nonpolitical registered Democrat who had been, in turn, a public defender and prosecutor in Philadelphia, assistant director of the President's Crime Commission, and a Massachusetts assistant attorney general specializing in organized crime.

The Administration's choice of associate administrators displayed political pragmatism. Richard W. Velde is the son of former Rep. Harold H. Velde (R., Ind.), remembered in Congress chiefly as chairman of the House Un-American Activities Committee in 1953–54. As counsel to Republicans on the McClellan subcommittee that worked on the LEAA legislation, Velde is philosophically dedicated to the block-grant concept. As an astute politician (and protégé of Senator Hruska) he also "knows how to talk to the Hill," in the words of an LEAA official. Says another: "Velde is an insurance policy for McClellan and Hruska. He's not going to let LEAA get into areas that would offend these two guys." Velde told me he sees his mission as "striking a balance" between the statutory state autonomy and "the need for Congress, LEAA managers and taxpayers to know whether the money is being spent in the most effective manner."

The other associate administrator, Clarence M. Coster, got his job because he had been police chief in Bloomington, Minn., which is in the home district of Rep. Clark MacGregor, second ranking Republican on the House Judiciary Subcommittee that oversees LEAA. Coster, as a former police chief, can talk tough with cops—and others—and get away with it. His standing orders to LEAA speech writers are "let it rip," and he regularly says unpleasant things. For instance, he recently chewed out a convention of burglar-alarm dealers for their absurdly high false-alarm rate—from 91 to 100 per cent for sixteen firms surveyed in Los Angeles alone—and told them to shape up if they were serious about their business.

Sen. Sam J. Ervin, second-ranking Democrat on the Senate Judiciary Committee, also has his man inside LEAA. He is general counsel Paul Woodward, formerly Ervin's legislative assistant and at one time assistant counsel to the subcommittee on criminal laws and procedures.

Rogovin had the top title, and the largest salary ($37,000; an associate administrator gets $35,000) and he thought, for a while at least, that his would be the authoritative voice inside LEAA. Before taking the post, Rogovin read the LEAA authorizing legislation, and spent several hours talking with Attorney General Mitchell. Nonetheless, he concedes now, he made a basic mistake—that of assuming Mitchell had given him the *authority* as well as the *responsibility* for running LEAA. But he never asked, directly, that Mitchell define his powers. "You are appointed to do a specific job," Rogovin said to me, "and assume you will be permitted to do it. Most of the conversation was about the ideas I had for LEAA, and what I thought we could and should do."

The Cops Move In

Daniel Skoler, director of LEAA's Office of Law Enforcement Planning (OLEP), which processes both block and discretionary grants, says that when the state governments got wind of the Safe Streets money they "responded . . . with the zeal of ballplayers just offered cold beer." And, unfortunately, with about as much coordination.

"What Congress envisioned was a process through which local requirements would filter up to the top and be put into one big mosaic by the state planning agency," says a former Congressional aide involved in writing the Safe Streets Act. "Congress had confidence in local government; it also felt the states would be strong enough to bring all these ideas together into a kind of meaningful plan."

In fact, however, most of the SPAs and the 450-odd regional planning groups created under their auspices are dominated by law-enforcement agencies. The International City Management Association, in a late 1969 survey, found that only 13 per cent of the members of the SPAs were local policy-making officials, and that only 15 per cent were classed as "citizens" representative of the general community. The rest were either state or law-enforcement functionaries. Mississippi's twenty-seven-member board includes only three persons who are not police or public officials: one of the law-enforcement members is Roy K. Moore, special agent in charge of the FBI office in Jackson. The boards of New Jersey (fourteen members) and North Carolina (twenty-six) are all criminal justice professionals; so are twenty-six out of twenty-nine members on Florida's board. An Urban Coalition survey of the twelve largest states found that 62 per cent of the 302 persons on SPA boards were criminal justice officials—only 5 per cent represented "citizen and community interests."

The result is that reform of the criminal justice system has become the responsibility of persons with institutional loyalties to the existing system. Few outside voices are present to suggest fundamental changes in the way things are done. Cop rule does not contribute to developing a meaningful "comprehensive" plan, but it does insure that rural countries and hamlets enjoy disproportionate access to the police pork barrel.

At the regional level, the law-enforcement weight is often even heavier.

In Florida, each of the seven regional boards is composed of four police chiefs, four sheriffs, a fiscal officer and a hired planner. A Georgia official, responding to a National League of Cities/U.S. Conference of Mayors survey, said regional boards there are picked by "political philosophy rather than competence." North Carolina's regional boards have 383 members: 233 are law-enforcement officers; 130 are from local government; only twenty speak for the general public. Minorities are poorly represented, even outside the South. Until April 1970, Massachusetts' SPA was all white. LEAA used quiet diplomacy, its officials insist, to attempt to get at least one black on each Southern SPA. Mississippi flatly refused. The Lawyers Committee for Civil Rights Under Law asked the Justice Department to file suit. Justice declined, saying the LEAA statute was mute on minority representations. The committee is now suing Mississippi on its own.

Cities receive short shrift in many states. New York State's SPA has twenty-seven members, only nine of them from New York City (the police commissioner and Dist. Atty. Frank Hogan). Gary, largest city in Indiana, is not represented on the Indiana State Criminal Justice Planning Agency. The Republican state administration in Michigan lumped Democratic-run Detroit and Wayne County—with 40 per cent of Michigan's population, and half its crime—into a region with six other counties. Less populous Lansing (which is Republican) is in a two-county region. Cleveland is in a seven-county region in which two urban counties have five votes each; five rural counties, three votes each. Houston has two-thirds the population in the area covered by its regional board, and one-twelfth the votes.

Sharing the Wealth

The regional system also means that LEAA planning funds are distributed over many states in the form of a thin dew. Minimum allocations to each region, regardless of population or crime rate, can be defended as necessary for planning competence, but the National League of Cities suggests that regions are gerrymandered to put money into low-crime areas. For example, in its 1969 plan, Kentucky listed three major urban areas as accounting for 70 per cent of its major crime. Nonetheless, the state was split into sixteen regions, each of which received a basic planning grant of $5,000, and rural regions received twice as much money per capita as did Louisville. Similarly, Colorado earmarked $2,000 in base grants to each of fourteen regions, although half the state's population and 70 per cent of its major crimes are concentrated in Denver. . . .

For local police, however, there is a most compelling reason for regionalism: money. Put federal Safe Streets planning money into every fork of every creek. Support Sheriff Jones's request for a new squad car, and he'll work for your video recorder. Use Washington's money to buy, for the tank town police, the very basic police equipment—patrol cars, side arms, uniforms, even office furnishings—that most cities routinely purchase with general tax revenues. *States include such items in their "comprehensive" plans as "crime prevention and detection" equipment, and LEAA doesn't flinch.* Some examples:

Colorado's "equipment acquisition" category for 1970 calls for forty-eight subgrants to cities, six of them for less than $100; twenty-nine for less than $1,000. The federally financed items range from twenty patrol cars and four snowmobiles down to "personal uniforms, office equipment and rescue equipment . . . too broad to quantify."

Mississippi's 1970 allocation was $2.117 million, of which $582,389 was earmarked for "purchase of basic equipment"—first-aid kits, service weapons, uniforms and furnishings, radios, fifteen automobiles, eighteen night sticks, six pairs of handcuffs, two station wagons for Parchman, the state prison. Equipment expenditures in other categories, chiefly riot control and training, push Mississippi's hardware bill past $1 million, more than half its Safe Streets money.

Georgia lists equipment grants for no less than 268 local police departments; its comprehensive plan, in effect, is a police shopping list: 569 mobile radio units, eighty-five automobiles, fifty fingerprint and ID kits, fifty-seven cameras, nine typewriters, sixty-four firearms of unspecified caliber, eight Mace units, eighteen pairs of handcuffs, forty-one fire extinguishers, eight evidence lockers, fourteen helmets. By 1975, Georgia states, it wants federal aid in buying a total of 1,300 police cars. It adds, with an apparently straight face, "Care has been taken to avoid indiscriminate distribution of equipment to departments that have little use for it."

Ohio's Law Enforcement Planning Agency offers tortuous arguments against concentrating spending in high-crime areas: "among other things, conceivably, [this] could drive crime from one area into another." Ohio also says "situation practicalities"—by which it means political pressures—require that Safe Streets funds go into small towns.

Daniel Skoler is the LEAA official who must see to it that state comprehensive plans make a semblance of sense. Skoler is finding that "comprehensive" is a word that lends itself to highly subjective interpretation. Under LEAA guidelines, a comprehensive plan must include projects in these areas: upgrading law-enforcement personnel; crime prevention (including public education); prevention and control of juvenile delinquency; improvement of detection and apprehension of criminals; improvement of prosecution and court activities, and law reform; increase in effectiveness of correction and rehabilitation (including probation and parole); reduction of organized crime; prevention and control of riots and civil disorders; improvement of community relations and research and development.

The official line at LEAA—one which Skoler will recite upon request—is that the 1969 comprehensive plans were pretty wretched, a shortcoming excused on the ground that the states had only about five months to produce them. In 1970, the plans were much better, although there is still need for improvement. In middle echelons, the comments are considerably more direct: Wilbur Brantley, a retired Los Angeles homicide detective who works in the LEAA regional office in San Francisco, says California's 1969 plan—more than 5,000 pages in twenty-five volumes, weighing 48 pounds—was "a pile of shit." The 1970 plan, while more concise, earns the same description. California's shortcoming, according to Brantley, is that the plans never get around to saying exactly what the state intends to accomplish, or where it will spend its Safe Streets money. "Hopelessly general," he told me. . . .

Feeding the Computers

"The year past was an excellent one for the vendors of electronic equipment," stated an LEAA internal document circulated in July. "*Communications and information systems alone accounted for more than $20 million within the police programs area,*" one of the OLEP divisions.

As an LEAA official somewhat testily replies, $20 million is a mere tinkle of coins for the mammoth electronics industry. Nonetheless, it is $1 of every $9 of LEAA's total action-grant budget of $182.75 million for 1970. Further, according to one authoritative estimate, spending for electronic gear in other areas—*computerized "intelligence systems" for civil disorders and organized crime, and command and control gear—push the overall electronic budget to nearly $50 million.* Garlan Morse, president of the Sylvania Electric Projects division of General Telephone and Electronics Corporation, predicted to *The New York Times* in April that law-enforcement agencies will be spending $500 million a year on electronic gear by 1975. Morse credits LEAA pilot projects with starting the boom.

That LEAA has no precise figures on how much of its money goes for electronics is a comment on how little LEAA actually knows of what the states are doing in the field. *Yet the electronic projects that LEAA is financing pose direct and basic threats to the privacy, liberty and personal security of the American citizen.* We are not talking about burglar alarms and car radios but of gear that a decade ago would have been dismissed as science fiction.

A recent LEAA document said the "explosive growth of computerized information systems" was one of the "most dynamic areas in law-enforcement and criminal justice" at all levels—police, corrections, courts, parole, probation and prosecution. More than thirty states, plus the District of Columbia, are developing statewide systems, a threefold increase since LEAA began funding such projects. Further, LEAA reports:

> Many small police departments and sheriffs' offices now have or will have immediate access to vital information through terminals on state networks. A rapidly growing number of cities and urban counties are developing computer systems for law enforcement. Regional systems comprising several units and levels of local government are emerging.

All of the state systems, LEAA says, "are designed to interface with the FBI's National Crime Information Center (NCIC) and several systems will be linked to those in adjoining states. . . . Almost all city and regional systems are interfaced with their respective state system where they exist. . . . In all states, the initial emphasis has been on police applications. . . ." The computers are linked physically by Bell System long-distance wires and microwave transmitters. TV-type display screens are replacing manual terminals for print-outs of transmitted data.

Police are finding a variety of information to put into these computers. One "organized crime" setup in New England is loaded with material on Mafia figures. Juveniles who get into trouble in the San Francisco Bay Area land in the computers (officials say they can "clear the innocent" more quickly when a youngster has a scrape away from his home community). A system based in Florida is intended to log suspected mob figures in and out of Caribbean islands known to be targets of organized crime. Bankruptcy data, business foreclosures, commercial frauds—these and more are going into the computer tapes.

In addition to financing local and state systems, LEAA is directing a project aimed at tying many—and potentially all—of the individual components into a national network. The project is known as SEARCH, an acronym for System for Electronic Analysis and Retrieval of Criminal Histories. The California Council on Criminal Justice (CCCJ) is coordinating SEARCH for LEAA.

Fifteen states are now involved as participants or observers, working with $1,429,460 provided by LEAA and $1,087,368 from state matching funds. Each state is converting 10,000 "criminal histories" into electronically accessible form. The subjects are felons with at least two arrests and one court disposition. The histories consist of "public record data" on criminal activities, basic biographical and physical data (including visible scars, marks, tattoos, amputations and deformities); "miscellaneous identifying numbers, skin tone, address, and occupation." Each state will maintain its own "bank" of subjects—thus persons involved in SEARCH argue that it is not a national data bank. Nevertheless, a *central* index, now being developed by the *Michigan state police,* will be directly available to each state and will contain summarized data on each state-held file. . . .

Some safety guidelines have been proposed by SEARCH task force headed by Dr. Robert Gallati, director of the New York State Identification and Intelligence System. The key provisions are that data supplied for use in SEARCH "must be limited to that with the characteristics of public record," and must be systematically verified for accuracy. Direct access would be restricted "to public agencies which perform, as their principal function, crime prevention, apprehension, adjudication, or rehabilitation of offenders." Users must sign nondisclosure agreements, and "should be instructed that their rights to direct access encompass only requests reasonably connected with their criminal justice responsibilities." Specifically excluded are data on juvenile, misdemeanor drunk and traffic arrests, and "unverified data such as that emanating from intelligence sources." The task force wrote: "The intent here is to avoid the use of data resulting from tips, rumors, or second-hand allegations that have not been formally substantiated or derived from official criminal justice proceedings. . . ."

SEARCH, when operative, will make police files instantaneously interchangeable. And many of the states involved in SEARCH are coincidentally developing computerized intelligence systems for material far removed from violent crime: "to analyze the potential for disorders," as stated in an LEAA internal document. The California Council on Criminal Justice, fascinated by the wonders of electronics, describes its desired system as follows:

> The state will have an operating intelligence system for the collection, analysis, interpretation, and dissemination of information relative to the prediction, detection, prevention, suppression and control of riots and disorders. This system will provide for necessary exchange of information at state and local levels, thus furnishing urgent and necessary coordination and cooperation.

Similar language is found in other state comprehensive plans. The type of intelligence useful to such systems is "raw" in the purest, or foulest, sense of the word. It deals with the political attitudes and activities of persons motivated by a diversity of reasons. Legitimate dissenter and terrorist will go on the tapes together.

Under the Gallati guidelines, such information would not get into the SEARCH system—so we are told. Cops, like generals, have a very human characteristic: they feel compelled to use fancy gadgetry once it is at hand. The computer systems designed to store information on organized crime and civil disorders are interfaceable with the SEARCH apparatus, and local police are already outspokenly angry with the Justice Department over alleged failures to provide information about potential terror bombers in the Middle West. SEARCH's mere existence, in an era of intensifying national paranoia, is an invitation to abuse. An action brought by the Oklahoma Civil Liberties Union contends that the state's *Office of Interagency Coordination* has prepared a black list of 6,000 Oklahomans who are regarded as "actual or potential troublemakers." The compilation of the list was made possible in large part by a grant of the LEAA in the amount of $29,953.

One early proposal that zipped through initial screening at CCCJ would have made the California Department of the Military a central repository for collecting, evaluating and disseminating "intelligence" on civil disorders for the benefit of cops, public officials and the National Guard. Then Dr. William W. Herrmann, chairman of CCCJ's task force on riots and disorders, made the mistake of giving a silly interview to the *Los Angeles Times. A retired Los Angeles policeman, Dr. Herrman is a "counterinsurgency specialist" for System Development Corporation, a think tank which does much military work.* Herrmann told the *Times* that a good computer intelligence system would "*separate out* the avowed dedicated activists bent on destroying the system," then find programs "to win the hearts and minds of the people." To Californians, Herrmann's ideas sounded too much like what the U.S. military has been trying on the South Vietnamese this past decade, and they raised such a fuss that Governor Reagan told the military to drop the project. Still alive, however, is a scheme of the Los Angeles police department (which wants $681,000 in LEAA money) to "develop 'intelligence' indicators of social and community problems that may lead to trouble. . . . This requires a center for receiving, analyzing and interpreting many different and diverse sources of information that might aid materially in the diagnosis of the build-up of social pressures that could possibly lead to a civil disturbance."

An Eye on Us All

. . . Another form of electronic apparatus, equally popular with technology-minded cops, poses a more immediate threat to the privacy of citizens. As is true with much of the new crime-fighting gear being developed in LEAA projects, the stated purpose is laudable; the byproduct is sobering. The equipment in question is cameras—still, movie and television—operated from surreptitious locations as a substitute for or adjunct to police patrols. They are intended to record activities of criminals; unfortunately, they also catch the innocent.

On June 30, LEAA awarded $150,000 to the Delaware Agency to Prevent Crime (that state's SPA) to create a special twenty-five-man unit to combat street crime. Much of the money is to go for equipment that will permit officers to make surreptitious nighttime movies and video tapes. One TV system includes an infrared zoom lens ($3,300); a video recorder capable of preserving infrared pictures ($2,000), and a searchlight with an infrared converter "to use when no light is available" ($500). The grant includes $3,800 for rentals of civilian trucks for the police.

> [The rental trucks] are to be used as the basis on which patrol is to be conducted under covert conditions: e.g., uniforms of dry cleaners, salesmen, public utilities, etc., make it possible to be in a neighborhood without being obvious.
>
> [The infrared equipment] will make nighttime and daytime surveillance of persons and places possible without disclosing the fact that this is being done.
>
> [The photographic and TV equipment] will be used by the patrolling forces to take pictures of persons whose activities are suspicious in nature, and of groups and activities whose nature dictates that police incidents may occur as a result thereof; e.g., if a mugging should occur, pictures taken in the area and about the time of occurrence will be shown to victims. At times, TV pictures will be required; at other times, simple photography will suffice.

In addition to the rented civilian trucks the Wilmington police are also buying an "anti-sniper van" which has photography portholes. In the van are to be four AR-18 .223 caliber rifles, four twelve-gauge shotguns and four .243 caliber carbines, and three tear gas kits, purchased at a cost to LEAA of $2,120. LEAA is also buying the Wilmington cops 1,750 rounds of rifle bullets and 250 rounds of double-ought buckshot, known to law-enforcement specialists as a "killer load."

The Delaware Agency to Prevent Crime sees no invasion of privacy in use of the covert equipment. Indeed, it expects a "significant deterrent impact" on crime "without breaching constitutional guarantees," because police will be able to saturate high-crime areas without being visible. The grant application quotes a finding by the President's Crime Commission that one of five persons frisked on public streets is apt to be armed. "The police cannot afford to make four enemies for every 'hit' in the ghetto area" of Wilmington, the agency wrote. "More aggressive patrol in the traditional sense is unacceptable to a large segment of citizens as involving unwarranted invasion of privacy. Aggressive patrol aggravates community resentment, which in turn offsets the deterrent influence over the very behavior this type of patrol was intended to accomplish." The prospectus does not discuss community attitudes toward covert surveillance.

A *surveillance system* being developed in Tampa, Fla., uses computers to control a network of video tape recorders and alarms placed in "convenience" grocery stores, overlooking parking lots, and atop warehouses in high-crime areas. STAVS (for sensitized transmitted alarm video system) is an expanded version of the cameras long used by banks. According to Florida's prospectus, no pictures actually will be made unless a crime is attempted. Activation of the camera then causes broadcast of a prerecorded radio signal to roaming squad cars or helicopters. A high-intensity light comes on atop the target building. The Florida prospectus states:

> The possibility of immediate apprehension of a criminal while in commission of a crime is the ultimate of evidence for prosecution. In the event im-

> mediate apprehension is not effected, then the [police] department would have video tape evidence of the crime and positive identification of the culprit while in the act of committing the crime.

Tampa police said they realized that "the use of the STAVS would be publicly known after it has been in operation for some time." Nonetheless, they said, the fact that the unit is compact, "affording efficient installation and secretiveness," means that "a potential criminal would have no knowledge as to which establishment has a STAVS unit installed in it." A central monitor, installed at police headquarters, will enable officers to observe what is happening in some fifty Tampa locations—without ringing bells to alarm the populace.

Tampa citizens will also be subject to covert surveillance even before they enter a business house. The Florida plan states: "The video-recording camera is installed overlooking a shopping center parking lot. The camera surveillance is watched on monitors. When suspicious activity occurs, the operator can utilize the affected camera's zoom lens for a close-up. . . ."

Arresting the Symptoms

Judge A. Leon Higginbotham, Jr., vice chairman of the National Commission on the Causes and Prevention of Violence, criticized LEAA's civil disorders work before a House subcommittee last spring. He expressed "great fear . . . that we get more expertise on getting Mace and riot guns than we have on community relations." He noted that the Safe Streets Act "gives a disproportionate advantage if you are chasing riot equipment than if you are working on community relations. I think that somehow or other we have to start turning the corner on that point."

Yet LEAA has been moving in exactly the opposite direction, and at an accelerating pace the past four months, for these reasons:

The troika ruling LEAA could not agree on broad program approaches. Coster and Velde are hard-nosed about unrest; their immediate interest is to develop a police ability to curb disturbances, rather than to develop long-range community relations projects. Rogovin, while administrator, took an opposite stance, and they were in a stalemate. "Charlie fought, and lost, some of his biggest battles in trying to get disorders programs approved," says a close observer. And many of his victories are being reversed, now that he is out of LEAA. For instance, there was for a time a pilot project to give police sensitivity training. "Coster saw no sense in this whatsoever, and he wouldn't let it continue," says a person now out of LEAA.

The Justice Department's Community Relations Service, in an unpublished critique circulated last summer, blamed the predominance of police on state and regional planning boards for the slipshod programs drafted by the states. Quotations from two CRS consultants in the Midwest are illustrative:

> This program is a one-way street. Demands will be made of citizens. However, there are no admonitions or demands placed upon law-enforcement officials to deal constructively . . . and justly with citizens. . . .
>
> There has been no input from minorities. Crime tremendously affects minorities and jeopardizes the health of these communities.

In 1969 riot-jittery states made heavy allocations of Safe Streets funds for prevention and control of civil disorders—*22.5¢* of every dollar. A special section of the Safe Streets Act directed LEAA to make riot grants in advance of approval of state comprehensive plans—a means of getting equipment to cops in a hurry. And much of these funds went for hardware items—tear gas, firearms, protective gear, floodlights, Louisiana's tank (described officially as a command-and-control vehicle). Once the police were armed, however, state interest in civil disorders dropped markedly. In fiscal 1970 the states allocated only 3.9 per cent of their block-grant money for civil disorders. "It's easier to buy a bunch of gas cannisters and masks than to find a sensible way to spend civil disorders money," said an official in LEAA's Western regional office. Yet enough riot money remains to make LEAA a minor bonanza for police hardware manufacturers. . . .

The Price of Safety

During the past two years the police have demonstrated that money for training and equipment can give them technical and tactical expertise—the basic professionalism in physical skills that army recruits attain in advanced infantry school. And now that the scientists are sniffing around law enforcement, the level of police technology is due for a quantum jump. More and more cops will be attending criminology classes and advanced professional programs under LEAA sponsorship (if only to get away from home for a few weeks), and the universities are recognizing law enforcement as a new area of grantsmanship. (However, Police Chief James Ahern of New Haven, Conn., says this program has "resulted in . . . a crop of new courses designed more to attract federal dollars than to be relevant to the student's needs. The money spent on those efforts has produced a second-rate system that has more training than education. In fact, the police science courses supported have tended to segregate police on campuses and limit severely their educational experience.")

The American people deserve something better for their money. The various Presidential commissions of the mid-1960s—crime, Kerner and violence—said quite specifically that the basic structure of the police agencies is unsound, a condition demonstrated through their failure to perform their basic mission. Nonetheless, LEAA is devoting its energy (and great sums of money) to buttressing up the existing institution, rather than stepping back for a critical look and asking, "Shouldn't we start from the ground up?"

An example: Asked for a concrete accomplishment of LEAA, Associate Director Coster points to the District of Columbia, whose crime rate has dropped during the past year. LEAA's role was to supply money to increase the police force by 1,000 to 5,100. The conditions that caused the crime remain untouched.

Edward T. Anderson, of the Friends Committee on National Legislation, suggests a different role for the federal government:

> The LEAA, instead of encouraging the formation of a dangerous national system of communications and interlocking computer banks, should rather be acting to force entrenched white-dominated police departments to give up some of their monopolistic power of life and death over poor and black and radical youth, so that power be responsible and tempered, not repressive and brutal. The struggle is already on between aggrieved local groups and the police. The LEAA must mediate and lead in this, not encourage the excesses of those in power now.

"The LEAA program has no place for anyone with dreams of repression," Richard Velde told an IACP meeting in 1969. "It is designed to make a safer America, a more just America for everybody—black and white, poor and rich." But LEAA has chosen sides; it is a program for cops, not for criminal justice, and the men in charge are insuring that it remains just that.

II

POLICING THE EMPIRE

In order to fully understand the police in the United States it is necessary to examine the police within an international context; the interrelationship between U.S. imperialism and the export of police advisors and equipment must be made explicit. The changing nature of imperialism, from the wholesale domination of foreign countries to more covert control, has not altered the essential economic basis of imperialism. The demands for enlarged consumer markets, low production costs through the use of cheap foreign labor, and increased economic dependency of Third World countries on the U.S. continues. The protection of the dominant position and the security of financial investments are imperatives of American imperialism.[1] Covert domination and control does not reduce the pervasiveness of this dependency. Manipulation of the international market through foreign policies and foreign aid programs facilitates and maintains dependency relationships,[2] protecting the economic and political investments of the United States. This protection takes different forms, varying according to the specific circumstances of individual African, Asian, Middle Eastern, and Latin American countries.

In Vietnam the response has been a full-scale commitment of armed forces; in Latin America, the Near East, and Africa the commitment has generally been much more subtle, taking the form of police and military advisors, special training for local police, providing a variety of sophisticated equipment, and designing programs for the individual needs of the countries.

One of the major conduits for funneling money, arms, and advisors into counterinsurgency operations, has been the Office of Public Safety (OPS).

1 Harry Magdoff, *The Age of Imperialism* (New York: Monthly Review Press, 1969), and "Imperialism: A Historical Survey," *Monthly Review* (May, 1972); see also K. T. Fann and Donald C. Hodges, eds., *Readings in U.S. Imperialism* (Boston: Porter Sargent Publisher, 1971).

2 See, for example, Susanne Bodenheimer, "Dependency and Imperialism: The Roots of Latin American Underdevelopment," and Theotonion Dos Santos, "The Structure of Dependency," in Fann and Hodges, loc. cit.

In 1962, OPS was expanded from a relatively small program of police assistance into one of the most powerful departments within the Agency of International Development (AID). OPS was given major responsibilitites for protecting the various overseas investments of the United States. With authorization and funding from Congress, OPS received an operating budget of $26 million for 1971–72.[3]

AID has described its policy of assistance to civil security forces, as administered through the OPS.

> Plainly, the U.S. has very great interests in the creation and maintenance of an atmosphere of law and order under humane, civil concepts, and control, in countering Communist efforts in all forms. When there is a need, technical assistance to the police of developing nations to meet their responsibilities promotes and protects these U.S. interests. This is the function of the AID Public Safety Program . . .[4]

Much of the money and equipment supplied by OPS is awarded to the police of designated countries.

> Arguing that the police constitute the "first line of defense" against insurgency and subversion, the United States has established a massive program of police assistance closely paralleling the military assistance program. Between 1961 and 1969, the U.S. spent over $236 million on this program to provide Third World police forces with modern communication equipment, intelligence systems and anti-riot gear.[5]

Mike Klare points out that Latin America alone has received approximately $29 million from OPS. Vietnam has received over half of OPS's annual budget, and since 1955, a steady supply of advisors and technicians. Between 1961 and 1969, countries in Africa received a total of $19,155 in police assistance. During that same period, countries in the Near East (Greece, Iran, Jordan, Lebanon, Pakistan, and Turkey) received $12,873 from OPS.[6]

The Vietnamese National Police, with arbitrary powers of arrest, imprisonment and torture, were primarily organized, trained and armed by OPS. The OPS-designed program of national registration for the Vietnamese people resulted in a totalitarian apparatus of population control,

[3] "A.I.D. Police Programs for Latin America 1971–72," *NACLA Newsletter* 5, no. 4 (July–August, 1971): 4.

[4] "A.I.D. Assistance to Civil Security Forces," *NACLA Newsletter* 6, no. 5 (September, 1970): 22.

[5] Mike Klare, "The Mercenarization of the Third World: U.S. Military and Police Assistance Programs," *U.S. Military and Police Operations in the Third World* (Berkeley: North American Congress on Latin America, 1970), p. 21.

[6] Joe Stork, "World Cop: How America Builds The Global Police State," *Hard Times* (August 10–17, 1970), p. 2.

as well as a multi-million dollar contract for Systems Development Corporation of Santa Monica, California.[7]

In Latin America the programs and advisors of OPS, while teaching torture techniques,[8] help to protect the interests of the United Fruit Company in Guatemala, Standard Oil and Gulf in Venezuela, and International Telephone and Telegraph Corporation in Brazil. The four Latin American countries receiving the largest U.S. police-aid grants in 1970—Guatemala, Brazil, Uruguay, and the Dominican Republic—have powerful right-wing terrorist groups. These quasi-clandestine groups, frequently working in conjunction with the police, beat, torture, and assassinate local subversives. The "Death Squad" in Brazil killed an estimated 500 to 1000 people between 1964 and 1970. The *Miami Herald* quoted a Brazilian judge's description of the 'Death Squad': "The members of the Death Squad are policemen . . . and everyone knows it." [9]

In Uruguay, February 1972, a police intelligence agent, Nelson Bardesio, was kidnapped by the Tupamaro guerrillas. Bardesio made detailed statements about the use and operations of the Uruguayan death squadron. He identified three of the principal organizers of the group: "Oscar Delegaa, a police subcommissioner who worked with the Office of Information and Intelligence; Navy Captain Ernesto Motto Benvenuto; and former Under Secretary of the Interior Armando Acosta y Lara." [10] Bardesio also described various death squadron attacks of which he had been a part.

In Guatemala one OPS project described its goal: "To promote a stable environment conducive to orderly social, political, and economical development in Guatemala." This would be primarily accomplished by improving the capabilities of the police to fight insurgency and terrorism.[11]

OPS officials in Venezuela had very friendly relations with various corporations located there. These "officers meet monthly with private security companies and officers of the oil firms and mining companies for dealing with insurgency and guerrilla warfare; therefore, playing a direct role in protecting selected private sectors of the economy and in determining military policy." [12]

The militarization of Costa Rica has taken place primarily under the direction of OPS. Prior to 1966, Costa Rica had a small police organiza-

[7] Ibid.

[8] "Para-Police Terror Squads," *NACLA Newsletter* 5, no. 4 (July–August, 1971): 7.

[9] Ibid.

[10] "Uruguay Police Agent Exposes U.S. Advisors," *NACLA's Latin American and Empire Report* 6, no. 6 (July–August, 1972): 20.

[11] "Summary of FY 1972 Program by Function," *NACLA Newsletter* 5, no. 4 (July–August, 1971): 24.

[12] Nancy Stein, "Command and Control: U.S. Police Operations in Latin America," *NACLA Newsletter* 6, no. 1 (January, 1972): 15.

tion and no standing army. Since 1966, the police have been restructured and enlarged, primarily through the efforts of AID. The majority of the Costa Rican high-level police officers have been trained by the United States, with a special emphasis on counterinsurgency operations.[13]

An important aspect in the export of law and order is police training. Much of this training takes place at the International Police Academy (IPA), conveniently located in Washington, D.C. According to Joe Stork, by 1970 over 3,000 high ranking foreign police officers had been trained at the Academy. Learning a strong pro-American ideology, high-level police commanders can take a course in "police organization, management, operation, planning, and research; communications, investigation, and counterinsurgency." Middle-level police commanders take a more general course that covers topics such as: "police administration, organization and operations; internal security; counter-insurgency and counter subversion, riot control; scientific and technical aids; firearms, narcotics law enforcement; border patrol, and customs." This course is offered in Spanish, English, and French.[14]

The main objectives of this program, in the language of AID's 1971–2 Police Plan, are "to strengthen the capability of civil police and para-military forces to enforce the law and maintain public order with the minimum use of physical force, and to counter Communist inspired or exploited subversion and insurgency." [15] With the growth of revolutionary movements around the world and the ineffectiveness of massive military intervention, the police are now looked upon as the first line of defense. According to General Maxwell Taylor, speaking at the 1965 graduation exercises of the IPA, "the outstanding lesson [of Vietnam] is that we should never let another Vietnam-type situation arise again. We were too late in recognizing the extent of the subversive threat. . . . We have learned the need for a strong police force and strong police intelligence organization to assist in identifying early the symptoms of an incipient subversive situation." [16]

The United States export of police, primarily through the OPS, has a two-fold purpose. On the one hand, it provides a viable and absolutely necessary means for protecting American investments and influencing foreign policy favorable to the United States. On the other hand, the experiences and practices of counterinsurgency programs abroad can be quickly translated and imported for domestic use. As Mike Klare noted, "[f]rom a military point of view, counterinsurgency in U.S. ghettoes poses the same problems as counterinsurgency in any hostile environment in

[13] John Saxe-Fernandez, "The Militarization of Costa Rica," *Monthly Review* 24, no. 1 (May 1972): 60–70.

[14] "Police Training Centers in the U.S.," *U.S. Military and Police Operations in the Third World* (Berkeley: North American Congress on Latin America, 1970), p. 23.

[15] "A.I.D. Police Programs for Latin America 1971–72," op. cit., p. 13.

[16] Ibid., p. 2.

which the occupational forces are outnumbered by potential insurgents."[17] The hostile environment ranges from Vietnam, Cambodia, and Uruguay to Watts, Detroit, and Harlem. In the final analysis, programs such as OPS are doomed to failure because they underestimate the pervasiveness of popular resistance and the growing determination of oppressed people to create a system of government and justice which is responsive to their needs.

Suggested Readings

"A.I.D. Police Programs for Latin America." *NACLA Newsletter* 5, no. 4 (July–August, 1971): 1–31.

FANN, K. T. and HODGES, DONALD, eds. *Readings in U.S. Imperialism.* Boston: Porter Sargent Publisher, 1971.

GOULDEN, JOSEPH. "Guatemala: Terror in Silence." *The Nation,* March 22, 1971, pp. 365–68.

GREEN, FELIX. *The Enemy: What Every American Should Know About Imperialism.* New York: Vintage Books, 1971.

KLARE, MICHAEL T. *War Without End: American Planning for the Next Vietnams.* New York: Knopf, 1972.

Middle East Research and Information Project. *U.S. and Jordan: The Trice-Rescued Throne* (February 1972).

PORTER, D. GARETH. "Saigon's Secret Police." *The Nation,* April 27, 1970, pp. 498–500.

ROCKEFELLER, NELSON. *Rockefeller Report on the Americas: Official Report of a Presidential Mission for the Western Hemisphere.* Chicago: Quadrangle, 1969.

SANFORD, DAVID. "Agitators in a Fertilizer Factory." *New Republic,* February 11, 1967, pp. 16–18.

"Uruguay Police Agent Exposes U.S. Advisors." *NACLA's Latin American and Empire Report* 6, no. 6 (July–August, 1972): 20.

U.S. Military and Police Operations in the Third World. Berkeley: North American Congress on Latin America, 1970.

[17] Mike Klare, "Bringing It Back: Planning for the City," *Police on the Homefront,* op. cit., p. 68.

MICHAEL T. KLARE

Policing the Empire

The now familiar panacea for domestic ills, "law and order," has long been used to describe American objectives in the troubled areas of Africa, Asia and Latin America. While the Federal Government did not start aiding local U.S. police agencies until 1968 (under the Omnibus Crime Control and Safe Street Act), we have been supplying the police of selected underdeveloped nations with equipment, arms and training since 1954. U.S. funds have been used to construct the National Police Academy of Brazil, to renovate and expand the South Vietnamese prison system, and to install a national police communications network in Colombia. The Agency for International Development (AID) estimates that over one million foreign policemen have received some training or supplies through the U.S. "Public Safety" program—a figure which includes 100,000 Brazilian police and the entire 85,000-man National Police Force of South Vietnam.

U.S. foreign aid programs in the underdeveloped "Third World" call for a modest acceleration of economic growth, to be achieved wherever possible through the normal profit-making activities of U.S. corporations and lending institutions. It is obvious, however, that an atmosphere of insecurity and rebelliousness does not provide an attractive climate for investment. In the rapidly urbanizing nations of the Third World, civil disorders have become a common phenomenon as landless peasants stream to the cities in search of economic and cultural opportunities. Since most of these countries cannot satisfy the aspirations of these new city-dwellers under present economic and social systems, built-up tensions are increasingly giving way to attacks on the status quo. After his 1969 tour of Latin America, Nelson Rockefeller noted in his report to the President that while Latin armies "have gradually improved their capabilities for dealing with Castro-type agrarian guerrillas," it appeared that

---

From Commonweal, *September 18, 1970, pp. 456–61. Reprinted with permission of the author and publisher. Michael T. Klare is a staff member of North American Congress on Latin America (NACLA), and author of* War Without End: American Planning for the Next Vietnams *(New York: Knopf, 1972).*

"radical revolutionary elements in the hemisphere [are] increasingly turning toward urban terrorism in their attempts to bring down the existing order." This prediction has already been borne out in Brazil and Uruguay, where urban guerrillas have staged spectacular bank robberies and kidnappings.

Since the late 1950's a paramount concern of American policymakers has been the preservation of social stability in countries deemed favorable to U.S. trade and investment. U.S. military planning has been shaped by the need to provide, on a moment's notice, trained counterinsurgency forces that can be flown to the aid of friendly regimes threatened by popular insurrection. The Military Assistance Program has been used to upgrade the capabilities of indigenous forces to overcome rural guerrilla forces. Finally, on the premise that the police constitute the "first line of defense against subversion," the Agency for International Development has funneled American funds and supplies into the hands of Third World police forces.

During hearings on the foreign assistance appropriations for 1965, AID Administrator David Bell described the rationale behind U.S. police assistance programs as follows:

> Maintenance of law and order including internal security is one of the fundamental responsibilities of government . . . .
>
> Successful discharge of this responsibility is imperative if a nation is to establish and maintain the environment of stability and security so essential to economic, social, and political progress . . . .
>
> Plainly, the United States has very great interests in the creation and maintenance of an atmosphere of law and order under humane, civil concepts and control . . . When there is a need, technical assistance to the police of developing nations to meet their responsibilities promotes and protects these U.S. interests.

The Public Safety program is not large in comparison to the military aid program—but its supporters can muster some impressive arguments in its favor. It is argued, for instance, that the police—being interspersed among the population—are more effective than the military in controlling low-scale insurgency. Supporters of the police assistance program also point out that police forces are cheaper to maintain than military forces, since they do not require expensive "hardware" like planes, tanks and artillery.

These arguments, advanced by men like Col. Edward Lansdale of the CIA, received their most favorable response from President John F. Kennedy and his brother Robert, then the Attorney General, in the early 1960's. Presidential backing was responsible for a substantial expansion of the Public Safety program in 1962, and for the centralization of all U.S. police assistance activities in AID's Office of Public Safety (OPS). The State Department memorandum establishing OPS is noteworthy for its strong language—the memo, issued in November 1962, declared that AID "vests the Office of Public Safety with primary responsibility and authority for public safety programs and gives that Office a series of powers and responsibilities which will enable it to act rapidly, vigorously, and effectively. . . . powers greater than any other technical office or division of AID." The two Kennedys also gave enthusiastic support to the creation of an Inter-American Police Academy in the Panama Canal Zone. (In order to open the Academy to police officers from other countries, it was later moved to Washington, D.C. and reorganized as the International Police Academy.)

The Office of Public Safety is empowered to assist Third World police organizations in three ways: (1) by sending "Public Safety Advisors" who provide "in-country" training for rank-and-file policemen; (2) by providing training at the International Police Academy and other U.S. schools for senior police officers and technicians; and (3) by shipping weapons, ammunition, radios, patrol cars, jeeps, chemical munitions and related equipment.

Using Latin America to measure the scope of these activities, we find that 90 Public Safety Advisors are stationed in 15 countries, and that some 2,000 Latin police officers have received training at the International Police Academy. Total OPS expenditures in these 15 countries reached an estimated $39 million by July 1, 1970 (outlays in individual countries ranged from the $1–$2 million spent in Bolivia, Costa Rica, El Salvador, Guyana, Honduras, Uruguay and Venezuela, to $3 to $4 million subsidies to Colombia, the Dominican Republic, Ecuador, Panama and Peru). The leading beneficiary of the Public Safety program in Latin America was Brazil, which received $7.5 million in OPS funds by the middle of 1970. AID's *Program and Project Data Presentations to the Congress for Fiscal Year 1971* noted that "through December 1969, the Public Safety project in Brazil has assisted in training locally over 100,000 federal and state police personnel. Additionally, 523 persons received training in the U.S." The AID document added that the project "has supported a substantial increase in police telecommunications" and that "substantial increases in police mobility have been achieved, primarily through funding for Brazilian manufactured vehicles."

In providing this kind of assistance, OPS notes that most countries possess a unified 'civil security service' which, "in addition to regular police include paramilitary units within civil police organizations and paramilitary forces such as gendarmeries, constabularies, and civil guards which perform police functions and have as their primary mission maintaining internal security." The AID program is designed to encompass all of these functions. According to OPS:

> Individual Public Safety programs, while varying from country to country, are focused in general on developing within the civil security forces a bal-

ance of (1) a capability for regular police operations, with (2) an investigative capability for detecting and identifying criminal and/or subversive individuals and organizations and neutralizing their activities, and with (3) a capability for controlling militant activities ranging from demonstrations, disorders, or riots through small-scale guerrilla operations.

As noted in the 1962 State Department memo, OPS possesses unique powers not granted to other AID bureaus. These powers enable OPS to "act rapidly, vigorously and effectively" in aiding Latin regimes threatened by popular uprisings. When a crisis develops in a Latin capital, OPS officials often stay up "night after night" in their Washington, D.C., office to insure that needed supplies—including radios and tear gas—reach the beleaguered police of the friendly regime.

Several instances of such rapid action by OPS can be identified. In 1962, when the government of Venezuela (then headed by President Romulu Betancourt) came under heavy pressure from urban guerrillas of the Armed Forces of National Liberation (FALN), President Kennedy launched a crash program to improve police operations in Caracas. A Public Safety Advisor named John Longan was secretly flown into the Venezuelan capital to head a team of police instructors. Using techniques developed by Special Forces instructors, Longan and his assistants provided Venezulan police with intensive training in riot-control operations. According to Peter T. Chew, a journalist sympathetic to OPS, Longan's men "persuaded Venezuelan police to favor the old-fashioned shotgun and showed how shotguns, firing buck-shot and gas grenades, could be effectively used against terrorists." OPS advisors were also brought into the Dominican Republic after the 1965 insurrection to give crash courses in crowd-control techniques. In the space of a few months, thousands of Dominican police were schooled in the handling of anti-riot chemical agents, large quantities of which were presumably supplied by AID.

AID officials insist that Public Safety assistance is "not given to support dictatorships." But there *are* apparently exceptions to this rule: Administrator Bell told a Senate Committee in 1965 that "it is obviously not our purpose or intent to assist a head of state who is repressive. On the other hand, we are working in a lot of countries where the governments are controlled by people who have shortcomings." Not wanting to embarrass AID or any of the people we support who have "shortcomings," Bell did not mention names.

It is entirely possible that one country Bell was referring to is Brazil—a country which enjoys a substantial OPS contribution despite well-documented reports that political prisoners are regularly being tortured by the police. In justifying continued OPS aid to such regimes, Bell explained that ". . . the police are a strongly anti-Communist force right now. For that reason it is a very important force to us." It is no surprise that these men should consider a small amount of (allegedly) Communist-led terrorism to be sufficient reason to subsidize the repressive apparatus of a totalitarian regime.

AID officials are fully aware that in many countries receiving OPS aid the police are regarded with suspicion and resentment by the native population because of a tradition of brutality and oppression. Since provocative police behavior frequently inspires anti-government campaigns, "the development of responsible and humane police administration and judicial procedures" is an important aspect of the Public Safety program. Students at the various OPS schools are advised to "stay out of politics" (i.e., to support whatever regime happens to be in power), and are trained in the techniques of "non-lethal crowd control" (i.e., the massive use of riot gases). The main objective of this approach, according to OPS Director Byron Engle, is to prevent situations in which "an oppressive police force drives a deep wedge between the people and their government." As a successful application of this philosophy, OPS cites the case of the Dominican Republic, where—after intensive training in the use of chemical agents—"police action against the Communists was so effective that the insurgents did not even end up with the body of a dead comrade to drag through the city in false martyrdom."

"Public Safety" in Vietnam

The Public Safety program in South Vietnam is the largest and one of the oldest U.S. police assistance programs—half of AID's Public Safety Advisors and more than half of OPS's annual budget are committed to Vietnam operations. The Vietnam program began in 1955, when Michigan State University received a contract from the International Cooperation Administration (AID's predecessor agency) to assemble a team of police experts to advise the government of Ngo Dinh Diem. Ultimately 33 advisors served in the Police Division of the now famous Michigan State University Group (MSUG); of this group, at least a few are known to have been CIA agents. The police division supervised the reorganization of Vietnam's decrepit police system, provided training in a variety of police skills, provided small arms and ammunition, and helped establish a modern records system for filing data on political suspects.

The MSUG effort was superseded in 1959 by a Public Safety Division (PSD) under direct U.S. management. In keeping with President Kennedy's call for increased counterinsurgency initiatives, the program was vastly expanded in 1962. Beginning with a staff of six in 1959, the PSD mission in Vietnam increased to 47 in 1963, and to 204 by mid-1968. Total support of the PSD program had reached $95,417,000 by the end of fiscal year 1968, and has continued at the rate of about $20 million a year;

(some of these funds are supplied by the Department of Defense rather than by AID).

From the very start of the Vietnam conflict, the National Police (NP) of South Vietnam has been regarded by our government as a paramilitary force with certain responsibilities related to the overall counterinsurgency effort. In the Foreword to a manual on *The Police and Resources Control in Counter-Insurgency* (Saigon, 1964), Chief Frank E. Walton wrote that "the methods included in this text are emergency procedures not utilized in a normal peace-time situation. They are stringent, *war-time* measures designed to assist in defeating the enemy . . ." In order to upgrade Vietnamese police capabilities to carry out its wartime responsibilities, PSD supervised the consolidation of all regional, provincial and specialized police agencies under the directorate of National Police in 1962, and subsequently prepared a "National Police Plan" for Vietnam in 1964. Under the plan, the NP's personnel strength grew from 19,000 men in 1963 to 52,000 by the end of 1965, 70,000 in 1967, and 85,000 by the end of 1969. To keep pace with this rapid growth, the plan provided for a vast increase in U.S. technical assistance, training and commodity support. Public Safety Division aid and management have become so extensive, that the National Police might more properly be considered a U.S. mercenary force than an indigenous institution.

Specific Functions

The specific counterinsurgency functions performed by the police—resources control, identification, surveillance and pacification—are spelled out in an OPS brochure on *The Role of the Public Safety in Support of the National Police of Vietnam* (Washington, D.C., 1969), and in AID's *Program and Project Data Presentations to the Congress for Fiscal Year 1971.*

Resources Control is defined by Public Safety Advisor E. H. Adkins Jr. as "an effort to regulate the movement of selected resources, both human and material, in order to restrict the enemy's support or deprive him of it altogether . . ." In order to prevent the flow of supplies and people to and from villages loyal to the National Liberation Front (NLF), 7,700 members of the National Police currently man some 650 checkpoints at key locations on roadways and waterways, and operate mobile checkpoints on remote roads and trails. By 1968, more than 468,456 persons had been arrested in this program, of whom 28,000 were reported as "VC suspects." AID reported that "Resources control efforts in 1969 resulted in nearly 100,000 arrests including more than 10,000 known or suspected VC. Confiscations included 50,000 units of medicine/drugs and 6,000 tons of contraband foodstuffs."

The *National Identity Registration Program* is described by OPS as "an integral part of the population and resources control program." Under a 1957 law, amended in 1967, every Vietnamese 15 years and older is required to register with the Saigon government and carry identification cards; anyone caught without the proper ID cards is considered a "VC suspect" and subject to imprisonment or worse. At the time of registration, a full set of fingerprints is obtained from each applicant, and information on his or her political beliefs is recorded. By 1971, 12,000,000 persons are to have been reached by this identification/registration program. "Once completed," AID explains, "the identification system will provide for a national repository of fingerprints and photographs and biographical data. It will be one of the most complete national identification systems in the world, and one of the most badly needed."

Surveillance of persons and organizations suspected of harboring anti-government sentiments is the responsibility of the NP's Special Police Branch (SP). The Special Branch is nothing more or less than Vietnam's secret police; originally the Indo-Chinese branch of the French *Surété*, the SP was known as the Vietnamese Bureau of Investigation during the Diem regime. According to the 1962 decree establishing the National Police, the SP was given the responsibilities of: "Gathering information on political activities," and "carrying out undercover operations throughout the country, searching for, investigating, keeping track of, and prosecuting elements indulged in subversive activities." OPS documents state that "SP agents penetrate subversive organizations," and "use intelligence collection, political data [and] dossiers compiled from census data . . . to separate the bad guys from the good." AID has nothing to say about the criteria used to separate the "bad guys" from the "good guys"; anyone familiar with the Vietnamese scene knows, however, that the SP's major responsibility is surveillance of non-Communist groups that could pose a political challenge to the regime in power. Persons who advocate negotiations with the NLF are routinely picked up by the Special Police and sentenced to stiff prison terms.

Pacification usually brings to mind "good-will" projects like school construction and free medical care; in Vietnam, however, the paramount task of the U.S. pacification effort is the identification and neutralization of the local NLF administrative apparatus—in Pentagon nomenclature, the "Viet Cong Infrastructure" (VCI). The counter-infrastructure campaign was initiated by the CIA in July 1968 as the "Phung Hoang" program—better known in English as Operation Phoenix. This program, incorporated into the Civil Operations and Revolutionary Development Support (CORDS) effort, is described by American officials as "a systematic effort at intelligence coordination and exploitation." In the *intelligence* phase, all allied intelligence services—including South Vietnam's Special Police Branch and America's CIA and military intelligence organizations

—are supposed to pool the data they have collected (or forcibly extracted) from informers and prisoners on the identity of NLF cadres. It is for this ultimate purpose that most of the other police functions described above —interdiction, identification, registration and surveillance—are carried on. In the *exploitation* phase of Phoenix, members of the paramilitary National Police Field Forces, sometimes assisted by the Army, make secret, small-scale raids into contested areas to seize or eliminate persons who have been identified by the intelligence services as "VCI agents." In testimony before the Senate Foreign Relations Committee, the head of CORDS, ex-CIA agent William E. Colby stated that in 1969 a total of 19,534 suspected VCI agents had been "neutralized"—of this amount 6,187 had been killed, 8,515 arrested, and 4,832 persuaded to join the Saigon side. Colby insisted that Phoenix did not constitute an "assassination" or "counter-terror" operation.

Each of the counterinsurgency programs described has been accompanied by an expansion of the prison population of South Vietnam. Since prison management is considered a major task of the overall police responsibility, the U.S. Public Safety program includes substantial assistance to the Directorate of Corrections—the Saigon agency ultimately responsible for the operation of South Vietnam's 41 civil prisons. U.S. aid has enabled the Directorate to enlarge the prison system from its 1967 capacity of 20,000 prisoners to the present capacity of 33,435 inmates.

From 1967–1969, OPS expenditures in support of prison maintenance have totaled $1.6 million. Specific project targets in 1969, according to AID's *Program and Project Data Presentations to the Congress,* include: "The renovation and expansion of selected correction centers, the addition of up to 1,000 trained personnel to administer correction centers . . . and the implementation of a plan for relocating prisoners in order to reduce overcrowding and provide greater security from VC attacks." To achieve these targets, "AID will provide technical advisors to help supervise relocations and to train new recruits . . . [and] will provide supplies for prison security . . ." One of the facilities selected for the relocation program was the dread prison of Con Son Island with its now-notorious "tiger cages."

In order to upgrade the administrative capabilities of the Corrections Directorate, AID regularly provides training to Vietnamese prison officials "outside of Vietnam." Although AID does not divulge any details, the ten officials receiving such training in fiscal year 1969 are probably among the 60 Vietnamese police officers brought to the U.S. to attend special courses. According to the AID manual on *Public Safety Training,* foreign police personnel can attend an 18-week course in "Penology and Corrections" at Southern Illinois University in Carbondale. The Southern Illinois program includes instruction in such topics as: "disposition of convicted offenders and juveniles; philosophy and practice of correctional institutional management; methods of correctional staff training and development." The program also includes a course on "Correctional Institute Design and Construction."

One begins to appreciate the breadth of the Vietnam program by reading AID's 1971 budget request—$13 million is being sought to achieve the following "Project Targets":

> . . . provision of commodity and advisory support for a police force of 108,000 men by the end of FY 1971; . . . assisting the National Identity Registration Program (NIRP) to register more than 12,000,000 persons 15 years of age and over by the end of 1971; continuing to provide basic and specialized training for approximately 40,000 police annually; providing technical assistance to the police detention system including planning and supervision of the construction of facilities for an additional 8,000 inmates during 1970; and helping to achieve a major increase in the number of police presently working (6,000) at the village level.

This presentation, it must be remembered, only represents programs under AID authority; missing from this prospectus are NP activities financed by the CIA and the Defense Department. Military Assistance funds are used to finance the activities of the paramilitary National Police Field Forces (NPFF), which, by January 1969, constituted a small army of 12,000 men organized into 75 companies (our expansion plans call for a total complement of 22,500 men and 108 companies by the end of 1970). Because of the "military commonality" of their equipment, all commodities support to the NPFF is provided by the Pentagon. The extent of CIA contributions to the National Police is of course impossible to determine; it is known, however, that the CIA has been involved in modernizing Vietnam's secret police files since 1955. One does not have to invoke the sinister image of the CIA, however, to establish beyond a doubt that the United States is intimately involved in every barbarous act committed by the South Vietnamese police on behalf of the Saigon government.

At Home Application

In studying the U.S. Public Safety program abroad, one is sooner or later struck by the extent to which the goals, doctrines and practices of this program have been adopted by the authorities here as an answer to our own internal difficulties. Thus when Administrator Bell tells us that "public safety forces have done and can do much to prevent conspiracy and the development of disruptive situations, and to insure an environment of law and order which supports the orderly social, economic, and political development of emerging nations," one can easily picture Ronald Reagan or Spiro Agnew speaking in the same terms of our own police apparatus. AID spokesmen have in fact made a determined effort to advise other government officials of the domestic application of techniques developed by OPS for use abroad. In September, 1967, Public Safety Director Byron Engle told the National Advisory Commission on Civil Disorders (Kerner Commission) that "in working with police in various countries . . . we have acquired a great deal of experience in dealing with violence ranging from demonstrations and riots to guerilla warfare." Much of this experience, he asserted, "may be helpful in the United States." Among the specific recommendations made by Engle for the control of urban disorders were: the massive use of chemical munitions, stringently enforced curfews, and the establishment of special tactical police units available on a 24-hour stand-by basis. Precisely the same recommendations were made to President Johnson by former Pentagon aide Cyrus Vance, and were later put into effect in Washington, D.C., when rioting broke out following the death of Martin Luther King, Jr. and when, in the wake of this rioting, Congress passed the Omnibus Crime Control and Safe Streets Act, a principal feature of the Public Safety program—Federal assistance to local police forces—became an established mechanism for domestic law enforcement.

JOE STORK

World Cop: How America Builds the Global Police State

Public Safety operations in Vietnam have been largely obscured from publicity by the more blatant military operations. Throughout the rest of the Third World, and notably in Latin America, the Office of Public Safety plays a similarly low-profile but proportionally much more crucial role in promoting the effective counter-insurgent role of national police forces in defending US and local elite interests. Through the activities of the OPS, the notion of the US as world policeman is transformed from a metaphor to a reality.

OPS traces itself back to the first Indochina programs in 1955, but the United States has engaged in a police-support role at least since the end of World War II, particularly in Germany, Japan, and the Truman Doctrine countries, Turkey and Iran. From rather humble, supplemental beginnings, the Office of Public Safety has attained a special status within the AID administration, with considerable autonomy and powers of review over the other AID programs as they relate to political developments.

Public Safety's unique status and privilege is rooted in the shift under the Kennedy brothers to developing an invincible counter-insurgency capability for coping with wars of national liberation. Institutions and programs from the Green Berets to the Peace Corps were initiated under the premise that the struggle against International Communism would be lost or won in the arena of the Third World. After Communism lost, "internal stability" became a typical watchword of the New Frontier. At the foreign assistance hearings in 1965, AID director David Bell sketched the rationale for OPS:

"Plainly, the United States has very great interests in the creation and maintenance of an atmosphere of law and order under humane, civil concepts and control. When there is a need, technical assistance to the

---

From Hard Times, *no. 85 (August 10–17, 1970), pp. 2–4. Reprinted in edited form with permission of the author and publisher. Joe Stork is currently working with the Middle East Research and Information Project. Research for this article was also provided by Mariette Wickes.*

police of developing nations to meet their responsibilities promotes and protects these US interests."

The "humane, civil concepts" advocated by AID are purely utilitarian. During the recent "election" campaign in the Dominican Republic, dozens were killed on the streets by the police. Last month the Organization of American States meeting was moved to Washington because of the propensity of the Dominican police to shoot into crowds, violating the Public Safety maxim against providing "martyrs" to the Left. In Colombia, on the other hand, sophisticated telecommunications and gifts, including police helicopters, helped prevent opposition crowds from getting out of hand in a "professional" manner. Volatile situations around an election were handled effectively to accomplish the same political end: the preservation of the US-supported regime and the maintenance of a "favorable investment climate." Out in the countryside, official violence operates discreetly with the help of human sensors, mobile strike units and other Vietnam spinoffs to eliminate the burgeoning guerrilla movement. (Caring enough to use the very best, the Justice Department is already employing the human sensors along the Mexican border in the campaign against pot smuggling and illegal immigration.)

More typical than Colombia is Guatemala, where the prime beneficiaries of law and order are United Fruit and assorted comprador elites. A Mexican journalist describes the Guatemalan police as "aggressive and incompetent," with a basic repertoire of tortures including electric shocks and rubber truncheons. The new Minister of "Gobernacion" commented recently that new AID agreements would be welcome in "strengthening our security system and combatting delinquency." Under the rubric of Public Safety, AID would have the police become aggressive and competent, and in Venezuela OPS successfully overcame a local tradition that made the police subject to manslaughter charges for shooting students and other "Communists."

The strategic import of the Public Safety program is reflected in the Operations Report submitted to Congress after every fiscal year, one of the few documents available to the public which even suggests the existence of the Office of Public Safety. Although the figures given are known to understate the actual expenditures, due to covert funding by the Department of Defense and the CIA, in 1969 (the last year for which figures are available), $35 million was spent by the Office of Public Safety. Of that, $29 million was spent in East Asia. More than half of the rest was spent in Latin America, in the countries most crucial to US corporate interests: Brazil, Dominican Republic, Venezuela, Colombia and Guatemala. In Africa, the pattern is the same, with the Congo, Liberia and Ethiopia getting most of the assistance. The Ethiopian figure is deceptively low nonetheless, since most of its military and police assistance is channeled by the US through Israel.

In Brazil, former Public Safety trainees hold positions such as Director of Training or Director of Investigations in several large states. The scope of the program has increased enormously since the pro-US coup in 1964. AID boasts that it has trained over 100,000 police over the same period that the Brazilian economy has been ripped off by US firms, including Hanna Mining, Pfizer Drugs, and Standard Oil. Brazil has been and continues to be one of the largest recipients of Public Safety funds, nearly $8 million since 1959, or more than 20 percent of the total spent in Latin America. The International Commission of Jurists recently accused the regime of "systematic and scientifically developed torture," including "plunging a prisoner's head into buckets of excrement until near suffocation and electric shocks on sensitive parts of the body." While AID claims that "support is not given to dictatorships," former AID administrator Bell considered it "desirable and proper to continue to assist in the improvement of the efficiency of the civilian police force. The police are a strongly anti-Communist force right now. For that reason, it is a very important force for us."

In the event of political crisis, large amounts of highly sophisticated equipment, especially telecommunications, vehicles, and lethal and non-lethal armaments, are rushed to Third World countries, sometimes funded by the Department of Defense or the CIA. ("In order to deal with the dynamics of internal security situations," AID administrator Bell explained at another point in his Congressional testimony, "the Public Safety program has developed and utilized methods to deliver to threatened countries, in a matter of days, urgently needed assistance, including training, equipment, and technical advice.") This capacity has been exercised several times over the past few months. In both Colombia and the Dominican Republic, rush orders of vehicles and arms were sent down just before their respective elections, in which the US had a special interest in seeing who won. In the Dominican Republic, Balaguer even used AID trucks to transport his campaign around the country. In South Korea in 1968, demonstrations against the third-term decision of Pres. Chung Hee Park were met with national police vehicles that still had the AID stickers on them.

In actual practice, OPS stresses the need for developing countries to have large amounts of the latest gadgetry. According to a report from a Chief (US) Public Safety Advisor in Venezuela, the host country had spent over a five year period, "the equivalent of some $6 million for US-manufactured items recommended specifically by the Public Safety Advisors." OPS has, in fact, helped to set up a police-industrial network. The Technical Services Division constitutes an important part of OPS's mandate: "the responsibility for developing new equipment and for modifying existing items to meet special field needs." OPS cites its real strategy at Congressional hearings: not to give equipment to recipient countries, but to train foreign personnel to need US equipment by standardizing vehicles and electronic gear to require purchases from the US even after the Advisors leave.

Venezuela also affords a glimpse into another feature of the symbiosis between OPS and US business interests overseas. According to a paper written by a former Public Safety Advisor, "The Chief and Deputy Chief Public Safety Advisors meet monthly with security officers of all major oil companies operating in the country and the security officer for the leading mine company." OPS trains Liberian police, who are actually security employees of Firestone Rubber. In Indonesia, any Public Safety assistance is hidden in a general technical assistance budget, but it is worth mentioning that fortunate political prisoners are hired out as chattel labor to the Goodyear plantations there. Last fall in the Dominican Republic, a strike by sugar cane cutters was brutally suppressed by the national police at the behest of the La Romana fields, owned and operated by the Gulf and Western conglomerate.

One important asset in the campaign to orient Third World police to the US in ideology—and supplies—is the International Police Academy in Washington, D.C. Due to Robert Kennedy's benevolence after the Bay of Pigs and the independent status of OPS, a special school, the Inter-American Police Academy, was set up in Panama in 1962 (by classified Presidential directive), near the Green Beret base at Fort Gulick. The next year it was moved to Washington and appropriately renamed. To date, more than 3,000 carefully-screened ranking police officers have gone through a variety of courses that all contain a high dosage of "Marxism" as interpreted by the FBI, as well as technical and administrative training: from setting up a beat system to running through mock riots and demonstrations in the game room known as the Police Operations Control Center.

The general course that most candidates take lasts about three months, is given in English and Spanish, and culminates in an elaborately banal graduation ceremony with the Marine Corps band, celebrities like Maxwell Taylor and William Bundy, and valedictory exhortations to support your international police. Each class presents a trophy or plaque to the Academy director as a class memento. The course includes arms training in the basement in one of the finest ranges in the world, according to connoisseurs, CBW training at "a nearby Army installation," three days at the John F. Kennedy School of Special Warfare at Fort Bragg, N.C., and a tour of Washington's own Con Son, Lorton Reformatory. Each student submits a "thesis" which is kept in the IPA library. Like most information about the Academy or OPS, such documents, even when unclassified, are unavailable to anyone not working within police circles. The theses are declared inviolable on the grounds of "academic freedom"; it would violate the students' confidences to open them to the public.

Another 2,000 higher-ranking officers have come for special courses, either at IPA, the FBI Academy in Quantico, Va., or specialized university courses in criminalistics, ballistics, and the like. All visitors end their stay with an eight-day bus tour of Middle America. AID assures everyone that "the best majority of the visiting officers find America-in-the-raw of irresistible warmth." Indeed, one of the selling points of the Public Safety program is the claim that 90 percent of the participants come away strongly pro-American. This figure, no doubt, is a statistical average, including one Colombian participant who claimed that he was a "200 percent supporter of the US."

The director of the International Police Academy is Michael McCann, a former assistant professor in police administration at Indiana University, until he joined the Public Safety program in Iran for several years beginning in 1951. He was in Teheran for the CIA's first successful attempt to subvert a nationalist government. One of the organizers of the coup against Mossadeq was Gen. Norman Schwartzkopf, former head of the New Jersey State Police. McCann regards the IPA as an "international forum" for police. A more effusive but accurate AID blurb calls it the "West Point of the police of the non-Communist arising world."

McCann's boss is Public Safety Director, Byron Engle, a former advertising man turned cop. His first overseas position was with the MacArthur regime in Tokyo, where he was Chief Police Administrator from 1946 to 1955 except for two years in Ankara, Turkey.

Basic direction and overview of OPS and IPA comes from an interagency board; besides Engle, it consists of Gen. William Du Puy, Special Advisor to the Joint Chiefs of Staff on Counter-Insurgency, representatives from the FBI and the CIA, and the State Department's officer in charge of Internal Defense Policy and Politico-Military Affairs.

Besides channeling ideological and technical training to Third World police, the whole OPS program has provided a laboratory for testing concepts, programs and weapons. General Du Puy, in a graduation address in October, 1968, pointed out how well the police-military coordination stressed by the Academy has come to be practiced at home: The military now share intelligence on "subversive groups" with the police, he said. After Martin Luther King's assassination, military command posts were set up, in every case, at metropolitan or precinct police stations in the US. He also cited the incentives of shortened Armed Forces service used to recruit military personnel to join local police forces, and the way that police departments are giving week-long Army training courses in civil disturbance control. Another example of the OPS-fostered police-military partnership is the "Civil Disturbance Steering Committee," which has been meeting weekly after Newark and Detroit in 1967, and is made up of officials from all the military services and the Justice Department. Army teams have been sent to several hundred cities to study with local police street layouts and vital installations. This and other information is stored in the Pentagon's "domestic war room."

The International Police Academy itself has been directly involved in domestic policing. According to a former student, inservice training once included mingling with local and federal counterparts in controlling the "counter-inaugural" demonstrations in Washington in January, 1969. Mayor Daley reportedly turned down a request of the State Department to send IPA trainees to Chicago for the Democratic Convention. Another report has it that IPA's Police Operations Control Center was put to domestic use to plot strategy for the Washington police and National Guard during the disorders in response to the closing of Resurrection City (called Insurrection City by OPS officials). In his recommendations to the Kerner Commission in September, 1967, Byron Engle recommended the use of chemical munitions as one of "the most effective weapons . . . *if used properly and in quantity*" (his emphasis).

One need not go farther afield than the International Police Academy itself to find a mutually supporting relationship between OPS and a successful corporate elite. The building which houses IPA in Georgetown is rented from O. Roy Chalk for $220,000 per year. (Chalk owns the D.C. Transit Company and built his domestic and foreign business operations on the backs of the Capital colony's bus riders—most of them poor and black. The IPA Review sometimes donates a commercial to Roy by suggesting that "the participants can ride inexpensive public buses—itself an orientation into American life." Until recently, Chalk owned Trans-Caribbean Airlines. He is a director of International Railways of Central America, which transports the produce of United Fruit Company.)

These ties, while important in their own right, strikingly point up the common interest of the military, the national-security-conscious New Frontiersman, and the traditional robber-businessman in maintaining an identical kind of law and order at home and overseas. Maintenance of the empire demands the same vigilance towards "internal security" in Washington, D.C., Rio de Janeiro, Saigon, Seoul and Santo Domingo. The threat of liberation to one is a threat to all, and the repression of one has lessons for the repression of all. The Kennedys wanted to enforce the stability of the status quo on all the Third World. They succeeded in bringing the tensions and threats of revolution home to the United States.

III

POLICE-INDUSTRIAL COMPLEX

Technological solutions to social, economic, and political problems have become one of the predominant characteristics of modern capitalist systems. Emphasis is placed on expanding research and inventing more technically sophisticated and specialized equipment under the belief that technology is capable of alleviating such problems as crime, inequality, and poverty, without altering the basic structure of the political economy. The result is a commitment to the existing social system, never challenging or questioning such basic factors as the unequal distribution of wealth or the existence of racist institutions in society.

The multiplying uses of technology, the importance of research, and the development of innovative machinery and equipment have long been recognized by both industry and the military. The agencies of the criminal justice system have only recently found technology to be particularly useful. Some brief examples of the new experimental uses include: telemonitoring of parolees by implanting electrodes in their brains in order to monitor and control behavior; tiny electronic devices for tapping telephone wires and "bugging"; video cameras mounted on city streets for following the movement of automobiles and pedestrians. The rationale for the use of these and other new devices is based on the assumption that technology is to be the primary method of solving economic and political problems.

Within the criminal justice system, the police have long neglected the development of technological resources. One of the strongest criticisms made by the 1967 President's Commission on Law Enforcement and Administration of Justice was that there was no scientific commitment to the development of sophisticated equipment by law enforcement agencies. The report noted that "more than two hundred thousand scientists and engineers are helping to solve military problems, but only a handful are helping to control the crimes that injure or frighten millions of Americans each year." [1]

[1] President's Commission on Law Enforcement and Administration of Justice, *The Challenge of Crime in a Free Society* (Washington, D.C.: U.S. Government Printing Office, 1967), p. 245.

A special task force on Science and Technology, under the direction of the Institute for Defense Analyses, was established by the Commission to look at the problem. The goals of the task force were to discover "how the resources of science and technology might be used to solve the problems of crime." [2] The final recommendations of the task force [written with the assistance of three International Business Machines (IBM) employees] were extensive, ranging from special projects for police, court, and correctional operations, to establishing specific information systems for all aspects of the criminal justice system. All of the suggested changes and improvements were based on criteria of efficiency and expediency, rarely focusing on the question of justice for the accused or the imprisoned.

Science and industry have quickly responded to the call for assistance. The police and other agencies of law enforcement have become stable, reliable, and wealthy customers of industry. Large proportions of law enforcement budgets are used solely for the purchase and maintenance of a wide array of technological innovations for aiding and improving police detection and apprehension of criminals. The result has been a financial bonanza for segments of industry. As Lee Webb points out in his article, total profits for the law enforcement industry are increasing at a high rate; in 1972 the estimate was well over 1.5 billion dollars. The estimate for 1973 is much higher. The Electronics Industry Association assessed the market for electronic equipment to be over $400 million a year.[3] The expansion of this industry has taken up much of the slack created by the diminishing aerospace industry and by the very gradual winddown of the full-scale armed forces commitment to war in Southeast Asia.

Vince Pinto documents the importance of the war in Vietnam as a reliable testing ground for many of the new weapons, chemical agents and crowd control tactics that are currently being imported for use by police departments throughout the country. Another writer, Robert Barkan, has described the war in Vietnam as being "Vietnamized" and the war's technology as being "Americanized." [4] For example, in Vietnam the MacNamara Line, an electronic fence, was set up in 1967 to trace troop supply movements along the Ho Chi Minh Trail. Today the same electronic system of detection is being used along the United States-Mexican border for drug and alien traffic. Sylvania Electronic System is now producing the ground sensors used in this system for the Department of Justice and the Customs Department, instead of for the Department of Defense.[5]

The computer industry also profits handsomely from the police-indus-

[2] Ibid.

[3] Robert Barkan, "War's Technology is a Peacetime Spy," *San Francisco Chronicle*, January 19, 1972, p. 8.

[4] Ibid.

[5] Ibid.

trial complex. *Datamation,* a magazine published by the computer industry, noted in June 1970 that "The FBI and other law enforcement agencies are in a great debt to the computer industry for putting at their disposal so many new weapons in the war on crime." [6] In California alone there are thirty-five computerized systems aiding the police. These systems range from the Police Information Network (PIN) in Alameda to Autostatis, a computer storage program for the California Highway Patrol.[7]

Accompanying computers in assisting the police are helicopters, special infrared lights for night surveillance, and lethal and nonlethal weapons. All of this equipment supplies law enforcement agencies with a large arsenal of sophisticated machinery for their policing activities, and improves the capacity of the police to control dissent and protest.

The variety of new equipment and arms being designed for, and supplied to, the police raises important ethical questions concerning the uses of technology. The use of technology per se is not what is being challenged. Technological achievements for improving the quality of life, e.g. the reduction of crime, transportation, sanitation, medical care, etc. are encouraged. What is forcefully challenged, however, is the application of much of the new technology against Third World, poor, and young people protesting the inadequacies and failings of this society. The emphasis on technological and scientific research and development suggests that inequities, injustices, and other "social problems," can be eliminated or altered through the application of technological solutions rather than through political struggle. The result is ameliorative reforms and changes, such as streamlining courts and prisons or equipping the police, but not a change in the basic conditions that give rise to social problems. The proliferation of technological devices of social control is designed to develop social integration and undermine popular insurgency without requiring a massive display of force and troops. Just as the Office of Public Safety is attempting to create new sophisticated forms of counter-insurgency in countries where the United States has economic interests, so the domestic law enforcement agencies are busy improving their surveillance and control of popular movements at home.

Suggested Readings

The Council on Economic Priorities. *Efficiency in Death: The Manufacturers of Anti-Personnel Weapons.* New York: Harper and Row, 1970.

Gerth, Jeff. "The Americanization of 1984," *Sundance,* April–May, 1972, pp. 58–65.

[6] "The FBI's Computer Network," *Datamation* 16: 146, cited in Denise Drachnik, "Data Banks, Technology, and the Criminal Justice System" (unpublished article, School of Criminology, University of California at Berkeley, June 1973).

[7] Denise Drachnik, op. cit., p. 1.

HERSH, SEYMOUR. "Your Friendly Neighborhood MACE," *New York Review of Books,* March 27, 1969.

NEILANDS, J. B. "Vietnam in Berkeley." *The Spokesman,* April, 1970, pp. 21–24.

The President's Commission on Law Enforcement and Administration of Justice. *Task Force Report: Science and Technology*. Washington, D.C.: U.S. Government Printing Office, 1967.

WEBB, LEE. "Back Home: The Campus Beat." National Action/Research on the Military-Industrial Complex. *Police on the Homefront.* Philadelphia: American Friends Service Committee, 1971.

WELLS, ROBERT. "Vietnamization on Main Street." *The Nation,* July 20, 1970, pp. 38–41.

WILLS, GARY. "Weapons." *The Second Civil War,* pp. 87–105. New York: Signet, 1968.

LEE WEBB

Repression—A New "Growth Industry"

Wall Street has its eyes on a big new growth industry. It's not computers, aerospace or oceanography this time. To blacks, chicanos, students or workers who have the law stacked against them it's known as repression. To the ruling class it's called the "law enforcement industry."

According to Equity Research Associates, a Wall Street research firm, total private and public expenditures on security services and law enforcement equipment will top $1 billion this year. By 1972, Equity estimates the market will grow to $1.5 billion. Earnings and profits of firms that sell to this market will rise "20% a year" for the next five to 10 years, according to Equity.

It has reached the point where a police-industrial complex appears to be forming as the motor behind the growing industry the way the military-industrial complex propels the defense establishment. And, as in most big industries in the U.S., the federal government is playing a key role in subsidizing and promoting the repression industry.

It is sizeable by any standards. There are nearly 400,000 employees of police departments across the country with budgets totalling $2.5 billion. Adding the prisons and corrections institutions, the prosecution and the court system, the entire total of what is called the "criminal justice system" amounts to a $4.2 billion industry.

In the past, this "market" did not excite industrial interests. First of all, it was fragmented into nearly 40,000 different police departments, making marketing and standardization a nightmare. Secondly, tight-fisted civic and business groups were reluctant to spend local tax money on beefing up police departments. But the black and student revolts of the 1960s and new Congressional legislation pumping federal money into police departments have stimulated old businesses and brought many new companies into the industry. Conveniently, federal, state, local and industry officials argue the "criminal justice system" must be enlarged.

From The Guardian, *December 27, 1969, p. 6. Reprinted with permission of the author and publisher.*

Speaking for these interests, the National Commission on the Causes and Prevention of Violence issued a report on Law Enforcement (Nov. 1, 1969), calling for "a solemn national commitment to double our investment in the administration of justice and the prevention of crime as rapidly as such an investment can be wisely planned and utilized."

The Commission described law enforcement as "underfinanced" since it took up less "than 2% of all government expenditures." Comparing law enforcement with other government programs, the Commission complained the U.S. spent "less each year than federal agricultural programs and little more than we do on the space program." The Safe Street and Crime Control Act of 1968 was singled out for praise by the Commission as an important step towards a "bigger and better" law enforcement system.

This Act and its operative agency—the Law Enforcement Assistance Administration (LEAA)—has two purposes. The first is to stimulate increased expenditures by state and local governments on police and criminal justice. The second is to modernize and professionalize the police by encouraging new police technology and science. Grants-in-aid to states for planning, demonstration projects, special units and others are designed to encourage matching state and local commitments, much like the federal highway program.

The money coming down the federal pipeline is big and getting bigger. In fiscal 1969, the LEAA received $63 million in appropriations. In fiscal 1970 it got $268 million to boost law enforcement. The agency's 1971 request has yet to be presented, but an appropriation of $650 million is not unexpected.

The Safe Streets Act was a piece of liberal legislation. It was the Congressional liberal's response to the conservative demand for more nightsticks and "tougher"—more brutal—police suppression. The liberal modernization and professionalization of the police will use computers, high-speed communication equipment and more sophisticated equipment to accomplish the same objective. The massive federal financing also means a nationally coordinated, locally led police force which is different in name only from a national police force.

Modernization of the police means more science and technology. Police departments are no longer willing to take hand-me-down technology from the Agency for International Development's Office of Public Safety, which had been doing most of the research and development in police technology up until just a few years ago. Speaking to a Congressional committee, Quinn Tamm, executive director of the International Association of Chiefs of Police, called for "inter-disciplinary teams of mathematicians, computer scientists, electronic engineers, physicists, biologists and other natural scientists . . . and psychologists, sociologists, economists and lawyers . . ." to work on raising the level of police technology.

In another speech, this time to the executives of Western Electric,

Tamm asked for their help on technology. "You gentlemen probably know better than I," Tamm said, "that industry spends huge sums on research and development. Unfortunately, an almost negligible portion of this is directed towards law enforcement because the market is so small and what little there is is greatly fragmented. Without a profitable market, industry logically has little interest in devoting any major portion of its research resources to police needs."

Since Tamm spoke last year, the police-industrial complex has pushed a lot of money into research and development, confident—as a result of the Safe Streets Act—that a profitable market is waiting to be tapped. The industry includes everyone from firms renting factory and bank guards, to those who sell burglar alarms, Mace, armored cars, pistols, uniforms and high-powered rifles.

The new conglomerates are also jumping into the law enforcement industry. The Bangor Punta Corporation has organized a Law Enforcement Division through acquisition of six companies. Another conglomerate entering the industry in a big way is Walter Kidde and Co. through its Globe Security System which offers a "total product and service package concept" of security. Kidde's board chairman Fred Sullivan, in a speech to the Los Angeles Society of Financial Analysts, recently noted that "with the conclusion to the [Vietnam] war, federal spending would be more directed to domestic programs, including the war against crime."

The established corporate giants are also out for a hunk of this growing market. Chrysler already has 40% of the police car market but is encouraging efforts to modernize the police by making them more mobile in hopes for more sales. Computer firms like IBM and Sperry Rand as well as radio makers like Motorola are after the big profits they see in information and communication systems.

As with the logic of defense expenditures, it is obvious that now the police are acquiring all this equipment, they are going to have to find a use for it.

VINCE PINTO

Weapons for the Homefront

The convergence of two related combat technologies—one developed for the jungles and hamlets of the Third World continents, the other for the ghettos and campuses—is taking place rapidly. Both abroad and at home the U.S. Government sees active or potentially active insurgent populations. Nowhere is there a front line of combat; engagements are episodic, occurring at unpredictable times and places. No large-scale troop and equipment movements telegraph intentions to the other side. While the preponderance of force is on one side, as is the manpower and technology, this very advantage is a drawback compared with the self-reliance and flexibility of the insurgent. Conventional forms of warfare a generation or two old have become obsolete.

Of course, there are also many important dissimilarities between Vietnam and an urban or campus trouble spot in the United States. Though the two struggles are not identical, it should not be surprising to find the same weapons and techniques developed for combat in Vietnam used to quell domestic struggles for liberation. Gas, helicopters, infrared detection, tanks, armored vehicles, barbed wire and hand grenades have been used both in Vietnam and the United States.

But domestic counterinsurgency weapons and methods have lagged behind those developed for international applications. Up until recently the standard arsenal for the patrolman was the sidearm and nightstick. Occasionally a labor strike was met with riot guns and gas bombs. Today's rapid expansion in the variety of the police arsenal illustrates the rapid expansion of domestic counterinsurgency planning. Today's police can employ a number of different gas dispensing devices, from shotguns to helicopters; carry individual two-way radios; fire machine guns on the practice range and high-powered rifles from moving aircraft; wear helmets and body armor; carry MACE in their belts; engage in mock confrontations; as well as use computers to sort out large quantities of infor-

---

From National Action/Research on the Military-Industrial Complex, Police on the Homefront *(Philadelphia: American Friends Service Committee, 1971), pp. 74–88. Reprinted with permission of the author and publisher.*

mation in seconds. Recently, for instance, the Pentagon announced plans to provide $20 million worth of riot control equipment to the National Guard—including face shields, batons, protective vests, shotguns, floodlights, public address systems, radios and tear gas.[1]

The hardware for a beefed-up police network is avidly supplied by a cabal of equipment manufacturers. Naturally, the strongest supporters of law and order, some of these companies provide think-tank contingency plans, or work closely with organizations like the Institute for Defense Analyses. Papers delivered at an Annual Symposium on Law Enforcement, Science and Technology in Chicago's Statler Hilton Hotel show the interest of military aerospace and electronics companies in police work. RCA representatives delivered a paper titled "Night Surveillance Systems for Law Enforcement." The company is working on a number of surveillance units for the Defense Department, as well as making components for the SAM missile system. Jet Propulsion Laboratory contributed "Evaluation of Helicopter Patrols." The man from Motorola spoke about "New Concepts of Portable Radio Communication." Motorola makes miniature circuits for a 2.75-inch antipersonnel rocket fuse ordered by the military. The Stanford Research Institute looked to the future with "Application of Aerospace Technology to Law Enforcement Problems."

GAS

The featured weapon in today's police arsenal is tear gas. Apart from guns, gas is the most commonly stocked item; training in its use is elaborate; reports of its use in actual confrontations are now practically routine.

Police expenditures on tear gas and other "non-lethal" weapons have skyrocketed in the past few years. The *Washington Post* reported January 13, 1969, that domestic law enforcement agencies spent $22 million for anti-riot weapons in 1968, compared to $1 million in 1967. The major U.S. suppliers of riot-control gases are the Lake Erie Corp. (a subsidiary of the Smith and Wesson Company, which in turn is a subsidiary of the Bangor Punta Corp.) and Federal Laboratories, Inc. (a subsidiary of the Breeze Corp.). The Federal Government has also been purchasing large quantities of such weapons. In January 1969, the Army purchased $10 million worth of CS anti-riot gas from the Thiokol Chemical Corp., and another $1 million worth of CS grenades from Federal Laboratories.

Police often consider gases to be valuable not only against mass demonstrations but also against an unruly individual in the station house; one squirt of chemical MACE in the face is enough to incapacitate. The writer of one "riot control" textbook feels, "This development is the first significant breakthrough in individual police weapons since the advent of

1 Dana Adams Schmidt, "Laird Authorizes More Guard Arms and Riot Drilling," *New York Times*, November 11, 1970, p. 1.

the hand gun. Currently, over 4,000 law enforcement departments are making increasing use of chemical MACE to control individual violence and civil disturbances, usually without the necessity of resorting to other means of force such as the gun or nightstick." [2] A shell filled with liquid CS gas and fired from an ordinary shotgun can penetrate the barricade of a sniper. A tear gas fixture which screws into an ordinary light bulb socket can be tripped by photo-electric cell or other alarm device and is normally used to protect bank vaults and restricted areas.

It is easy to defend the use of chemical weapons as humane simply by comparing them to weapons whose effects are designed to be lethal. Moreover, even though there are no clear-cut guidelines, the public generally believes lethal weapons occupy the last position on an escalating-degree-of-force scale. When guns are used by the police, many believe the "peacekeepers" had no other recourse. For chemical weapons there is not even this vague and weak restriction. Even the victims of a gas attack on a non-violent sit-in may be uncertain that the police had used excessive force in halting the action. Political censure caused by the indiscriminate rain of bullets—such as Jackson and Kent State—can be avoided by the smooth tactical use of gas. On August 13, 1968, the Attorney General of the United States spelled it out:

> Although they are not universally adaptable to all police uses, nonlethal chemical agents represent the best immediate alternative to the use of deadly force—or no force at all. They are now proven to be the most effective, safest, and most humane method of mob control. Used with caution when the need arises, they will reduce death, physical injury, and property loss to a minimum.[3]

The Federal Government advocated use of gas after the Newark and Detroit riots, according to Colonel Rex Applegate, a pioneer in the field of riot control. He says, "Emphasis on the non-lethal chemical weaponry aspects of individual command and riot control is expected to be extremely heavy in the years ahead." [4]

The most commonly encountered gas in U.S. demonstrations is designated CN. Mild in effect, it was used to train soldiers in World War I to wear their masks correctly.

CS gas is more violent and is named for Corson and Stoughton, two scientists who concocted it in 1928. Its effects are stronger and last longer; according to Applegate, ". . . CS is normally recommended for use in the escalating-degree-of-force scale after the milder CN has failed, and/or just prior to the use of firearms." [5] The morality of shooting gassed people is not mentioned.

[2] Col. Rex Applegate, *Riot Control Materiel and Techniques* (Harrisburg, Pa.: Stackpole Books, 1969), p. 196.

[3] *Ibid.*, p. 128.

[4] *Ibid.*, p. 129.

[5] *Ibid.*, p. 132.

DM gas causes vomiting and severe distress, and unlike the other two mentioned, normally requires medical attention. DM will poison water and open food in the area around which it has been released. Because it takes a few minutes to work, it is usually mixed with CS to insure an immediate effect.

All these gases and chemical irritants come packaged in a variety of ways and can be delivered and disseminated in different ways.

The SKITTER by Brunswick Corp., and JET SPIN by Lake Erie Chemical, are both gas grenades that jump and wiggle so that they can't be thrown back. The TRIPLE CHASER by Federal Laboratories breaks into three smoketrailing sections, each taking off on an unpredictable path, spewing gas and smoke.

The gas grenade disperses its material either by burning, which presents a fire hazard, or by exploding and creating a shrapnel hazard and serious injury if it explodes in the hand. The third method, pressurized release, is slower but safer and is disadvantageous to the police since it can be thrown back easily.

Gases come in visible or invisible form. Invisible gas can not be photographed by the press nor easily avoided by those gassed. For Colonel Applegate, this is a decided advantage: "The psychological panic-producing effect of invisible gas on rioters is relatively much more pronounced. This is one reason dust, micro-fine particles of CS and CN agents are more tactically flexible and generally used."

Even though deaths from the mild CN gas have been reported in medical journals,[6] the riot control manual just quoted assures its readers,

> The world reputation and successful use of CN-type tear gas as a nonlethal riot-control agent is well established. During the past four decades, under normal street and field conditions, it has been proven a reliable, nontoxic chemical agent during thousands of incidents involving people of all age groups and physical condition.

Reliance on chemical weapons will be "extremely heavy in the near future," as Applegate stated.

Some rapid changes in gas grenade technology were made in 1963 at the request of the Agency for International Development (AID). Since AID has been the largest single purchaser of tear gas weapons in the last five years, its request for a new model was not taken lightly.

The Agency's Office of Public Safety sent a memo to U.S. manufacturers of gas weapons describing the kind of grenade they wanted. In about thirty "under-developed" countries around the world AID was, and still is, helping to train civil police forces in riot and insurgent control, and the grenade's specifications were based on real tactical experience. The AAI Corporation of Baltimore came up with the desired model, a blast-type hand- or rifle-launched 3" x 6" weapon encased in color-

[6] *Journal of Forensic Sciences,* vol. 9, no. 3, July 1964.

coded DuPont DELRIN plastic. Advantageous because it eliminated the need for a special 37mm gas gun, and storable in a temperature range from 0° to 120°, it was designated MPG (Multi-Purpose Grenade). AAI corporation guarantees the weapon for six years.

In addition to chemical irritants such as CN, CS, and MACE, domestic police forces have used or experimented with and stocked a number of other civil disturbance weapons.

SMOKE

Smoke is a very ancient weapon, used in warfare at least as early as the Crusades. Both offensive and defensive, it can be used to create confusion and cover troop movements. Today the employment of smoke to control civil insurrections has a new twist. In *Riot Control Materiel and Techniques* Applegate states:

> Colored smoke concentrations produce greater initial psychological and panic effect than white smoke. Certain colors have a more dramatic impact than others. Caucasians are said to have a greater repugnance to brilliant green smoke, which is associated with disagreeable personal experiences such as seasickness, bile and vomit. Negroids (*sic.*) and Latins are declared to be most adversely affected by brilliant red.

He goes on to say,

> Rioters confronted with strong concentrations of colored smoke feel, instinctively, that they are being marked, or stained, and thus they lose anonymity. Colored particles of volatilized dye in the smoke cloud adhere to persons, objects and clothing, etc., and produce in the presence of moisture and perspiration, indelible stain. Such stains will be especially noticeable on neckbands, collars, and shirt cuffs. These stains are often of assistance to the police in later identifying mob participants.[7]

These smoke munitions are manufactured by the same companies that make chemical irritants.

SOUND

Sound as a weapon is even more ancient, according to the Biblical account of the battle of Jericho. Our modern version, called the CURDLER, is for use not against fortification, but against people. The CURDLER (also called SUPERSOUND and PEOPLE REPELLER) is usually used as an ordinary speech amplifier by police or firemen on a rescue mission, but it can deliver 350 watts of modulated shrieks and screams when needed. The noise produced is rated at 120db at 30 feet, like being next to a jet engine at take-off. Ordinary speech projected over this weapon can be understood *two and one-half miles away*. Apart from causing its victims to drop what they have to cover their ears, its weird effect pro-

[7] Applegate, pp. 188–9.

duces disorientation and nausea. Usually the CURDLER is mounted on an armored personnel carrier or helicopter, although its manufacturer, Applied Electro Mechanics of Alexandria, Va., also makes a portable version. Purchasers include New York City police and fire departments, E. I. DuPont Company, Allegheny Airlines, the Navy, Air Force, Coast Guard and Marines of the United States, and the police of Madrid.

OTHER "NON-LETHAL" WEAPONS

Tear gas, smoke, and noise will soon be joined by several new products in the crowd-control armory. "RioTrol" (also known as the "instant banana peel") is a by-product of the petroleum industry that has potential for use in the ghetto. Heretofore, the powdery white polyethylene oxide was used as lubricant for oil-drilling equipment. When 2 kilograms of the substance are spread over 600 square feet of sidewalk and watered down, the area becomes more slippery than ice. According to a sales brochure, police officers, equipped with special boots and gloves, would be able "to go amongst writhing bodies and remove riot ringleaders." One danger to unpadded victims—what about concussions from the resulting falls? The product, which sells for $5.95 a pound, is manufactured by the Western Co. of Richardson, Texas.

Another proposed tactic for the control of hostile crowds is the use of dense foam to immobilize and confuse rioters. The origin of this material is the foam sprayed on airfields to cushion the touchdown of damaged aircraft. The use of this product for control of crowds presents certain already-demonstrated dangers, however—recently a salesman for the Defensor Protective Equipment Corp. of Media, Pennsylvania (manufacturer of the "Defensor" High Volume Foam Generator) was asphyxiated when he slipped and fell into the foam during a demonstration of its potential riot-control applications.

A proposed incapacitating agent which is still in the experimental stage is the long-barreled tranquilizer gun using drugged darts. The device was developed by Dr. William C. Conner, a psychiatrist at Emory University Hospital in Atlanta. Dr. Conner has been experimenting with darts that are ordinarily used to subdue wild animals for capture or tagging. In the tests, a pistol-shaped gun uses a carbon dioxide cartridge to propel the darts, which are composed of a needle three-fourths of an inch long attached to a cylindrical projectile syringe containing sleep-inducing drugs. The missile, which has a range of about 30 feet, injects automatically on impact. The device used in the test was manufactured by the Palmer Chemical and Equipment Co. of Douglasville, Ga., which manufactures tranquilizer guns for use against animals.

Hypodermic darts of the type tested in Atlanta could be used to disable fleeing rioters and looters when it is deemed undesirable to fell them by gunfire. The problem with such drugs, however, is that each individual reacts differently to them. A dose which would knock out a 200-pound man could endanger the life of someone weighing half as much. The darts might also strike the eyes or other vulnerable points, and thus cause permanent damage.

GUNS

Despite all the talk about non-lethal weapons, every urban police force has an abundant supply of lethal anti-riot weapons, i.e., guns. The Philadelphia police force carries its armories around on wheels to be handy in case of trouble—each of the mobile armories, known as Stakeout cars, carries the following armament:

2 M-70 Winchester rifles, 30/06 cal., with BalVarscope, sling, case and 200 rounds ammunition;

2 M-12 Winchester shotguns, 12 gauge with case and 100 rounds .00 buck ammunition;

1 Thompson submachine gun, .45 cal., with 500 rounds ammunition;

1 M-1 carbine, .30 cal., with 200 rounds ammunition.

This list of guns is hardly exceptional. In Detroit, for instance, the police have purchased 500 new carbines, 300 shotguns and 150,000 rounds of ammunition.

The standard anti-riot gun is the 12-gauge shotgun, because of its wide field of fire. The .00 buck charge is a favorite shell, because the nine ball bearings in the load umbrella out in broad fanning patterns. With a charge like that, a policeman can just point the gun and fire—and be sure of hitting one or more persons. Among new shotguns, the favorite is High Standard's Model 10, a semi-automatic, five-shot weapon, with lightweight plastic stock and a searchlight on top. Anything the light covers will be in the shot pattern, so aiming at night is an easy matter. The Model 10 uses a 12-gauge, 12-pellet high-velocity magnum load. Police departments favor the gun because it can be fired with one hand like a pistol.

Like other categories of anti-riot weaponry, new guns are now being developed for use in urban counterinsurgency. Most prominent among the gunsmiths working on this problem is Edward Stoner, inventor of the Army's new M-16 rifle. Stoner has developed a new high-velocity assault rifle that can penetrate a brick wall. The Stoner gun, made by the Cadillac Gage Company, is being purchased in substantial quantities by police agencies for use as an anti-sniper gun. According to the rifle's manufacturer, "the *proper* way to shoot a sniper is through the wall." With the addition of various interchangeable parts, the Stoner rifle can be converted into a carbine, submachine gun or medium machine gun.

DUMDUM BULLETS

Dumdum bullets are soft lead rounds with a hollow, slotted nose. Since 1899 they have been outlawed for use in international warfare because of the terrible wounds they cause. When the bullet strikes the flesh it flattens out to twice its size, virtually causing a small explosion in the body. The wound is almost always fatal. In 1909 the United States Congress adopted the Hague Conference Declaration against their use between warring countries.

Despite the fact that the use of dumdum bullets is a war crime, they are standard ordnance in almost half the police departments in the United States, among them the sheriffs of Los Angeles County and police in Kansas City, Miami, St. Louis, Tucson and Nashville. The U.S. Treasury Department, the Secret Service, the Bureau of Narcotics and the White House police are some of the Federal purchasers.

At least two large companies make the bullet, Super-Vel Cartridge Corp. of Shelbyville, Indiana and Remington Small Arms Company in Bridgeport, Connecticut (Remington is controlled by DuPont).

Smaller manufacturers of the bullet are Norma Projetilfabrik, a Swedish company with offices in South Lansing, New York; the Dutch Speer Ammunition Company in Lewiston, Idaho; and Winchester-Western, a division of Olin-Mathieson.[8]

BARBED TAPE

Once the police have rounded up rioters and other law-breakers, their problems are not over. The mass arrests which usually follow the outbreak of ghetto disturbances place tremendous logistical and manpower demands on the anti-riot forces at a time when they need all available resources for continued operations in the ghetto. Thus the police must devise procedures for the detention under guard of thousands of prisoners with the minimum outlay of manpower.

One solution to the problem of guarding prisoners was recently devised by the U.S. Army Mobility Equipment Research and Development Center at Fort Belvoir, Va. The Army's contribution is the "instant obstacle" —barbed tape. A substitute for conventional barbed wire, this tape is thin, razor-sharp stainless steel, 64% lighter and more compact than barbed wire. One 40-pound package of the tape forms a barbed-wire fence 75 feet long and 2-1/2 feet high; the tape can be rolled out from the back of a jeep in a matter of minutes. The instant barbed wire has several applications to anti-riot operations in addition to the detainment of prisoners. If enough of it were available, an entire ghetto could be cut off from the rest of the city to halt the spread of violence to the "white" part of town, and to prevent the inflow of weapons and other supplies. In addition, the tape could be used to protect police stations and other targets of mob activity *inside* the conflict area.

[8] Robert Wells, "Vietnamization on Main Street," *The Nation,* July 20, 1970, pp. 38–41.

ARMORED CARS

A number of U.S. firms have begun producing smaller heavily-armored wheeled or tracked vehicles for use in city streets. Cadillac Gage Company, Detroit, makes a wheeled model called the COMMANDO. Accommodating 12 men, it travels 60 mph on the highway, 4 knots on the water. Vertical gun ports allow firing hand guns even at high targets. The armor will protect against any small arms fire, and is angled to deflect bullets. Twelve COMMANDOS were in operation during the Detroit riot in 1967.

Bauer Ordnance Company of Warren, Michigan produces a wheeled vehicle built on a Chevrolet truck chassis which looks very similar to a Brinks armored car. It weighs two tons and is equipped with a 360° turret for mounting a machine gun, riot gun, gas dispenser or water cannon.

Fiercest of all is a ten-ton track tank from B&H Enterprises, Leesburg, Fla. Slow but powerful, the model R2 can push down masonry walls. In addition to a crew of 3 it can carry 15 other men. Standard equipment includes "built-in Molotov cocktail protection." Tanks for tear gas are provided. An optional item is the CURDLER.

Some cities, under civilian pressure, have cancelled plans to buy tanks. But the press has reported at least two actual field uses, in raids on the Black Panther Party in New Orleans.[9] (The tank was purchased for the Louisiana police by the Justice Department's Law Enforcement Assistance Administration for $16,464.)[10]

In the competition for police appropriations, the armored car may ultimately lose out to a more versatile transport, the helicopter. The Chicago Police Department recently allocated $168,000 for three helicopters that will be used for an "anti-burglar patrol" as well as for mobile observation posts during riots. In the eyes of police officials, the helicopter has an outstanding attraction in that it can be used to spot snipers and keep them pinned down until apprehended by ground forces.

The Role of the Federal Government

The Law Enforcement Assistance Administration of the Justice Department is concerned with all aspects of police work. In addition to dispensing research and training grants to universities and think-tanks, LEAA is also engaged in establishing weapon and equipment standards and tests. Such standardization will aid what LEAA calls "the police officer as consumer" and will be beneficial to industry. At present, the word

[9] *New York Times,* September 16, 1970, and *Philadelphia Bulletin,* November 11, 1970.

[10] Joseph C. Goulden, "The Cops Hit the Jackpot," *The Nation,* November 23, 1970, p. 521.

is going out about the possibilities for profit. As was explained in *The Police Chief,* "LEAA, both through state grants and Institute funding, is fostering the recognition of police by industry as a specific market." [11]

LEAA's first report pointed out, "There is no central source at present to research and test product capabilities and set up minimum and optimum standards for police and other use." Such a source would "help overcome the fragmentation problem that besets industry in its dealings with law enforcement agencies," improve the effectiveness and lower the costs of standardized equipment.[12]

Accordingly, LEAA's National Institute of Law Enforcement and Criminal Justice has contracted with the National Bureau of Standards to plan (and eventually to establish and operate) a new Users Standards Laboratory for police equipment from fingerprint kits to prison door locks. As the second LEAA report describes it:

> The new laboratory will serve as the cornerstone of a "consumer testing service" for the nation's criminal justice agencies. It will: (1) define performance standards for equipment; (2) develop uniform procedures for measuring equipment quality; (3) inspect and certify commercial testing laboratories; and (4) develop standard design specifications so that equipment from different manufacturers can be used together easily and economically. . . . Quality standards will be proposed to industry for voluntary acceptance and compliance.[13]

Additionally, the Institute is supporting the development of a Police Weapons System Program by the International Association of Chiefs of Police. Its purpose is to (a) evaluate current policies and practices in the acquisition and use of offensive and defensive weapons, (b) survey current weapons systems research and development, (c) establish a central source of police weapons data. The IACP is to study "firearms, chemical weapons, batons, explosives and protective equipment . . . . nonlethal chemical weapons will receive special emphasis." [14]

LEAA's job was summed up dramatically by Dr. Alfred Blumstein:*

> Think of where military technology would be if each battalion commander were responsible for his own research and development. A national agency was needed to represent the combined interests of police departments across

[11] Walter Key, "A Report from the National Institute," *The Police Chief,* November 1969, p. 15.

[12] *First Annual Report of the Law Enforcement Assistance Administration* (Washington, D.C.: U.S. Department of Justice, 1969), p. 27.

[13] *Second Annual Report of the Law Enforcement Assistance Administration* (Washington, D.C.: U.S. Department of Justice, 1970), p. 91.

[14] *Ibid.,* p. 210.

* Dr. Blumstein was the Institute for Defense Analyses' director of the Science and Technology report to the President's Commission on Law Enforcement and Administration of Justice. He left IDA to become director of the Urban Systems Institute at Carnegie-Mellon University.

the nation. The creation of the Law Enforcement Assistance Administration, and especially its research and development arm, the National Institute of Law Enforcement and Criminal Justice, was an important step in that direction.[15]

In its present form LEAA looks like a baby Department of Defense, beginning to engage in the same pattern of activity practiced by its bigger brother. It is creating the framework around which a national police force can easily be built, and an important part of that framework will be the growing police-industrial complex.

[15] Dr. Alfred Blumstein, "Science and Technology for Law Enforcement," *The Police Chief*, December 1969, p. 61.

IV

COUNTERINSURGENCY

Counterinsurgency operations have always been one of the major concerns of modern law enforcement agencies in the United States. The police are officially responsible for preventing any insurgent threat to the power, property, and wealth of America's ruling class. Under the direction of those in power, the police use counterinsurgency strategies to attack and defeat popular movements seeking to transform fundamental economic and political relationships in the society. In the United States, this means counterinsurgency has been practiced against labor organizations, socialist and other progressive political groups, radical feminists, and Third World organizations—any groups that challenge capitalism, imperialism, sexism, and racism.

Under the guise of "national security" and "suspected subversion," counter-insurgency is aimed at defeating popular movements by political or military means, and at discrediting their ideas and principles. The tactics of repression vary, depending on the popularity and ingenuity of the target movement, available technology, and specific political and environmental conditions. Politically, efforts are made to publicly ridicule or isolate an organization or its leaders by spreading false rumors, fabricating evidence of misconduct or corruption, or charging foreign support. Thus, members of the Black Panther Party are identified as "thugs," Martin Luther King is branded an "adulterer," anti-war activists are characterized as "hippies," and the Vietnam Veterans Against The War are dismissed as "crazies." Political tactics of counter-insurgency are supported by an array of sophisticated hardware and military strategies, including wiretaps, electronic bugging devices, harassment and surveillance, informers, agents provocateurs, and murder.

Research and planning are important components of law enforcement counterinsurgency activities. Mike Klare's essay analyzes the relationship between foreign and domestic counterinsurgency operations, noting the role played by universities and "think-tanks" such as the Defense Research Corporation (DRC), the Center for Research in Social

Systems (CRESS), and the Institute for Defense Analyses (IDA) in formulating new methods of social control.

The pervasiveness of counterinsurgency within the United States is not fully known. However, recent disclosures of the Watergate "bag of tricks," the publication of FBI documents (stolen from an FBI office in Media, Pennsylvania, in March 1971), and occasional exposés and autobiographies provide some insight into its organization and programs.

From its beginning in 1908, the FBI has played an important role in the suppression of political movements. One of their first major repressive actions was a series of nationwide raids in 1919–1920. These notorious "Red Raids" imprisoned and deported thousands of aliens who had been members of various labor organizations in the United States. The "alien radical division" of the FBI, directed by J. Edgar Hoover, in cooperation with the Immigration Bureau, using information supplied by informers, systematically arrested members of the I.W.W., the Union of Russian Workers, the Communist Labor Party and the Communist Party.[1] These groups had been vocally and politically active in their attempts to radicalize America, by altering the unequal and oppressive relationship between labor and industry.[2] Using informers to gain information, and then "[i]ndiscriminate arrests of the innocent with the guilty, unlawful searches and seizures by federal detectives, intimidating preliminary interrogations of aliens held incommunicado, high-handed levying of excessive bail, and denial of counsel," [3] the government was able to arrest and deport thousands of politically active people.

An independent committee of lawyers, outraged by the government's blatant violation of the Bill of Rights, investigated the raids, and found "federal agents guilty of using third-degree tortures, making illegal searches, seizures, and arrests, using agents provocateurs, and forcing aliens to incriminate themselves." [4]

Labor organizing in the 1930s was similarly opposed by big business using police, informers, species, and agents provocateurs. Senator La Follette, in his committee's investigation of violations of workers' civil liberties by cmployers, uncovered the widespread use of spies by organized business. "Great interstate corporations maintained private espionage systems which rivaled the detective agencies in scope and in ruthlessness." [5] Between January 1933 and April 1937, Pinkerton, a nation-

[1] William Preston, Jr., *Aliens and Dissenters* (New York: Harper Torchbooks, 1963), pp. 208–37.

[2] See, for example, Preston, loc. cit., and Alan Wolfe, *The Seamy Side of Democracy: Repression in America* (New York: David McKay, 1973).

[3] Preston, op. cit., p. 221.

[4] Ibid., p. 222.

[5] E. David Cronon, ed., *Labor and the New Deal* (Chicago: Rand McNally, 1963), p. 40.

wide private detective agency, supplied 1,228 spies to industry. These spies/informers became members of almost every trade union in the country, including company unions.[6]

The counterinsurgency activities of the FBI did not stop after the Red Raids; they became more organized and sophisticated. In the mid-1930s, a division of "national security" was formed to maintain surveillance of radical political organizations. In the 1940s, a "racial intelligence" division was organized to deal with violations of civil rights. And, by the 1960s, with the increase of urban insurrections, civil disobedience and unrest, black militancy, antiwar and student protest, "internal security" had become a major preoccupation of the FBI.[7]

Robert Wall's short autobiographical sketch of his work in the FBI provides valuable insight into the ideology of the FBI and other law enforcement agencies. Dissent and protest are defined by the FBI as illegal, illegitimate forms of voicing disagreement. The organizing of oppressed groups, especially Third World people and political movements, are watched electronically with wiretaps and bugs, or personally with informers harassed, provoked into illegal actions by agents, and sometimes murdered.

The use of informers and agents provocateurs has recently been exposed in (1) the trial of Philip Berrigan and Mary McAlister, (2) the trial of a group of Catholics in Camden, New Jersey, who had raided a draft board office, and (3) the trial of black militants who had been charged with attempting to blow up the Statue of Liberty. In all of these cases, the informers were provocateurs hired by the FBI and the police to provoke political activists into illegal and even violent actions.

> In the Berrigan case, Boyd Douglas, who had been previously convicted of passing bad checks, theft, and escape from custody, was hired to spy on Berrigan while both were in a federal prison. After becoming a friend of Berrigan's, Douglas suggested the use of guns and explosives for antiwar activities. Manuals on explosives, given to him by the FBI, were then handed over to Berrigan and his friends.[8]
>
> Robert Hardy was the chief prosecution witness against a group of Catholic antiwar activists in Camden, New Jersey. With the help and advice of the FBI, Hardy supplied details and tools for a raid on a local draft board. Hardy admitted under oath that the group would not have acted if he had not encouraged them to do so.[9]
>
> Raymond Wood, an undercover police officer working for the New York City Police Department, was the instigator of an alleged plot by black mili-

[6] Ibid., p. 41.

[7] See, John Elliff, "The Scope and Basis of FBI Domestic Intelligence Data Collection," in Pat Walters and Stephen Gillers, eds., *Investigating the FBI* (New York: Doubleday, 1973).

[8] Paul Jacobs, "Informers" (unpublished article, Center for the Study of Law and Society, University of California at Berkeley, 1972), p. 1.

[9] Ibid., p. 2A.

tants to blow up the Statue of Liberty. Immediately after exposing the plot, Wood was promoted to the rank of detective.[10]

The Black Panthers, designated by J. Edgar Hoover as the "greatest single threat to the security of the country" have been the victims of a nationwide campaign of repression. Between May 1967 and December 1969, an average of one Black Panther was arrested every day. Arrest charges ranged from illegal possession of weapons, disorderly conduct, attempted murder, murder, theft, robbery, resisting arrest, leafletting and selling newspapers, to jay walking, profanity and obscenity, no identification, curfew violations, etc. The total bail for arrested Panthers during this period was $4,890,580. Arrests were made all over the country, ranging from Berkeley and Victoria, B.C., to Milwaukee, Denver, Chicago, and Des Moines.[11] Among the more blatant actions against the Panthers were the murders of Fred Hampton and Mark Clark, leaders of the Chicago Black Panther Party.

In Chicago the Panther Party had become one of the most powerful independent organizations. Their free breakfast programs, plans for a free medical clinic, newspaper, and community organizing were seen as specific threats to the firmly established political power of the Daley machine, and generally as threats to the established economic and political system of the country. Along with Hoover's identification of the Black Panther Party as a national threat, Attorney General, John Mitchell, labeled the Panthers "a subversive threat to the national security."[12] Both the FBI and the Justice Department assigned numerous agents to investigate, wiretap, and surveil the Panthers.

Using an informer's misinformation, the State's Attorney Police, armed with submachine guns and shotguns, entered Fred Hampton's apartment on the pretext of searching for unauthorized and unregistered weapons. After more than 200 shots were fired, Hampton and Clark were dead, four others seriously wounded, three arrested unharmed, and one policeman was wounded slightly.

The use of sophisticated electronic equipment and computers has made political surveillance of the Black Panther Party and other political movements even more intense and pervasive. With computers, dossiers are easily compiled and information disseminated. In 1966, a survey of federal executive departments and agencies found over 3.1 billion personal files. These files included: "264.6 million police records, 342 million medical histories, 279.6 million psychiatric records, and 187.8 million 'security or other investigative reports.'"[13]

10 Paul Jacobs, "Informers: The Enemy Within," *Ramparts*, August–September, 1973, p. 52.

11 Alan Wolfe, op. cit., pp. 48–51.

12 Christopher Chandler, "Black Panther Killings in Chicago," *New Republic*, January 10, 1970, p. 23.

13 Vern Countryman, "Computer and Dossiers," *The Nation*, August 30, 1971, p. 146.

The FBI has fingerprints or data on over one-third of the U.S. population.[14] And, the latest computer system, Project SEARCH (System for Electronic Analysis and Retrieval of Criminal Histories), to be in full operation by 1975, will provide a national computerized "criminal justice information center." [15]

Dossiers are not only compiled by local, state, and federal law enforcement agencies. A classified Army document, made public in 1971, documented the widespread use of a special Army domestic surveillance system. Using over 1,500 domestic intelligence agents and 300 regional offices, the Army compiled about 18,000 dossiers between 1968 and 1970.

The Army's Civil Disturbance Information Plan, written in 1968 following the ghetto rebellions, was designed to supply information for the prevention and control of major civil disturbances. The domestic spy system was expanded in 1969 to include a wide variety of surveillance targets: anti-war and anti-draft activities; militant organizations; "extremists" in the armed forces; demonstrations, rallies, parades, marches, conventions, conferences and picketing; foreign participation or influence in civil disturbances; strikes and labor disputes; subversion and terrorism.[16] Information was primarily gathered on radicals, militant Third World organizations, and anti-war activists. Due to public and congressional opposition to the Army's discovered spy operations, the Department of Justice has now assumed the functions of Army intelligence. Dossiers, frequently filled with inaccurate information supplied by informers and based on political criteria, have not been destroyed but simply reassigned to another governmental agency.

The Watergate "bag of tricks" further documents the use of counterinsurgency methods to manipulate and control dissent. Not only were telephones and private conversations taped by the White House, but burglaries (for example, the raid on Daniel Ellsberg's psychiatrist's office) were authorized, phony letters and false documents supplied to the media, and violent demonstrations were encouraged by the White House.

These and other counterinsurgency operations have become important tactics used to suppress, repress, and control political movements in the United States. Using intelligence units specializing in covert political espionage and overt military maneuvers, law enforcement agencies protect ruling-class domination. Any challenges to the established order are defined as illegal, and attempts to make the society more progressive are attacked. Counterinsurgency operations are needed and used when the legitimacy of the existing economic and political relationships are ques-

[14] Jeff Gerth, "The Americanization of 1984," *Sundance* 1, no. 1 (April–May, 1972): 60.

[15] Ibid.

[16] Richard Halloran, "Army Spied on 18,000 Civilians in Two Year Operation," *New York Times*, January 19, 1971; Vin McLellan, "Surveilling Civilians: Old Dossiers Never Die," *The Village Voice*, November 11, 1971, p. 10.

tioned and challenged. Tactics of repression are used out of the state's desperation and weakness, when other less blatant forms of social control fail.

Suggested Reading

BITTNER, EGON. "The Police on Skid-Row: A Study of Peace Keeping." *American Sociological Review* 32, no. 5 (October, 1967).

BLAUNER, ROBERT. "Internal Colonialism and Ghetto Revolt." *Social Problems* (Spring, 1969).

BROWNING, FRANK. "They Shoot Hippies, Don't They?" *Ramparts,* November, 1970.

Department of the Army Field Manual. *Civil Disturbances and Disasters,* March 1968.

FONER, PHILIP S., ed. *The Black Panther Speaks.* New York: J. B. Lippincott Co., 1970.

HALLORAN, RICHARD. "Army in '68 Feared Civil 'Insurgency.'" *New York Times,* February 28, 1971.

———. "Army Spied on 18,000 Civilians in 2 Year Operation," *New York Times,* January 18, 1971.

———. "Dissidence Unit Has Dossiers on 14,000." *New York Times,* April 2, 1971.

HEUSSEMSTAMM, F. K. "Bumper Stickers and the Cops." *Trans-action,* February, 1971.

JACKSON, GEORGE. *Blood in My Eye.* New York: Random House, 1972.

JACOBS, HAL, *ed. Weatherman.* Palo Alto, Calif.: Ramparts Press, 1970.

JACOBS, PAUL. "Informers: The Enemy Within." *Ramparts,* August–September, 1973.

JANOWITZ, MORRIS. *Social Control of Escalated Riots.* Chicago: University of Chicago, Center for Policy Studies, 1968.

KLARE, MICHAEL. *War Without End.* New York: Knopf, 1972.

LEWIN, NATHAN. "Justice Cops Out." *New Republic,* June 6, 1970.

LOUGH, THOMAS. *Urban Disarmament.* Kent, Ohio: Kent State University, Center for Urban Regionalism, 1969.

MCLELLAN, VIN. "Surveilling Civilians: Old Dossiers Never Die." *The Village Voice,* November 11, 1971, pp. 9–10, 50.

MORALES, ARMANDO. "Police Deployment Theories and the Mexican-American Community." *El Grito,* Winter, 1970.

"Police Infiltration of Dissident Groups." *The Journal of Criminal Law, Criminology and Police Science* 61, no. 2, June, 1970.

PRESTON, WILLIAM JR. *Aliens and Dissenters.* New York: Harper, 1963.

ROWEN, JAMES. "Law and Slaughter: Quick Triggers in New Mexico." *The Nation,* June 19, 1972.

SMITH, R. DEAN and KOBETZ, RICHARD W. *Guidelines for Civil Disorders and Mobilization Planning.* Washington, D.C.: International Association of Police Chiefs, 1968.

WOLFE, ALAN. *The Seamy Side of Democracy: Repression in America.* New York: David McKay, 1973.

MICHAEL T. KLARE

Bringing It Back: Planning for the City

Counterinsurgency research has been accorded the status of a science only within the past few decades; its purpose, however, is centuries old. Historically its role has been to maintain dominion over a colonial population with a limited allocation of the military strength of the home country. The duration and breadth of any empire is ultimately determined by the ability of its armies to maintain order in colonial territories without overtaxing the manpower and financial resources of the homeland.

The occupation army of an imperial power is always outnumbered by the indigenous population of a colony; in order to maintain hegemony, therefore, it must maintain a supremacy in armament and organization that outweighs its numerical inferiority. When a nationalist movement has secured the active support of the population, in sufficient numbers to offset the technological advantage of occupying forces, colonialism is doomed.

Since the end of World War II, the United States has assembled the largest empire in the history of mankind. (The term "empire" as commonly used today means American cultural, political, and economic hegemony over other countries.) For the most part, it has tried to exercise its influence over the internal affairs of its "allies" and satellites through economic and political sanctions. The security of this empire has been threatened, however, by the periodic outbreak of national liberation movements. Vietnam has shown the U.S. that the price of empire can be very costly indeed, that Che Guevara was probably right in proposing that the American Empire could be destroyed by the simultaneous creation of "two, three . . . many Vietnams."

The U.S. government has responded to the danger posed by national

---

From *National Action/Research on the Military-Industrial Complex,* Police on the Homefront *(Philadelphia: American Friends Service Committee, 1971), pp. 66–73. Reprinted with permission of the author and publisher.*

liberation movements by accelerating its preparations for counterinsurgency operations in "remote areas." Our scientific and technical resources have been mobilized for research aimed at improving the "kill effectiveness" of our expeditionary forces. American universities have undertaken the task of collecting and evaluating intelligence on the revolutionary process in underdeveloped areas.[1] Through the Military Assistance Program, the Defense Department has trained the armed forces of friendly nations for counterguerrilla operations, and provides them with specially-trained cadres from the Special Forces schools in the U.S. and the Panama Canal Zone.

Sophisticated research on counterinsurgency is one of the many innovations of the "McNamara Revolution" in national security policy. Soon after taking office in 1961, McNamara established "Project Agile" —a multi-million dollar program in counterinsurgency research—under the auspices of the Pentagon's Advanced Research Projects Agency (ARPA). Using the systems-analysis approach of the military think-tanks, Pentagon scientists provided the U.S. with a greatly enhanced capability to engage in counterguerrilla warfare in remote and relatively inaccessible areas.

In order to be successful in counterinsurgency operations, "remote" or domestic, the guardians of an empire must possess:

—a close-knit and highly disciplined organization which can compensate for the psychological effects of being surrounded by a hostile (and usually ethnically different) population;

—a comprehensive intelligence network which can penetrate insurgent organizations and identify their leadership;

—detailed knowledge of the physical and social characteristics of the territories being patrolled;

—superior mobility and communications, so that small units can outmaneuver large numbers of opponents;

—weapons whose superiority in firepower is directly proportional to the numerical superiority of opposing forces;

—the promise of help from the home country, in the form of supporting troops from a "strategic reserve" which can be brought in quickly when the local forces lose control of a situation.

Since the onset of the Vietnam war, America's think-tank intellectuals have been devoting increasing amounts of time to the development of techniques and devices to improve U.S. capabilities in these areas. Lightweight radios have been designed which can penetrate heavy jungle cover;

[1] Mike Klare, "Universities in Vietnam," *Viet Report* (January, 1968), pp. 12–14; see also, *The University-Military-Police Complex,* 1970, available for $1.25 from NACLA, P.O. Box 57, Cathedral Station, New York, N.Y. and P.O. Box 226, Berkeley, California, and Mike Klare, "The Military Research Network," *The Nation,* October 12, 1970.

new armored personnel carriers can travel through swamps or rice paddies; helicopter tactics have been advanced immeasurably; infrared surveillance techniques provide new data on enemy troop movements at night; special computers assign letter grades (A to E) on the "reliability" of every hamlet in South Vietnam. Research on counterinsurgency is continuing at special Pentagon laboratories in the U.S. and Thailand to prepare for the "Vietnams of the future."

WATTS, 1965: America woke up to discover that its domestic colony, the urban ghetto, was no longer secure and that the local garrison troops had been overwhelmed. Vietnam had come home.

Like any colony, Watts had been patrolled by a small occupation army, recruited from the white society outside and compliant blacks. When Watts rebelled, these forces were overrun, and regular troops had to be brought in. When this was repeated in Newark, Detroit and Chicago, it became clear that such domestic operations were going to strain America's manpower commitments abroad. Our domestic occupation forces would therefore have to be equipped with an advanced counterinsurgency capability in order to ease the burden of the overall strategic requirements of the empire. Every succeeding development in police technology is a manifestation of this requirement.

From a military point of view, counterinsurgency in U.S. ghettos poses the same problems as counterinsurgency in any hostile environment in which the occupation forces are outnumbered by potential insurgents; consequently, domestic operations must conform to the six principles cited above. Specifically, the anti-ghetto forces must be able to:

—move in disciplined formations in order to control the movements of rioters and hostile crowds, even when being severely taunted and provoked;

—infiltrate militant black organizations and identify their leaders for quick arrest when trouble begins;

—seal off entire sections of the ghetto in accordance with predetermined contingency plans, in order to contain rioting;

—maintain effective communications between anti-riot forces (i.e., municipal police, state police, National Guard, etc.), while blocking insurgent communications;

—spot, encircle and eliminate snipers and fire-bombers without suffering casualties;

—bring in National Guard and Army units which have been trained in anti-ghetto operations, and whose officers are familiar with the terrain and social characteristics of the conflict area.

Beginning in 1965, the Federal Government initiated a substantial research program in order to determine U.S. capabilities in the areas defined above. The officials involved were appalled to discover the primitive nature of standard police tactics during riot situations. Whereas throughout the Third World the U.S. has equipped local armies with a sophisticated capability for counterinsurgency operations, America's own garrison troops, the police, had been allowed to languish in nineteenth-century conditions. The weapons of domestic riot-control—billy-club, teargas and shotgun—hadn't undergone any technological innovations in fifty years, nor had any new tactics been developed for their use. Furthermore, no money was being spent on *new* weapons and anti-riot techniques. It was clear that the Federal Government would have to assume responsibility for this critical problem.

Not surprisingly, the government turned to its Vietnam-tested consultants when it undertook a major program of research on urban counterinsurgency. The Office of Public Safety of the State Department's Agency for International Development (AID) was already training police officials from the underdeveloped areas at the International Police Academy in Washington, D.C.; now this expertise would be used to develop training programs for domestic law enforcement officials. Selected universities would be asked to furnish strategies for a new pacification program in the home country.

Beginning in 1965, Project Agile—the Pentagon's principal counterinsurgency research program—was redirected to include studies of "urban disequilibrium." Using a cross-cultural approach that linked ghetto riots in the U.S. to urban rebellions in Latin America, Agile contractors sought to delineate the essential characteristics of urban insurgency and to suggest a workable strategy for urban counterinsurgency. As part of this effort, the Defense Research Corporation (DRC) of Santa Barbara, Calif., prepared a series of "Urban Insurgency Studies" which comprised "an inventory of urban insurgent and counterinsurgent techniques, tactics and doctrines." [2]

The Pentagon hurriedly appropriated additional funds for further research in this area. The Research Analysis Corporation (RAC) drew up a technical paper entitled "A Summary Report of Research Requirements for Sensing and Averting Critical Insurgent Actions in an Urban Environment." In this classified report "the special problems of insurgency in an urban setting are defined, and suggested tactics, techniques and hardware for counterinsurgent forces are examined." [3] In yet another program of "Urban Insurgency Studies," the Simulmatics Corporation of New York City conducted "an analysis of communications,

[2] John L. Sorenson, *Urban Insurgency Cases* (Santa Barbara, California: Defense Research Corporation, 1965).

[3] John M. Breit, Dorothy K. Clark, John H. Glover, and Bradish J. Smith, *A Summary Report of Research Requirements for Sensing and Averting Critical Insurgent Actions in an Urban Environment* (McLean, Va.: Research Analysis Corp., 1966), abstract.

coordination and requirements during the Watts Riots."[4] The Center for Research in Social Systems (CRESS), then at American University in Washington, D.C., contributed a "Selected Bibliography of Crowd and Riot Behavior in Civil Disturbances," and a handbook entitled "Combating Subversively Manipulated Civil Disturbances." The author of the handbook, Adrian H. Jones, described his report as follows: "A systematic study of the patterns of development of civil disturbances and the tactics of the subversive manipulators is made to identify countermeasures for controlling the subversive manipulation of civil disturbances."[5]

In 1966 the Institute for Defense Analyses (IDA), whose work on counterinsurgency has been discussed elsewhere,[6] was commissioned by the President's Commission on Law Enforcement and the Administration of Justice to organize a task force on Science and Technology in crime control. Members of the task force's Science Advisory Committee included Adam Yarmolinsky, a Harvard Law professor and former aide to Defense Secretary McNamara, and Dr. Robert L. Sproull, Vice President and Provost of the University of Rochester and currently chairman of the Defense Science Board. From IDA's own staff came Joseph Coates, an expert on chemical warfare.*

Emphasizing the advantages of a systems-analysis approach to police operations, the task force concluded: "The experience of science in the military . . . suggests that a fruitful collaboration can be established between criminal justice officials on one hand and engineers, physicists, economists, and social and behavioral scientists on the other. In military research organizations these different professions, working with military

4 Ithiel de Sola Pool, David J. Yates, Aprodicio Laquain, Richard Blum, and Michael Weatlake, *Report on Urban Insurgency Studies* (New York: Simulmatics Corp., 1966), abstract.

5 Adrian H. Jones, *Combating Subversively Manipulated Civil Disturbances* (Washington, D.C.: American University, Center for Research in Social Systems, 1966), abstract.

6 Cathy McAffee, "IDA: The Academic Conscripts," *Viet Report* (January, 1968), pp. 8–11.

* *Joseph Coates* subsequently prepared two special studies on police operations for IDA: "Non-Lethal Weapons for Domestic Law Enforcement Officers" (a paper presented at the First National Symposium on Law Enforcement Science and Technology 1967), and "The Police Function in Stability Operations" (IDA report no. TN-547, May 1968).

In the earlier paper, Coates argues that "chemical agents could provide the police with new graduated and controlled levels of force, and an opportunity to give more responses proportional to the needs of the situation. They also offer opportunities to deal with situations which hitherto have not been satisfactorily dealt with, such as . . . the apprehension of the fleeing youth or the immobilization of a number of people at the same time." A much condensed version of this paper appeared in the *New York Times Magazine* for Sept. 17, 1967 under the heading, "Wanted: Weapons That Do Not Kill."

officers in interdisciplinary teams, have attacked defense problems in new ways and have provided insights that were new even to those with long military experience. Similar developments appear possible in criminal justice." [7]

The bulk of the IDA report is devoted to suggestions for how modern communications and data-processing systems can be applied to the problems of domestic counterinsurgency, in order to increase the efficiency of local police agencies. Noting that most law enforcement agencies in the U.S. lacked the means for any kind of systematic research on anti-riot techniques, IDA later urged that the Federal Government establish a centralized crime research organization modeled on the Pentagon's Advanced Research Projects Agency. IDA subsequently received a $152,000 contract from the Justice Department to design a "National Program of Research, Development, Test and Evaluation on Law Enforcement and Criminal Justice."

Many of IDA's recommendations were incorporated into the Omnibus Safe Streets and Crime Control Act of 1968, which was passed by the Congress in the wake of the nationwide rioting which followed the assassination of Martin Luther King, Jr.[8]

A report on anti-riot operations prepared by Cyrus R. Vance* known as the "Detroit Book" is reported to have influenced government strategy during the April 1968 round of ghetto disturbances. A censored version of the secret report was subsequently made available to the press, a summary of which appeared in the *New York Times* for April 14, 1968. A principal feature of the Vance report is the recommendation that

[7] The Institute for Defense Analyses, *Task Force Report: Science and Technology* (Washington, D.C.: U.S. Government Printing Office, 1967), p. 2.

[8] The Omnibus Act superseded an earlier law, the Law Enforcement Assistance Act of 1965, which was signed into law by President Johnson on September 22, 1965 (shortly after the Watts riots). A complete list of projects supported by this law appears in *Grants and Contracts Awarded Under the Law Enforcement Assistance Act of 1965, Fiscal Years 1966–1968* (Washington, D.C.: Office of Law Enforcement Assistance of the U.S. Department of Justice, 1968).

* *Cyrus R. Vance* is one of the most conspicuous figures in the Federal Government's efforts to upgrade national strategies for the containment of ghetto rebellions. A former Deputy Secretary of Defense and principal aide to Robert S. McNamara, Vance served as McNamara's representative in Detroit during the disorders of 1967, and later as an assistant to President Johnson during the riots in Washington, D.C., which followed the assassination of Dr. Martin Luther King, Jr.

It was on Vance's orders that the Army's computerized data of information on civilian "troublemakers" was started. He wrote: "I cannot overemphasize the importance of such information, particularly when the Federal team has to make a determination as to whether the situation is beyond the control of local and State law enforcement agencies. . . . I believe it would be useful to assemble and analyze such data for Detroit, Newark, Milwaukee, Watts, et cetera." Quoted in U.S. House of Representatives, Committee on Appropriations, *Department of Defense Appropriations for 1971*, part 3, Hearings, 91st Congress, Second Session (Washington, D.C.: U.S. Government Printing Office, 1970), p. 156.

riot areas be inundated with police, National Guardsmen, and if necessary Army troops at the earliest outbreak of violence. Gunfire would be kept to a minimum, but the liberal use of tear gas encouraged. An early curfew, stringently enforced, was another key recommendation.

CONTROLLED RESPONSE

Both the IDA task force findings and Vance's report reflect a new pattern in urban counterinsurgency doctrine which will be familiar to those who have read Herman Kahn's manifestos or who have studied the air war against North Vietnam. Like the Air Force doctrine of "instrumental escalation," counterinsurgency strategy in the ghetto now encompasses a graduated series of phased escalations, whereby the government seeks to achieve its desired objective—the restoration of stability—through the minimum use of force. Thus whereas in Newark and Detroit excessive police violence at the early stages of the rioting provoked increased community resistance, the new strategy would conserve heavy firepower for later phases of an uprising in the hope that less violent tactics would achieve quicker results.

The principle of "controlled response" to urban disorders was introduced by William W. Herrmann* of the System Development Corporation at the Second National Symposium on Law Enforcement Science and Technology. In a paper entitled "Riot Prevention and Control: Operations Research Response," Herrmann explained:

> Insufficient, or inadequate, levels of response—whether offensive or defensive—are quite likely to result in the dissipation of resources with no significant effect other than a possible further weakening of the government's position. Overresponse, on the other hand, although it may accomplish a given tactical objective such as the neutralization of a specific individual, group of individuals, or "target," may do so at the expense of some other strategic objective. For example, overly aggressive tactics may effectively neutralize a given threat, but do so at the expense of more people becoming disaffected from the government and its aims and more closely allied with the dissident forces or causes.

This view is entirely in accord with the flexible response strategy advocated by former Defense Secretary McNamara for dealing with in-

* *William W. Herrmann* was one of the few professionals in the Los Angeles Police Department who had received his Bachelor's, Master's, and Doctor's degrees (in 1952, 1956, and 1960, respectively). His last assignment was Officer in Charge, Advanced Systems Development as well as patrol, investigative, intelligence and special civil disturbance control units. After he left the Police Department in 1967, he continued the same kind of work in Thailand as an advisor to the Thai National Police Department. In 1968 he transferred to South Vietnam and was awarded a Certificate of Appreciation for his service in support of counterinsurgency efforts. This information is from his "Curriculum Vitae" distributed at the Third National Symposium on Law Enforcement Science and Technology, April 1970.

surgencies in the Third World. In fact, U.S. government officials regularly apply McNamara's analysis to the domestic crisis. In 1967 the Treasury Department's Director of Law Enforcement Coordination, Arnold Sagalyn, remarked that, "Our obsolescent, 19th Century police weapons are . . . posing a danger to the peace and welfare of our urban communities. . . . For the police officer's basic weapon, his gun, lacks the *flexible response capability* needed to deal with the specific type of problem involved. The inability of the police officer to control the degree and deadliness of this physical force in proportion to the nature and quality of the threat has put him—indeed the entire community—in a critical dilemma." [9]

[9] Treasury Department press release, March 9, 1967, entitled "Remarks by Arnold Sagalyn . . . Before the National Symposium on Law Enforcement Science and Technology. . . ." (emphasis added).

ROBERT WALL

Special Agent for the FBI

I

In May of 1965, after serving as a naval officer for several years, I arrived in Washington, D.C. to begin my training for the position of Special Agent with the Federal Bureau of Investigation. I was both naïve and apolitical. I thought of myself as an intense idealist and was convinced that the FBI was an organization in which personal integrity was highly valued. To me the organization was above all a protector of the innocent public and only secondarily the relentless pursuer of wrongdoers. In short, I was an ideal candidate for the job. I would not question; I would simply learn to do as I was told, content to believe that the FBI would never direct me wrong.

This belief managed to survive my first two years in the bureau, during which I worked on criminal investigations and government job applications. It was when I was assigned to work in Internal Security in Washington, D.C., that I began to have my first serious doubts about the integrity of the organization, its motives, and its goals.

The Washington Field Office is the operating arm of the FBI in Washington, D.C. Like other field offices, we reported to the bureau's Washington headquarters, but our office was one of the largest. Assigned to the office were between five and six hundred agents, broken up into squads of from a handful to fifty or sixty. Two squads worked only on applications for government jobs and five or six handled criminal investigations. In addition, there were nine squads assigned to do "security" work. One of those nine was charged with investigating all of the various individuals and organizations that allegedly threatened the national security or that advocated the overthrow of the United States government by force or violence.

It was to this squad that I was assigned in May, 1967, shortly before

From The New York Review of Books, *January 27, 1972, pp. 12, 14–18. Reprinted with permission of the author and publisher.*

my second anniversary as an agent. I looked forward to the assignment because anything would have looked good to me after a few months spent investigating applicants for government jobs. But I realized that all my FBI experience until then had in no way prepared me for work in security. During the training course for new agents which I had undergone in 1965, instruction on "security" meant listening to stories of the bureau's great accomplishments, e.g., the capture of the Nazi espionage teams that landed in Florida and New England during World War II, and, of course, the apprehension of Colonel Rudolph Abel. We learned also that the bureau had been able to break up the Ku Klux Klan and the Communist Party.

But nothing in this training was meant to define how the FBI views national security or threats to it. We were told instead that only a handful of experienced and carefully picked agents, the "cream of the crop," were selected to work in this most difficult and challenging field. Furthermore, information about the security work of the FBI was supplied on a "need to know" basis only, and there was no immediate need to tell us much more.

Later, in September, 1967, I was sent to the FBI National Academy in Quantico, Virginia, for a two week in-service training in "Basic Security." But this consisted mainly of an elaborate rehash of the noninformation we had received during new agents training. Nonetheless, I was eager to learn more about the work of the squad and the men assigned to it.

The heyday of this squad was during the late Forties and early Fifties when those who were called Communists, pinkos, reds, Commie symps, fellow travelers, and sundry other names were being "discovered" and routed from all levels of American society. By the time I arrived on the scene the squad was jokingly referred to by some as "the graveyard," owing to the advanced age of some of the agents and the motionless manner in which they conducted their investigations now that their prime had passed. Of the dozen or so agents on the squad, all were near or past their twentieth year of service in the bureau. Most of them had spent the better part of their careers on the squad as "red chasers."

Each of the older agents would willingly relate how he had shared in the FBI's successful smashing of the Communist Party. The stories most often had the flavor of back fence gossip, for they concerned not some insidious plot to overthrow the government, but rather the clandestine love affairs of various Party members.

One agent told me that he spent twelve years of his bureau service in "lookouts." A lookout is a place where an agent can sit (sometimes stand, kneel, lie, or squat, but usually sit) unobserved and look out to see what the person under investigation is doing. One of these lookouts which he recalled fondly was in a hotel room across an airshaft from a room rented by a Communist Party "angel" in a downtown Washington, D.C., hotel. In fact this agent had spent some years of his life peering across the airshaft at his wholly innocuous subject. The blinds in the room he watched were never closed. He liked to tell of the lively sexual activities he had seen.. He seemed to think that, in the absence of other evidence, they confirmed that something subversive was taking place.

Another agent told of months spent watching the suburban home of a suspected "Commie" where the only information of value obtained was that after the suspect left for work in the morning his wife would signal to her lover, who lived two streets away, by switching on the back porch light. The lover would then jump in his car and race over for a morning visit. The agent's report indicated the time elapsed from the moment when the porch light went on until the lover arrived panting at the door, and then the length of his stay. The lover was not known to be a member of the Party, but was suspected of being a sympathizer, which may have been the justification used by the agents to account for the time they spent watching that particular house.

By 1967, the Communist Party in Washington, D.C., had only three members remaining. The main function of the squad then was to verify the residence and employment of the persons who once had been subjects of FBI investigation and who were still considered dangerous enough to keep track of, even though they were no longer active with the Party or any other subversive group, for that matter. Every three, six, nine, or twelve months the files on these persons would be reopened and assigned to an agent on the squad who would make certain that the individual still lived at the same address and worked at the same job.

To accomplish this task, the agent could use several methods. He could personally observe the subject at his home and follow him to work. Or he could request the agents handling one of the three remaining informants familiar with former Party members to ask the informants about the man in question. The latter method was usually chosen since it would eliminate any real work for the agent. After the informant had reported, the case could then be closed again. In closing the case, the agent could either certify that the subject was still worthy of the bureau's attention or try to give him a lower priority, thereby lengthening the interval before the file had to be reopened. It was simpler and required much less paperwork to certify that the subject still needed watching. Thus the investigations of hundreds of perfectly harmless people continued on through the years.

II

By 1967, the antiwar movement was growing from its lean beginnings to a movement of national significance. The response of the bureau was consistent with its history. It determined that the movement was a part of the larger Communist conspiracy to overthrow the United States government. Having decided this, the bureau set about to investigate the movement to show the existence of the conspiracy.

Proof sufficient to satisfy the bureau was readily available. For example, it was noted that among the thirty-five to forty thousand persons who took part in the march on the Pentagon in October, 1967, approximately twenty persons who had once been named as members, suspected members, or sympathizers of the Communist Party were reported to be in the crowd. A few among them had actually assisted in organizing the march. Although the bureau always insists that it neither draws conclusions nor makes recommendations from the facts that it gathers, the FBI report on the march on the Pentagon was leaked to the press and its impact was obvious: the thousands who marched to protest the war in Southeast Asia were publicly labeled as mere pawns in a Communist master plan to spread dissent throughout the nation. They had been duped into giving aid and comfort to the enemy and demoralizing our fighting men.

Had the bureau believed its own propaganda, it would have investigated only the "Communist agitators" in the antiwar movement. Instead we were directed to investigate all the leaders in all the local peace groups and to determine among other things the source of any money used to finance the movement. From there it was a simple step to the investigation of anyone connected to the peace movement in any way. The number of investigations was limited only by the time available and the problem of distinguishing the organizers and leaders of mass rallies from the passive followers.

To deal with the peace movement the FBI followed its usual practice of planting informants. It was easy to recruit young people to infiltrate the antiwar organizations and other groups in the so-called "New Left" since large numbers of volunteers were needed to hand out leaflets, run mimeo machines, answer phones, stuff envelopes, and similar chores connected with political organizing. All one of our FBI informants needed to do was walk into the office and state briefly that he was opposed to the war and wished to volunteer his services. He would seldom be challenged to prove his allegiance to the movement. Then, with little additional effort, he had access to mailing lists, names of contributors, copies of leaflets and handbills, and was able to report in detail on any organizational meetings that might take place.

Since an organization gave an informant a convenient base from which to operate, the bureau tried to place informants in all the organizations likely to participate in any mass march or demonstration. Then if a coalition of groups was formed to plan a large rally, at least one informant would, we hoped, be among those selected to represent a group when the coalition met to plan its activities. Frequently this was the case.

The informants were always directed to look especially for any indication that violence was being planned by any group or individual within a group. This was the rationale by which the bureau justified its infiltration of these political organizations, although during my three years working on radical groups I never found any evidence that would lead to a conviction for criminal violence.

But the bureau also had an active counterintelligence program which was titled "Cointelpro—New Left." This program was designed to develop means to thwart and undermine the activities of any organization that fell into the category of "New Left." A frequent tactic was to leak stories to the press and television shortly before any mass march or rally. This was easy enough to do. Agents in our offices would write often fanciful press releases warning that violence was expected on the day of the rally, or that the organizers of the march were in contact with Hanoi, or that some known Communists were active in organizing the march. Our superiors in the Internal Security Division at FBI headquarters would then pass on the information to conservative newspapers, which published it immediately. The purpose of such stories was not only to influence the general public but to scare away those whose commitment was weak and thereby reduce the number of persons who might otherwise attend.

Another purpose of the program was to create dissent among the various groups involved in the new left to prevent them from working together. In one case we addressed a letter to the leaders of the National Mobilization Committee (NMC) which said that the blacks of Washington, D.C., would not support the upcoming rally of the NMC unless a twenty thousand dollar "security bond" was paid to a black organization in Washington. At the same time we instructed some informants we had placed in the black organization to suggest the idea of a security bond informally to leaders of the organization. The letter we composed was approved by the bureau's counterintelligence desk and was signed with the forged signature of a leader of the black group. Later, through informants in the NMC, we learned that the letter had caused a great deal of confusion and had a significant effect on the planning for the march.

I should stress that such "counterintelligence" activities were carried on frequently, although some were quite absurd. For example, some of the agents in our office tried to confuse peace demonstrations by such collegiate tactics as handing out leaflets giving misleading information about the time and place when the marchers were supposed to meet.

The FBI claims to be a nonpolitical organization and asserts that it is not a national police force. But in its intelligence and counterintelligence work on the new left it was engaging in activity that clearly was political. Moreover, in trying to suppress and discourage a broad-based national political movement, it acted as a national political police.

III

The FBI has always been divided about college campuses. It wants to know what is happening on the campus, yet it is afraid of being charged with interfering with academic freedom. When the antiwar students began challenging the legitimacy of the Reserve Officers Training Corps (ROTC), the propriety of secret military research projects in colleges and universities, and the legality and morality of the draft, they turned their campuses into centers of political activity.

The bureau's first response to this student activism had a cautious note. We were instructed to investigate to determine who was responsible for the demonstrations and uprisings on the campuses, on the theory that they were organized by outside agitators traveling around the country, but not to conduct investigations on campus. We were told to plant informants in violence-prone student groups but not to use students themselves as informants. Then as campus activity increased we got the green light to recruit students again but were warned to choose only those who were "mature" and reliable. Those students selected were to be admonished strongly that the bureau was not interested in "legitimate campus activity" (a term as definable as "New Left").

I was understandably somewhat anxious when in November, 1967, I was assigned the case titled "Students for a Democratic Society (SDS)." Here was the organization that the bureau had singled out among all the other young activist groups for special attention. I was told that I had to prepare a comprehensive report on all SDS activities in the Washington, D.C., area in less than a month. Every campus SDS chapter was to be identified, as were the names and backgrounds of all officers of the various groups, the number of members in each chapter, the activities of each group, including especially any activity where violence or destruction of property took place.

The agent previously assigned to the case assured me that a brief letter to the bureau would suffice since there was no significant SDS activity in Washington, D.C., a fact that he had dutifully reported three times in the preceding year. (This particular agent was at the time moving up the ladder of bureau success to a supervisory position and I felt certain that his astute handling of the SDS case was largely responsible.)

With very little effort I was able to learn that there were already four campus SDS chapters in the city and an SDS regional office had just been set up. Realizing that it would be impossible in the time remaining to compile all the information demanded by the bureau, I chose to imitate my predecessor and reported that there was no significant SDS activity in the Washington, D.C., area. Shortly thereafter, when the squad was beefed up, I arranged to have the SDS case reassigned to one of the newcomers.

The bureau's ambivalence regarding campus unrest was apparent when the Washington Field Office received a request from then Assistant Director William Sullivan to analyze the activity on campuses, point out the causes, and recommend the appropriate FBI policy for dealing with student movements. Since our squad was closest to the problem, the job of preparing the position paper was turned over to us. Our squad supervisor elected to assign the task to an older agent who had recently been assigned to the squad. This agent had little experience with college matters but had as yet been assigned few cases and had more time available. He also had a reputation for being able to "write well," that is, to say what the bureau wanted to hear in the language to which it was accustomed.

When I learned of the choice I was disturbed. The agent chosen, if described by a friend, would have been called an extreme conservative. In the banter of the office I had hung the label "fascist pig" on him. He in turn called me the "Father Groppi" of the office, or "Grop" for short. I knew that he saw a conspiracy in every campus demonstration and felt that swifter police action was the first and best answer to any problem of disruption by college students. So I knew what tack he would take.

At this point I was still naïve enough to believe that the bureau was amenable to change and I saw this paper as an opportunity to "affect the bureau from within." So I went to my supervisor and asked for his permission to take over the assignment of preparing the paper for Sullivan. He refused because, in his words, "You're too young to place the SDS in proper historical perspective with the old guard Communist organizations." Undismayed, I "borrowed" the rough draft of my colleague's paper and proceeded to draft a reply and counterproposal. In essence I contended that university administrators needed to re-evaluate the role of the university in our society and take the initiative away from radical agitators by instituting needed changes before the demand for these changes became the rallying point for student discontent.

I concluded that if university administrators could recognize the issues behind the student uprisings, meet with student representatives, and be willing to compromise, they would generally be able to avert destructive confrontation. I recommended that the bureau keep its hands off the universities, even those that had already suffered disruption, because the FBI had no legal justification to intrude; any intrusion would, moreover, be taken by students as an indication of attempted repression by federal authorities.

When I dropped my paper on the supervisor's desk, he handled the situation with the skill of a diplomat. Rather than choose between the papers, he gave both to a third agent to prepare a compromise paper to be presented to Sullivan, setting out the principal points on both sides of the issue. He promised also that I would have the opportunity to make an oral presentation to Sullivan at a later date.

About two weeks later, I returned to the office unexpectedly in midmorning to discover that a meeting with Sullivan had been arranged at 1 P.M. that day. Angry at what appeared to be an attempt to keep me out, I went to the Coordinating Security Supervisor (my supervisor's supervisor) who had originally received the request from Sullivan that set the whole paper-writing flurry in motion. In his smooth Dixie manner he assured me that no slight had been intended. I had not been invited to the meeting merely because of an administrative oversight. Certainly I'd be allowed to have my say.

It seemed obvious to me then that they did not want me to attend the meeting but they didn't want to be too obvious about it. So I spent some time preparing an oral argument while I awaited the one o'clock meeting. At 12:45, just as I was bringing my shoes to a new luster, my phone rang. The Coordinating Supervisor on the other end advised me that unfortunately Mr. Sullivan's office had only four chairs for visitors and since I had been the last to request a part in the presentation and would be the fifth person, there was no choice but to exclude me. He tried to calm me with lavish praise for my initiative and willingness to tackle difficult problems, but he managed only a hollow laugh when I suggested that I'd accept standing room.

I was certain that my exclusion was just another example of how people on the lower levels of a bureaucracy act as a buffer for those higher up the ladder. They decided what the man at the top wanted to hear and they gave him just that. They had heard and read Mr. Hoover's statements that the SDS was a subversive group that traveled about the country seeking to destroy the institutions of higher learning and they could not make a presentation that deviated from that line.

The final result was an order directing intensified investigations of student agitators and expanded "informant penetration" of campus SDS groups. Predictably, the informants reported the names of hundreds of students who had done no more than say they were interested in SDS or had dropped in at a meeting. Our Washington squad alone opened dozens of cases on freshmen college students who attended orientation sessions sponsored by SDS on Washington, D.C., campuses. Soon we had so many new cases that we had to request additional agents to handle this new "threat to national security."

IV

While we were investigating antiwar groups and student activists, the squad also handled what were called "Racial Matters." This category was an absurdly and frighteningly broad one. Investigations on almost anything done by or for black people could be opened simply by labeling it a Racial Matter. Here, for example, are some of the "cases" we investigated.

—A group of teen-agers from the ghetto areas of Washington, D.C., who marched to the city council chambers and demanded restoration of funds for summer jobs for ghetto youth.

—Two busloads of steelworkers who picketed the Department of Labor to protest discriminatory practices at the Bethlehem Steel Sparrow's Point (near Baltimore) plant.

—A group of high-school students who staged a protest in their school cafeteria complaining that the food was not fit for human consumption.

—Two members of the Student Nonviolent Coordinating Committee (SNCC) who opened a bookstore on 14th Street in northwest Washington. The FBI quickly responded with an investigation titled "Drum and Spear Bookstore, Racial Matter."

When the poor people's march was organized to dramatize the plight of the poor in our nation and a camp was set up near the Washington Monument, this was a Racial Matter. More logically perhaps, investigations of the Ku Klux Klan, the American Nazi Party, and similar groups were also Racial Matters.

Clearly the bureau had no rational criterion for opening these investigations. The only consistent pattern that I found was that if an individual or group is black and does something to gain attention it is likely to be investigated.

Our guide to Racial Matters at the field office was the early edition of the Washington *Post*. A typical news item would read: "Police arrested six persons early this morning when a crowd gathered as detectives of the Metropolitan Police Department were attempting to arrest a suspected narcotics peddler at the corner of 14th and U Streets, N.W. Some rocks and bottles were allegedly thrown at police," etc. Inevitably, when such a story appeared, we would receive a call from the supervisor of the Racial Desk in bureau headquarters asking what we knew about the incident. It was his firm conviction that incidents of this type were a manifestation of the conspiracy by blacks to take over their community by driving out the police.

So that we would not be embarrassed when the supervisor called, it became standard practice for one of the early arrivers in the office to scan the paper for articles like the one above. He would clip the item, call the precinct to verify the names of the persons arrested, and then paraphrase the news item in a teletype message to bureau headquarters, advising them that we were following the incident and would report any further developments. A month or two later, the agent to whom the case was assigned would close it with a letter stating that the incident was apparently spontaneous and not part of a conspiracy, and giving an estimate of the damages, the names of those arrested, and the background of those who already had records in FBI files.

Often the supervisor on the Racial Desk at the bureau would request specific information about a case under investigation by the field office. The agent to whom the Drum and Spear Bookstore case was assigned received such a request. For months he had been investigating the bookstore, watching its operations, checking out its owners, looking into its bank records, trying to ascertain the source of its funds. He had found nothing connected with crime, conspiracy, or evil doings. Now he was instructed to go to the bookstore and purchase a copy of the "Little Red Book" containing the quotations of Chairman Mao Tse-tung. It was pointless to ask what purpose the purchase of this particular book would serve. It was obvious to us that the supervisor felt that the bookstore, by selling this book, was somehow implicated in the Oriental branch of the Communist conspiracy.

The agent dutifully made his way to the Drum and Spear where he learned that they had sold their last copy of the book. Rather than order a copy to be mailed to the supervisor, a cheeky solution which he admitted considering, he returned downtown, bought a copy at Brentano's, and duly passed it on to the bureau supervisor, just as if it had come from the Drum and Spear. Thereafter, the written description of the Drum and Spear contained the note that radical literature including the "Little Red Book" of Mao Tse-tung was obtainable there.

As I worked on Racial Matters in Washignton (a city whose black population comprises more than 70 percent of the total), the appalling racism of the FBI on every level became glaringly apparent to me. It seemed that every politically dissident black man was a candidate for investigation. Perhaps this racism was no worse than in other branches of government, but it was extremely discouraging to find it so firmly entrenched in an organization of supposedly educated, professional men charged with responsibility for investigating violations of the civil rights laws.

The documents stolen from the Media, Pennsylvania, office of the FBI demonstrate the endemic racism of the bureau. In one memo that J. Edgar Hoover directed to all offices of the FBI, he ordered that "all black student unions and similar organizations organized to project the demands of black students, which are not presently under investigation, are to be subjects of discreet preliminary inquiries, limited to established sources and carefully conducted to avoid criticism, to determine the size, aims, purposes, activities, leadership, key activists, and extremist interest or influence in these groups." The stated purpose for these investigations was that these groups are the "target for influence and control by violence prone Black Panther Party (BPP) and other extremists."

Only the fact that the organizations to be investigated were black could explain the horrendous abuse of logic that the bureau used to justify this invasion of campuses throughout the country. J. Edgar Hoover had publicly announced that the small and largely ineffectual Black Panther Party was the greatest single threat to the security of the country. Having itself created the threat, the bureau set out to neutralize it. Even if Hoover could have seriously documented his charges against the Panthers, which he never did, it was absurd to investigate hundreds of people whose only connection with the Black Panther Party was that the Party was trying to influence them. Hoover might similarly have justified an FBI investigation of every member of a "working class" union because the Communist Party directed its propaganda and organizing effort at workers, or an investigation of every college student organization because the SDS sought to influence and control students.

Nor was this assault on the black student unions an isolated incident. I could cite many similar ones, for example the FBI's interest in the Smithsonian Institute when it opened an annex in the largely black Anacostia section of Washington, D.C. One of the annex's first events was a program for Black History Week centered on the life and contributions of Frederick Douglass. The FBI actually paid informants to attend the program and report the contents of the speeches given during it.

In the case of Stokely Carmichael the FBI was particularly determined and vicious. When he moved to Washington, D.C., in December, 1967, our squad kept him under surveillance twenty-four hours a day, following him about the city from lookouts and cars, and on foot. The investigation became even more intense a few days after Martin Luther King was assassinated. When blacks in Washington, D.C., as well as in many other cities, outraged by the murder, rioted for a day and a half, in the Washington Field Office a fifty-man special squad was assembled to get Carmichael for inciting to riot. We were directed to gather evidence showing that Carmichael had plotted, planned, and directed the rioting, burning, and pillage that took place in Washington, D.C. Fifty agents spent their full time for over a month on this one case.

One man, who later admitted that he had "been mistaken and perhaps exaggerated a bit," claimed that Carmichael had a pistol which he fired into the air and then told the crowd to go home and get guns. A great many others stated firmly that Carmichael had urged the crowd not to dishonor Dr. King's memory by rioting and had politely asked shop owners to close their shops in his memory. Lacking any substantial evidence on which to base a charge, the bureau nevertheless submitted voluminous reports on the minute by minute activities of Carmichael that were heavily weighted to imply that he had actually incited the mobs. Had Carmichael not decided to leave this country and go to Africa, the FBI, I am confident, would eventually have found something with which to bring an indictment against him.

Quite by accident I learned that the Internal Revenue Service (IRS) was aiding in the hunt for something with which to pin a charge on so-called "Black Militants." In early 1969 I was checking the background of a former member of SNCC, a man I had been investigating for almost two years. On three occasions I tried to close the case because I could find no indication that the subject was doing anything that would warrant an FBI investigation. Each time permission was refused, his status as a former member of SNCC being sufficient justification for going on with the investigation. I learned that the IRS had requested his arrest record from the Identification Division of the FBI. When I went to the IRS I found it had secretly set up a special squad of men to investigate the tax records of a list of "known militants and activists," and that the FBI was supplying the names of the persons for the IRS to include in this list. After talking to several IRS officials I was sent to a locked sound-proofed room in the basement of the IRS headquarters in Washington where I found a file on my subject, among hundreds of others piled on a long table.

V

There are hardly any limits on the bureau's activities in compiling political information, particularly about the new left. A case in point is the Institute for Policy Studies, an organization set up by dissenting officials in Kennedy's administration to carry out independent studies in international and domestic questions. The Institute caught my attention shortly after I began investigating the new left. Reports from FBI informants showed that many of the leaders and spokesmen of antiwar and civil rights organizations called at the Institute when they visited Washington.

I reasoned that if there were a conspiracy that linked all these groups the Institute was the logical place to look for it. I drafted a memo to that effect and requested that a case on the Institute be opened and assigned to me. My supervisor quickly agreed: he was then trying to increase the case load of the squad to justify a request for an increase in manpower.

Most of the information about the Institute's work is easily available and I was soon able to accumulate a vast dossier on it including biographical sketches of its founders, sources of its financial support, a general idea of its day to day operation, and a pile of scholarly studies published by it. After analyzing this data I concluded that the Institute was not the secret mastermind of any conspiracy to overthrow the government but simply what I described in my report as a "think-tank of the Left," where a wide variety of current and former government officials, lawyers, journalists, radicals, and others were holding seminars, doing research, writing reports, etc. I closed the investigation. To do otherwise, incidentally, would have meant a mound of paperwork that would have occupied me full time for months.

About a year later another agent newly assigned to the squad came to see me with the closed file of the Institute and asked whether I thought the case ought to be reopened. This agent, like so many others, had strong right-wing views and could not believe that the Institute was merely sponsoring seminars and doing the other work I had described. It seemed necessary to him to think that a grand new left conspiracy existed. In spite of my opposition, he had the case reopened and began a full-scale investigation of the Institute. He began monitoring the checking account of the Institute to determine where its money was going. He asked for telephone company records and compiled a list of the Institute's long distance telephone calls. He attempted to place informants in the Institute as student interns and gathered every available paper published by it. Individual investigations were then opened on the people who worked for or received money from the Institute.

When I left the bureau in April, 1970, the case on the Institute was still being investigated with gusto, and a huge collection of papers and reports on it had accumulated. So far as I have been able to determine, the FBI has found no evidence whatever of any illegal activity by the IPS, but the Institute continues to be investigated.

My experience has shown me that the FBI in its pursuit of blacks, the antiwar movement, and college activists was not an impartial, disinterested finder of fact but rather a relentless guardian of orthodoxy, a police force which sought to cause harm to movements that boldly questioned the policies of the government. It engaged in these activities not simply because of the political prejudices of the director and his staff, but, to a large extent, to justify its own existence. Each attack on any outspoken critic of American institutions was intended to show the FBI as the indispensable protector of the public. To each slanderous name-calling or alarmist leak to the press, Hoover added a soft-spoken if tendentious appeal to Congress for more money and additional personnel. Enemies of the public were created to justify the bureau's role as defender of the "National Security" against domestic foes who sought, according to Hoover's propaganda, to subvert the country.

This is not to say that an effective federal investigative agency is not needed to deal with crimes or that the FBI itself has not done efficient and honest criminal work (altough it has for years been reluctant to act vigorously against organized crime). But my years in the FBI convinced me that most of what the bureau does in matters of internal security consists of investigations and rumor mongering that are foolish, pointless, and time-wasting so far as protection of the public from violation of criminal laws is concerned; while the agency is all too effective in harassing legitimate political activity. At the same time, all of the investigations I have referred to here have resulted in adding more names and dossiers to the millions in the FBI's files. The FBI is thus creating a proliferating store of secret police files on innocent people, often based on bizarre allegations and dubious information, and sometimes on nothing at all.

What I saw and did as an agent for the FBI exposed for me the wisdom of the old question: Who will watch the watchers? I have no easy answer to it.

V

POLICING MASS DISSENT

During the 1960s, scenes of mass protest and police brutality became a common event as we witnessed southern sheriffs with dogs and cattle prodders harassing civil rights marchers, soldiers shooting "looters" during ghetto rebellions, police beating white antiwar demonstrators, and sheriffs administering "street justice" to college students at Berkeley, Columbia, and other campuses. The horror stories of police illegality, brutality, and vindictiveness have been thoroughly documented by government commissions, journalists, and social scientists.[1] In this section we include two such accounts—the Kerner Commission's case study of the bloody 1967 Detroit riot and the Walker Report's celebrated analysis of the "police riot" at the National Democratic Convention in Chicago in 1968—plus an analysis of police ideology concerning mass dissent prepared by the Skolnick task force for the 1969 National Commission on the Causes and Prevention of Violence.

Although there is extensive documentation of illegal police actions against mass dissent, the conventional literature rarely attempts to analyze such behavior in a historical and political context. When there is analysis, it typically focuses on explaining the actions and psychology of rank and file officers, or on the internal dynamics of police organization.[2] Police violence is deplored and explained in terms of "bad apples" or individual police pathology, a lack of proper training, or poor planning and organization. For example, the Walker Report concluded that "some policemen lost control of themselves under exceedingly provocative circumstances . . ." And the Kerner Commission characterized police violence during the 1967 ghetto rebellions as "over-reaction."

1 See suggested further reading below.

2 See, for example, National Commission on the Causes and Prevention of Violence, *To Establish Justice, To Ensure Domestic Tranquility* (Washington, D.C.: U.S. Government Printing Office, 1969); President's Commission on Campus Unrest, *The Scranton Report* (Washington, D.C.: U.S. Government Printing Office, 1970); New York State Special Commission, *Attica* (New York: Bantam, 1972); and Rodney Stark, *Police Riots: Collective Violence and Law Enforcement* (Belmont, Calif.: Wadsworth, 1972).

The implication of this level of analysis is that police "mishandling" of mass dissent can be reformed through more elaborate screening devices for recruits, riot-control training, and more careful organization and planning. The Scranton Commission on Campus Unrest, for example, recommended that "peace officers be trained and equipped to deal with campus disorders, firmly, justly, and humanely. They must avoid both uncontrolled and excessive response. Too frequently, local police forces have been undermanned, improperly equipped, poorly trained, and unprepared for campus disturbances. We therefore urge police forces . . . to improve their capacity to respond to civil disorders." [3]

This kind of analysis ignores the history of police repression in the United States as well as the political and structural conditions under which the police operate. Police violence against mass protest is neither a new phenomenon nor simply a consequence of "over-reaction." In times of political crisis, police violence is extensive, systematic and planned rather than the result of individual excesses or poor organization.

The police generally do the job that they have been called upon to perform, after other forms of nonviolent repression (co-option, reform, etc.) have failed.[4] A cursory examination of the history of police violence in the United States supports this conclusion. Between 1870 and 1937, police and troops were regularly used against the labor movement and casualties typically resulted. For example, in 1873 a peaceful demonstration by unemployed workers in Tompkins Square, New York was attacked by police with clubs and horses. "It was an orgy of brutality," observed Samuel Gompers. "The attacks of the police kept up all day long—wherever the police saw a group of poorly dressed persons standing or moving together." [5] During the depression of 1877, striking railroad workers were attacked by police and militia, causing many deaths and hundreds of injuries. According to labor historians, Philip Taft and Philip Ross, "the widespread and ferocious reaction has no parallel in our history." [6] Official violence against workers and organizers continued through the first three decades of this century:[7]

[3] Quoted in Anthony Platt, *The Politics of Riot Commissions, 1917–1970* (New York: Macmillan, 1971), p. 484. For more extensive recommendations along the same line, see National Advisory Commission on Civil Disorders, *The Kerner Report* (Washington, D.C.: U.S. Government Printing Office, 1967), pp. 267–291.

[4] Alan Wolfe, "Political Repression and The Liberal Democratic State," *Monthly Review* 23, no. 7 (December, 1971): 18–38.

[5] Quoted in Richard Hofstadter and Michael Wallace, eds., *American Violence: A Documentary History* (New York: Vintage, 1971), p. 347.

[6] Philip Taft and Philip Ross, "American Labor Violence: Its Causes, Character and Outcome," in Hugh Davis Graham and Ted Robert Gurr, eds., *Violence in America: Historical and Comparative Perspectives* (New York: Bantam, 1969), p. 290.

[7] The following examples are documented in the essay by Taft and Ross, op. cit., pp. 281–395 and the book by Hofstadter and Wallace, loc. cit.

—in 1892, the Carnegie Steel Company used 300 Pinkerton detectives and 8,000 National Guard to crush a strike at the Homestead, Pennsylvania plant
—in 1894, over 14,000 police, militia, and troops responded to the Pullman strike, killing over thirty workers
—between 1900 and 1910, police and troops were frequently used to break strikes and unions in Pennsylvania and Colorado
—the Industrial Workers of the World or "Wobblies," as they were called, were a special target of official violence, suffering extensive casualties at the 1916 "Everett Massacre" and 1919 Centralia riot during their efforts to organize lumber workers in Washington
—in 1913–14, a strike in the Colorado mining fields at Ludlow was brutally repressed by hired thugs, sheriff's deputies, and the National Guard; during the course of the struggle, twelve children and two women were murdered in their tents
—after World War I, armed soldiers were often sent to trouble spots as a "precautionary measure" in order to prevent labor organizing and strikes
—official violence against labor continued into the 30s, as exemplified at the 1932 Dearborn, Michigan strike against the Ford Motor Company in which four workers were killed by local police armed with firehoses, pistols, and machine guns.

Official violence has been systematically employed not only against labor groups, but also against radical and progressive political organizations, as well as black and other Third World movements in this country. The description by the Walker Report of police activities during the 1968 National Democratic Convention is comparable to accounts of official violence against the Socialist Party at the beginning of this century. Contrast the Walker Report with, for example, the following description of police attacks on the 1919 May Day parade in Cleveland:

> " . . . A platoon of mounted police dashed into the melee, wielding clubs without discrimination upon men and women alike. Instantly, bedlam broke loose. Army trucks and tanks, police autos, ambulances and police patrol wagons were dashing helter-skelter through the crowds, overrunning and injuring many in an attempt to disperse the crowds." [8]

Official violence against people of color in the United States goes back to the slaughter of native Americans, the day-to-day exploitation of slaves, and the systematic domination by whites of all Third World people who were robbed of their lands or imported as cheap labor.[9] During this century alone, Black protests and rebellions received brutal repression, as the following examples indicate:[10] in the 1917 East St. Louis race riots, in which thirty-nine Blacks and nine whites were killed, the police and National Guard participated in the violence either by protecting or supporting attacks by whites on Blacks; in the

[8] Quoted in Hofstadter and Wallace, op. cit., p. 353.

[9] For a well-documented analysis of America's racial history, see Paul Jacobs and Saul Landau, *To Serve The Devil* (New York: Vintage, 1971).

[10] The following examples are documented by Platt, loc. cit.

1919 Chicago race riot, twice as many Blacks as whites were injured and arrested due to the fact that "there were instances of actual police participation in the rioting as well as neglect of duty:" [11] in the 1935 Harlem riot, reports of extensive police brutality were confirmed by a distinguished commission appointed by Mayor LaGuardia; in Detroit's bloody 1943 race riot, police and soldiers failed to provide proper protection to blacks and also supported attacks by whites; and in the ghetto rebellions of the 1960s in Watts, Newark, Detroit and many other cities, official violence was responsible for hundreds of deaths. In the following selection from the Kerner Report, it is reported that forty-three persons (thirty-three Blacks) were killed by the police and National Guard in the 1967 Detroit rebellion alone. And this estimate is probably low, according to reporter Garry Wills, who claims that many corpses were burned in destroyed buildings and puts the toll around 100.[12]

These varied examples indicate that violent repression by official authorities is a recurring phenomenon, decreasing when there is little active struggle by radical movements (the 1940s and 50s, for example) and increasing when mass dissent has popular support and cannot be undermined simply by political tactics (the 1870s and 1960s, for example).[13] Although the modern state apparatus has an enormous amount of violence at its disposal, there is often a hesitancy to use it because official violence can breed counterviolence, instability, and even revolutionary opposition.[14] The United States government learned this lesson in Vietnam.

When the police and other specialists in official violence are called upon to control mass dissent, it is clear to them that they are expected to use massive and decisive force. To require them to do this in a non-provocative and "legitimate" manner is an impossibility, given that their presence is in itself provocative, illegitimate, and a visible indication that the state protects established economic and political arrangements. So long as there is an economic system that benefits a few at the expense of the many and a political system that protects racial and sexual privileges, the greater the likelihood that popular movements by workers, people of color, women, and other exploited groups will arise. And in these confrontations, the police are called upon to repress such movements. The solution to police violence against mass dissent, therefore, lies not in better recruitment or training procedures but rather in the success of those movements that challenge the basic in-

[11] Finding by the Chicago Commission on Race Relations, quoted in Platt, ibid., p. 102.

[12] Garry Wills, *The Second Civil War* (New York: Signet, 1968), pp. 47–50.

[13] Wolfe, loc. cit.

[14] This point is elaborated by George Lukács, *History and Class Consciousness* (Cambridge: M.I.T. Press, 1971), pp. 256–71.

equalities in modern capitalist society. It is a contradiction to instruct the police to act with restraint and civility when their function is to protect property, profit, and privilege.

Suggested Reading

ARMISTEAD, TIMOTHY. "Police on Campus and the Evolution of Personal Commitment," *Issues in Criminology* 4 (1969): 171–84.

Chicago Commission on Race Relations. *The Negro in Chicago: A Study of Race Relations and a Riot.* Chicago: University of Chicago Press, 1922.

Cox Commission. *Crisis at Columbia.* New York: Vintage, 1968.

GRAHAM, HUGH DAVIS and GURR, TED ROBERT, eds. *Violence in America: Historical and Comparative Perspectives.* New York: Bantam, 1969.

HOFSTADTER, RICHARD and WALLACE, MICHAEL, eds. *American Violence: A Documentary History.* New York: Vintage, 1971.

JACOBS, PAUL. *Prelude to Riot.* New York: Random House, 1966.

MAILER, NORMAN. *Miami and the Siege of Chicago.* New York: Signet, 1968.

MARSHALL, THURGOOD. "The Gestapo in Detroit." *Crisis* 50 (1943): 232–33, 246–67.

MASOTTI, LOUIS H. and CORSI, JEROME R. *Shoot-Out in Cleveland.* New York: Bantam, 1969.

National Advisory Commission on Civil Disorders. *Kerner Report.* Washington, D.C.: U.S. Government Printing Office, 1967.

National Commission on the Causes and Prevention of Violence. *To Establish Justice, To Ensure Domestic Tranquility.* Washington, D.C.: U.S. Government Printing Office, 1969.

New York Civil Liberties Union. *Police on Campus.* New York: New York Civil Liberties Union, 1969.

New York State Special Commission. *Attica.* New York: Bantam, 1972.

PLATT, ANTHONY. *The Politics of Riot Commissions, 1917–70.* New York: Macmillan, 1971.

President's Commission on Campus Unrest. *The Scranton Report.* Washington, D.C.: U.S. Government Printing Office, 1970.

PRESTON, WILLIAM. *Aliens and Dissenters.* New York: Harper, 1963.

RUDWICK, ELLIOT M. *Race Riot at East St. Louis, 1917.* New York: Meridian, 1966.

SKOLNICK, JEROME H., director. *The Politics of Protest.* New York: Simon & Schuster, 1969.

Sparling Commission. *Dissent and Disorder.* Chicago: Chicago Civil Liberties Union, 1968.

STARK, RODNEY. *Police Riots.* Belmont, Calif.: Wadsworth, 1972.

WILLS, GARRY. *The Second Civil War.* New York: Signet, 1968.

WOLFE, ALAN. *The Seamy Side of Democracy: Repression in American.* New York: McKay, 1973.

Detroit 1967

On Saturday evening, July 22, 1967, the Detroit Police Department raided five "blind pigs." The blind pigs had had their origin in prohibition days, and survived as private social clubs. Often, they were after-hours drinking and gambling spots.

The fifth blind pig on the raid list, the United Community and Civic League at the corner of 12th Street and Clairmount, had been raided twice before. Once 10 persons had been picked up; another time, 28. A Detroit vice squad officer had tried but failed to get in shortly after 10 o'clock Saturday night. He succeeded, on his second attempt, at 3:45 Sunday morning.

The Tactical Mobile Unit, the Police Department's crowd control squad, had been dismissed at 3 a.m. Since Sunday morning traditionally is the least troublesome time for police in Detroit—and all over the country—only 193 officers were patrolling the streets. Of these, 44 were in the 10th precinct where the blind pig was located.

Police expected to find two dozen patrons in the blind pig. That night, however, it was the scene of a party for several servicemen, two of whom were back from Vietnam. Instead of two dozen patrons, police found 82. Some voiced resentment at the police intrusion.

An hour went by before all 82 could be transported from the scene. The weather was humid and warm—the temperature that day was to rise to 86—and despite the late hour, many people were still on the street. In short order, a crowd of about 200 gathered.

In November of 1965, George Edwards, Judge of the United States Court of Appeals for the Sixth Circuit, and Commissioner of the Detroit Police Department from 1961 to 1963, had written in the *Michigan Law Review:*

> It is clear that in 1965 no one will make excuses for any city's inability to foresee the possibility of racial trouble . . . Although local police forces gen-

From Report of the National Advisory Commission on Civil Disorders (*Washington, D.C.: U.S. Government Printing Office, 1968*), *pp. 47–61.*

> erally regard themselves as public servants with the responsibility of maintaining law and order, they tend to minimize this attitude when they are patrolling areas that are heavily populated with Negro citizens. There, they tend to view each person on the streets as a potential criminal or enemy, and all too often that attitude is reciprocated. Indeed, hostility between the Negro communities in our large cities and the police departments, is the major problem in law enforcement in this decade. It has been a major cause of all recent race riots.

At the time of Detroit's 1943 race riot, Judge Edwards told Commission investigators, there was "open warfare between the Detroit Negroes and the Detroit Police Department." As late as 1961, he had thought that "Detroit was the leading candidate in the United States for a race riot."

There was a long history of conflict between the police department and citizens. During the labor battles of the 1930's, union members had come to view the Detroit Police Department as a strike-breaking force. The 1943 riot, in which 34 persons died, was the bloodiest in the United States in a span of two decades.

Judge Edwards and his successor, Commissioner Ray Girardin, attempted to restructure the image of the department. A Citizens Complaint Bureau was set up to facilitate the filing of complaints by citizens against officers. In practice, however, this Bureau appeared to work little better than less enlightened and more cumbersome procedures in other cities.

On 12th Street, with its high incidence of vice and crime, the issue of police brutality was a recurrent theme. A month earlier, the killing of a prostitute had been determined by police investigators to be the work of a pimp. According to rumors in the community, the crime had been committed by a vice squad officer.

At about the same time, the killing of Danny Thomas, a 27-year-old Negro Army veteran, by a gang of white youths had inflamed the community. The city's major newspapers played down the story in hope that the murder would not become a cause for increased tensions. The intent backfired. A banner story in the *Michigan Chronicle,* the city's Negro newspaper, began: "As James Meredith marched again Sunday to prove a Negro could walk in Mississippi without fear, a young woman who saw her husband killed by a white gang, shouting: 'Niggers keep out of Rouge Park,' lost her baby.

"Relatives were upset that the full story of the murder was not being told, apparently in an effort to prevent the incident from sparking a riot."

Some Negroes believed that the daily newspapers' treatment of the story was further evidence of the double standard: playing up crimes by Negroes, playing down crimes committed against Negroes.

Although police arrested one suspect for murder, Negroes questioned why the entire gang was not held. What, they asked, would have been the result if a white man had been killed by a gang of Negroes? What if Negroes had made the kind of advances toward a white woman that the white men were rumored to have made toward Mrs. Thomas?

The Thomas family lived only four or five blocks from the raided blind pig.

A few minutes after 5 a.m., just after the last of those arrested had been hauled away, an empty bottle smashed into the rear window of a police car. A litter basket was thrown through the window of a store. Rumors circulated of excess force used by the police during the raid. A youth, whom police nicknamed "Mr. Greensleeves" because of the color of his shirt, was shouting: "We're going to have a riot!" and exhorting the crowd to vandalism.

At 5:20 a.m., Commissioner Girardin was notified. He immediately called Mayor Jerome Cavanagh. Seventeen officers from other areas were ordered into the 10th Precinct. By 6 a.m., police strength had grown to 369 men. Of these, however, only 43 were committed to the immediate riot area. By that time, the number of persons on 12th Street was growing into the thousands and widespread window-smashing and looting had begun.

On either side of 12th Street were neat, middle-class districts. Along 12th Street itself, however, crowded apartment houses created a density of more than 21,000 persons per square mile, almost double the city average.

The movement of people when the slums of "Black Bottom" had been cleared for urban renewal had changed 12th Street from an integrated community into an almost totally black one, in which only a number of merchants remained white. Only 18 percent of the residents were homeowners. Twenty-five percent of the housing was considered so substandard as to require clearance. Another 19 percent had major deficiencies.

The crime rate was almost double that of the city as a whole. A Detroit police officer told Commission investigators that prostitution was so widespread that officers made arrests only when soliciting became blatant. The proportion of broken families was more than twice that in the rest of the city.

By 7:50 a.m., when a 17-man police commando unit attempted to make the first sweep, an estimated 3,000 persons were on 12th Street. They offered no resistance. As the sweep moved down the street, they gave way to one side, and then flowed back behind it.

A shoe store manager said he waited vainly for police for 2 hours as the store was being looted. At 8:25 a.m., someone in the crowd yelled, "The cops are coming!" The first flames of the riot billowed from the store. Firemen who responded were not harassed. The flames were extinguished.

By midmorning, 1,122 men—approximately a fourth of the police department—had reported for duty. Of these, 540 were in or near the six-block riot area. One hundred eight officers were attempting to establish a cordon. There was, however, no interference with looters, and police were refraining from the use of force.

Commissioner Girardin said: "If we had started shooting in there . . . not one of our policemen would have come out alive. I am convinced it would have turned into a race riot in the conventional sense."

According to witnesses, police at some roadblocks made little effort to stop people from going in and out of the area. Bantering took place between police officers and the populace, some still in pajamas. To some observers, there seemed at this point to be an atmosphere of apathy. On the one hand, the police failed to interfere with the looting. On the other, a number of older, more stable residents, who had seen the street deteriorate from a prosperous commercial thoroughfare to one ridden by vice, remained aloof.

Because officials feared that the 12th Street disturbance might be a diversion, many officers were sent to guard key installations in other sections of the city. Belle Isle, the recreation area in the Detroit River that had been the scene of the 1943 riot, was sealed off.

In an effort to avoid attracting people to the scene, some broadcasters cooperated by not reporting the riot, and an effort was made to downplay the extent of the disorder. The facade of "business as usual" necessitated the detailing of numerous police officers to protect the 50,000 spectators that were expected at that afternoon's New York Yankees-Detroit Tigers baseball game.

Early in the morning, a task force of community workers went into the area to dispel rumors and act as counterrioters. Such a task force had been singularly successful at the time of the incident in the Kercheval district in the summer of 1966, when scores of people had gathered at the site of an arrest. Kercheval, however, has a more stable population, fewer stores, less population density, and the city's most effective police-community relations program.

The 12th Street area, on the other hand, had been determined, in a 1966 survey conducted by Dr. Ernest Harburg of the Psychology Department of the University of Michigan, to be a community of high stress and tension. An overwhelming majority of the residents indicated dissatisfaction with their environment.

Of the interviewed, 93 percent said they wanted to move out of the neighborhood; 73 percent felt that the streets were not safe; 91 percent believed that a person was likely to be robbed or beaten at night; 58 percent knew of a fight within the last 12 months in which a weapon had been employed; 32 percent stated that they themselves owned a weapon; 57 percent were worried about fires.

A significant proportion believed municipal services to be inferior:

36 percent were dissatisfied with the schools; 43 percent with the city's contribution to the neighborhood; 77 percent with the recreational facilities; 78 percent believed police did not respond promptly when they were summoned for help.

U.S. Representative John Conyers, Jr., a Negro, was notified about the disturbance at his home a few blocks from 12th Street, at 8:30 a.m. Together with other community leaders, including Hubert G. Locke, a Negro and assistant to the commissioner of police, he began to drive around the area. In the side streets, he asked people to stay in their homes. On 12th Street, he asked them to disperse. It was, by his own account, a futile task.

Numerous eyewitnesses interviewed by Commission investigators tell of the carefree mood with which people ran in and out of stores, looting and laughing, and joking with the police officers. Stores with "Soul Brother" signs appeared no more immune than others. Looters paid no attention to residents who shouted at them and called their actions senseless. An epidemic of excitement had swept over the persons on the street.

Congressman Conyers noticed a woman with a baby in her arms; she was raging, cursing "whitey" for no apparent reason.

Shortly before noon, Congressman Conyers climbed atop a car in the middle of 12th Street to address the people. As he began to speak, he was confronted by a man in his fifties whom he had once, as a lawyer, represented in court. The man had been active in civil rights. He believed himself to have been persecuted as a result, and it was Conyers' opinion that he may have been wrongfully jailed. Extremely bitter, the man was inciting the crowd and challenging Conyers: "Why are you defending the cops and the establishment? You're just as bad as they are!"

A police officer in the riot area told Commission investigators that neither he nor his fellow officers were instructed as to what they were supposed to be doing. Witnesses tell of officers standing behind sawhorses as an area was being looted—and still standing there much later, when the mob had moved elsewhere. A squad from the commando unit, wearing helmets with face-covering visors and carrying bayonet-tipped carbines, blockaded a street several blocks from the scene of the riot. Their appearance drew residents into the street. Some began to harangue them and to question why they were in an area where there was no trouble. Representative Conyers convinced the police department to remove the commandos.

By that time, a rumor was threading through the crowd that a man had been bayoneted by the police. Influenced by such stories, the crowd became belligerent. At approximately 1 p.m., stonings accelerated. Numerous officers reported injuries from rocks, bottles, and other objects thrown at them. Smoke billowed upward from four fires, the first since the one at the shoe store early in the morning. When firemen answered the alarms, they became the target for rocks and bottles.

At 2 p.m., Mayor Cavanagh met with community and political leaders at police headquarters. Until then there had been hope that, as the people blew off steam, the riot would dissipate. Now the opinion was nearly unanimous that additional forces would be needed.

A request was made for state police aid. By 3 p.m., 360 officers were assembling at the armory. At that moment looting was spreading from the 12th Street area to other main thoroughfares.

There was no lack of the disaffected to help spread it. Although not yet as hard-pressed as Newark, Detroit was, like Newark, losing population. Its prosperous middle-class whites were moving to the suburbs and being replaced by unskilled Negro migrants. Between 1960 and 1967, the Negro population rose from just under 30 percent to an estimated 40 percent of the total.

In a decade, the school system had gained 50,000 to 60,000 children. Fifty-one percent of the elementary school classes were overcrowded. Simply to achieve the statewide average, the system needed 1,650 more teachers and 1,000 additional classrooms. The combined cost would be $63 million.

Of 300,000 school children, 171,000, or 57 percent, were Negro. According to the Detroit superintendent of schools, 25 different school districts surrounding the city spent up to $500 more per pupil per year than Detroit. In the inner city schools, more than half the pupils who entered high school became dropouts.

The strong union structure had created excellent conditions for most working men, but had left others, such as civil service and Government workers, comparatively disadvantaged and dissatisfied. In June, the "Blue Flu" had struck the city as police officers, forbidden to strike, had staged a sick-out. In September, the teachers were to go on strike. The starting wages for a plumber's helper were almost equal to the salary of a police officer or teacher.

Some unions, traditionally closed to Negroes, zealously guarded training opportunities. In January of 1967, the school system notified six apprenticeship trades it would not open any new apprenticeship classes unless a large number of Negroes were included. By fall, some of the programs were still closed.

High school diplomas from inner-city schools were regarded by personnel directors as less than valid. In July, unemployment was at a 5-year peak. In the 12th Street area, it was estimated to be between 12 and 15 percent for Negro men and 30 percent or higher for those under 25.

The more education a Negro had, the greater the disparity between his income and that of a white with the same level of education. The income of whites and Negroes with a seventh-grade education was about equal. The median income of whites with a high school diploma was $1,600 more per year than that of Negroes. White college graduates made $2,600 more. In fact, so far as income was concerned, it made very little difference to a Negro man whether he had attended school for 8 years or for 12. In the fall of 1967, a study conducted at one inner-city high school, Northwestern, showed that, although 50 percent of the dropouts had found work, 90 percent of the 1967 graduating class was unemployed.

Mayor Cavanagh had appointed many Negroes to key positions in his administration, but in elective offices the Negro population was still underrepresented. Of nine councilmen, one was a Negro. Of seven school board members, two were Negroes.

Although Federal programs had brought nearly $360 million to the city between 1962 and 1967, the money appeared to have little impact at the grassroots. Urban renewal, for which $38 million had been allocated, was opposed by many residents of the poverty area.

Because of its financial straits, the city was unable to produce on promises to correct such conditions as poor garbage collection and bad street lighting, which brought constant complaints from Negro residents.

On 12th Street, Carl Perry, the Negro proprietor of a drugstore and photography studio, was dispensing ice cream, sodas, and candy to the youngsters streaming in and out of his store. For safekeeping, he had brought the photography equipment from his studio, in the next block, to the drugstore. The youths milling about repeatedly assured him that, although the market next door had been ransacked, his place of business was in no danger.

In midafternoon, the market was set afire. Soon after, the drug store went up in flames.

State Representative James Del Rio, a Negro, was camping out in front of a building he owned when two small boys, neither more than 10 years old, approached. One prepared to throw a brick through a window. Del Rio stopped him: "That building belongs to me," he said.

"I'm glad you told me, baby, because I was just about to bust you in!" the youngster replied.

Some evidence that criminal elements were organizing spontaneously to take advantage of the riot began to manifest itself. A number of cars were noted to be returning again and again, their occupants methodically looting stores. Months later, goods stolen during the riot were still being peddled.

A spirit of carefree nihilism was taking hold. To riot and to destroy appeared more and more to become ends in themselves. Late Sunday afternoon, it appeared to one observer that the young people were "dancing amidst the flames."

A Negro plainclothes officer was standing at an intersection when a man threw a Moltov cocktail into a business establishment at the corner. In the heat of the afternoon, fanned by the 20 to 25 m.p.h. winds of both Sunday and Monday, the fire reached the home next door within minutes. As residents uselessly sprayed the flames with garden hoses, the fire jumped from roof to roof of adjacent two- and three-story buildings. Within the hour, the entire block was in flames. The ninth house in the burning row belonged to the arsonist who had thrown the Molotov cocktail.

In some areas, residents organized rifle squads to protect firefighters. Elsewhere, especially as the wind-whipped flames began to overwhelm the Detroit Fire Department and more and more residences burned, the firemen were subjected to curses and rock-throwing.

Because of a lack of funds, on a per capita basis the department is one of the smallest in the Nation. In comparison to Newark, where approximately 1,000 firemen patrol an area of 16 square miles with a population of 400,000, Detroit's 1,700 firemen must cover a city of 140 square miles with a population of 1.6 million. Because the department had no mutual aid agreement with surrounding communities, it could not quickly call in reinforcements from outlying areas, and it was almost 9 p.m. before the first arrived. At one point, out of a total of 92 pieces of Detroit firefighting equipment and 56 brought in from surrounding communities, only four engine companies were available to guard areas of the city outside of the riot perimeter.

As the afternoon progressed, the fire department's radio carried repeated messages of apprehension and orders of caution:

> There is no police protection here at all; there isn't a policeman in the area. . . . If you have trouble at all, pull out! . . . We're being stoned at the scene. It's going good. We need help! . . . Protect yourselves! Proceed away from the scene. . . . Engine 42 over at Linwood and Gladstone. They are throwing bottles at us so we are getting out of the area. . . . All companies without police protection—all companies without police protection—orders are to withdraw, do not try to put out the fires. I repeat—all companies without police protection orders are to withdraw, do not try to put out the fires!

It was 4:30 p.m. when the firemen, some of them exhausted by the heat, abandoned an area of approximately 100 square blocks on either side of 12th Street to await protection from police and National Guardsmen.

During the course of the riot, firemen were to withdraw 283 times.

Fire Chief Charles J. Quinlan estimated that at least two-thirds of the buildings were destroyed by spreading fires rather than fires set at the scene. Of the 683 structures involved, approximately one-third were residential, and in few, if any, of these was the fire set originally.

Governor George Romney flew over the area between 8:30 and 9 p.m.

"It looked like the city had been bombed on the west side and there was an area two-and-a-half miles by three-and-a-half miles with major fires, with entire blocks in flames," he told the Commission.

In the midst of chaos, there were some unexpected individual responses.

Twenty-four-year-old E. G., a Negro born in Savannah, Ga., had come to Detroit in 1965 to attend Wayne State University. Rebellion had been building in him for a long time because,

> You just had to bow down to the white man. . . . When the insurance man would come by he would always call out to my mother by her first name and we were expected to smile and greet him happily. . . . Man, I know he would never have thought of me or my father going to his home and calling his wife by her first name. Then I once saw a white man slapping a young pregnant Negro woman on the street with such force that she just spun around and fell. I'll never forget that.

When a friend called to tell him about the riot on 12th Street, E. G. went there expecting "a true revolt," but was disappointed as soon as he saw the looting begin: "I wanted to see the people really rise up in revolt. When I saw the first person coming out of the store with things in his arms, I really got sick to my stomach and wanted to go home. Rebellion against the white suppressors is one thing, but one measly pair of shoes or some food completely ruins the whole concept."

E. G. was standing in a crowd, watching firemen work, when Fire Chief Alvin Wall called out for help from the spectators. E. G. responded. His reasoning was: "No matter what color someone is, whether they are green or pink or blue, I'd help them if they were in trouble. That's all there is to it."

He worked with the firemen for 4 days, the only Negro in an all-white crew. Elsewhere, at scattered locations, a half dozen other Negro youths pitched in to help the firemen.

At 4:20 p.m., Mayor Cavanagh requested that the National Guard be brought into Detroit. Although a major portion of the Guard was in its summer encampment 200 miles away, several hundred troops were conducting their regular week-end drill in the city. That circumstance obviated many problems. The first troops were on the streets by 7 p.m.

At 7:45 p.m., the mayor issued a proclamation instituting a 9 p.m. to 5 a.m. curfew. At 9:07 p.m., the first sniper fire was reported. Following his aerial survey of the city, Governor Romney, at or shortly before midnight, proclaimed that "a state of public emergency exists" in the cities of Detroit, Highland Park and Hamtramck.

At 4:45 p.m., a 68-year-old white shoe repairman, George Messerlian, had seen looters carrying clothes from a cleaning establishment next to his shop. Armed with a saber, he had rushed into the street, flailing away at the looters. One Negro youth was nicked on the shoulder. Another, who had not been on the scene, inquired as to what had happened.

After he had been told, he allegedly replied: "I'll get the old man for you!"

Going up to Messerlian, who had fallen or been knocked to the ground, the youth began to beat him with a club. Two other Negro youths dragged the attacker away from the old man. It was too late. Messerlian died 4 days later in the hospital.

At 9:15 p.m., a 16-year-old Negro boy, superficially wounded while looting, became the first reported gunshot victim.

At midnight, Sharon George, a 23-year-old white woman, together with her two brothers, was a passenger in a car being driven by her husband. After having dropped off two Negro friends, they were returning home on one of Detroit's main avenues when they were slowed by a milling throng in the street. A shot fired from close range struck the car. The bullet splintered in Mrs. George's body. She died less than 2 hours later.

An hour before midnight, a 45-year-old white man, Walter Grzanka, together with three white companions, went into the street. Shortly thereafter, a market was broken into. Inside the show window, a Negro man began filling bags with groceries and handing them to confederates outside the store. Grzanka twice went over to the store, accepted bags, and placed them down beside his companions across the street. On the third occasion he entered the market. When he emerged, the market owner, driving by in his car, shot and killed him.

In Grzanka's pockets, police found seven cigars, four packages of pipe tobacco, and nine pairs of shoelaces.

Before dawn, four other looters were shot, one of them accidentally while struggling with a police officer. A Negro youth and a National Guardsman were injured by gunshots of undetermined origin. A private guard shot himself while pulling his revolver from his pocket. In the basement of the 13th Precinct Police Station, a cue ball, thrown by an unknown assailant, cracked against the head of a sergeant.

At about midnight, three white youths, armed with a shotgun, had gone to the roof of their apartment building, located in an all-white block, in order, they said, to protect the building from fire. At 2:45 a.m., a patrol car, carrying police officers and National Guardsmen, received a report of "snipers on the roof." As the patrol car arrived, the manager of the building went to the roof to tell the youths they had better come down.

The law enforcement personnel surrounded the building, some going to the front, others to the rear. As the manager, together with the three youths, descended the fire escape in the rear, a National Guardsman, believing he heard shots from the front, fired. His shot killed 23-year-old Clifton Pryor.

Early in the morning, a young white fireman and a 49-year-old Negro homeowner were killed by fallen power lines.

By 2 a.m. Monday, Detroit police had been augmented by 800 State Police officers and 1,200 National Guardsmen. An additional 8,000 Guardsmen were on the way. Nevertheless, Governor Romney and Mayor Cavanagh decided to ask for Federal assistance. At 2:15 a.m., the mayor called Vice President Hubert Humphrey, and was referred to Attorney General Ramsey Clark. A short time thereafter, telephone contact was established between Governor Romney and the attorney general.

There is some difference of opinion about what occurred next. According to the attorney general's office, the governor was advised of the seriousness of the request and told that the applicable Federal statute required that, before Federal troops could be brought into the city, he could have to state that the situation had deteriorated to the point that local and state forces could no longer maintain law and order. According to the governor, he was under the impression that he was being asked to declare that a "state of insurrection" existed in the city.

The governor was unwilling to make such a declaration, contending that, if he did, insurance policies would not cover the loss incurred as a result of the riot. He and the mayor decided to re-evaluate the need for Federal troops.

Contact between Detroit and Washington was maintained throughout the early morning hours. At 9 a.m., as the disorder still showed no sign of abating, the governor and the mayor decided to make a renewed request for Federal troops.

Shortly before noon, the President of the United States authorized the sending of a task force of paratroops to Selfridge Air Force Base, near the city. A few minutes past 3 p.m., Lt. Gen. John L. Throckmorton, commander of Task Force Detroit, met Cyrus Vance, former Deputy Secretary of Defense, at the air base. Approximately an hour later, the first Federal troops arrived at the air base.

After meeting with state and municipal officials, Mr. Vance, General Throckmorton, Governor Romney, and Mayor Cavanagh, made a tour of the city, which lasted until 7:15 p.m. During this tour Mr. Vance and General Throckmorton independently came to the conclusion that—since they had seen no looting or sniping, since the fires appeared to be coming under control, and since a substantial number of National Guardsmen had not yet been committed—injection of Federal troops would be premature.

As the riot alternately waxed and waned, one area of the ghetto remained insulated. On the northeast side, the residents of some 150 square blocks inhabited by 21,000 persons had, in 1966, banded together in the Positive Neighborhood Action Committee (PNAC). With professional help from the Institute of Urban Dynamics, they had organized block clubs and made plans for the improvement of the neighborhood. In order to meet the need for recreational facilities, which the city was not providing, they had raised $3,000 to purchase empty lots for playgrounds. Although opposed to urban renewal, they had agreed to cosponsor with the Archdiocese of Detroit a housing project to be controlled jointly by the archdiocese and PNAC.

When the riot broke out, the residents, through the block clubs, were able to organize quickly. Youngsters, agreeing to stay in the neighborhood, participated in detouring traffic. While many persons reportedly sympathized with the idea of a rebellion against the "system," only two small fires were set—one in an empty building.

During the daylight hours Monday, nine more persons were killed by gunshots elsewhere in the city, and many others were seriously or critically injured. Twenty-three-year-old Nathaniel Edmonds, a Negro, was sitting in his backyard when a young white man stopped his car, got out, and began an argument with him. A few minutes later, declaring he was "going to paint his picture on him with a shotgun," the white man allegedly shotgunned Edmonds to death.

Mrs. Nannie Pack and Mrs. Mattie Thomas were sitting on the porch of Mrs. Pack's house when police began chasing looters from a nearby market. During the chase officers fired three shots from their shotguns. The discharge from one of these accidentally struck the two women. Both were still in the hospital weeks later.

Included among those critically injured when they were accidentally trapped in the line of fire were an 8-year-old Negro girl and a 14-year-old white boy.

As darkness settled Monday, the number of incidents reported to police began to rise again. Although many turned out to be false, several involved injuries to police officers, National Guardsmen, and civilians by gunshots of undetermined origin.

Watching the upward trend of reported incidents, Mr. Vance and General Throckmorton became convinced Federal troops should be used, and President Johnson was so advised. At 11:20 p.m., the President signed a proclamation federalizing the Michigan National Guard and authorizing the use of the paratroopers.

At this time, there were nearly 5,000 Guardsmen in the city, but fatigue, lack of training, and the haste with which they had had to be deployed reduced their effectiveness. Some of the Guardsmen traveled 200 miles and then were on duty for 30 hours straight. Some had never received riot training and were given on-the-spot instructions on mob control—only to discover that there were no mobs, and that the situation they faced on the darkened streets was one for which they were unprepared.

Commanders committed men as they became available, often in small groups. In the resulting confusion, some units were lost in the city. Two Guardsmen assigned to an intersection on Monday were discovered still there on Friday.

Lessons learned by the California National Guard two years earlier in Watts regarding the danger of overreaction and the necessity of great restraint in using weapons had not, apparently, been passed on to the Michigan National Guard. The young troopers could not be expected to know what a danger they were creating by the lack of fire discipline, not only to the civilian population but to themselves.

A Detroit newspaper reporter who spent a night riding in a command jeep told a Commission investigator of machine guns being fired accidentally, street lights being shot out by rifle fire, and buildings being placed under siege on the sketchiest reports of sniping. Troopers would fire, and immediately from the distance there would be answering fire, sometimes consisting of tracer bullets.

In one instance, the newsman related, a report was received on the jeep radio that an Army bus was pinned down by sniper fire at an intersection. National Guardsmen and police, arriving from various directions, jumped out and began asking each other: "Where's the sniper fire coming from?" As one Guardsman pointed to a building, everyone rushed about, taking cover. A soldier, alighting from a jeep, accidentally pulled the trigger on his rifle. As the shot reverberated through the darkness, an officer yelled: "What's going on?" "I don't know," came the answer. "Sniper, I guess."

Without any clear authorization or direction, someone opened fire upon the suspected building. A tank rolled up and sprayed the building with .50-caliber tracer bullets. Law enforcement officers rushed into the surrounded building and discovered it empty. "They must be firing one shot and running," was the verdict.

The reporter interviewed the men who had gotten off the bus and were crouched around it. When he asked them about the sniping incident, he was told that someone had heard a shot. He asked "Did the bullet hit the bus?" The answer was: "Well, we don't know."

Bracketing the hour of midnight Monday, heavy firing, injuring many persons and killing several, occurred in the southeastern sector, which was to be taken over by the paratroopers at 4 a.m., Tuesday, and which was, at this time, considered to be the most active riot area in the city.

Employed as a private guard, 55-year-old Julius L. Dorsey, a Negro, was standing in front of a market when accosted by two Negro men and a woman. They demanded he permit them to loot the market. He ignored their demands. They began to berate him. He asked a neighbor to call the police. As the argument grew more heated, Dorsey fired three shots from his pistol into the air.

The police radio reported: "Looters, they have rifles." A patrol car driven by a police officer and carrying three National Guardsmen arrived. As the looters fled, the law enforcement personnel opened fire. When the firing ceased, one person lay dead.

He was Julius L. Dorsey.

In two areas—one consisting of a triangle formed by Mack, Gratiot, and E. Grand Boulevard, the other surrounding Southeastern High School—firing began shortly after 10 p.m. and continued for several hours.

In the first of the areas, a 22-year-old Negro complained that he had been shot at by snipers. Later, a half dozen civilians and one National Guardsman were wounded by shots of undetermined origin.

Henry Denson, a passenger in a car, was shot and killed when the vehicle's driver, either by accident or intent, failed to heed a warning to halt at a National Guard roadblock.

Similar incidents occurred in the vicinity of Southeastern High School, one of the National Guard staging areas. As early as 10:20 p.m., the area was reported to be under sniper fire. Around midnight there were two incidents, the sequence of which remains in doubt.

Shortly before midnight, Ronald Powell, who lived three blocks east of the high school and whose wife was, momentarily, expecting a baby, asked the four friends with whom he had been spending the evening to take him home. He, together with Edward Blackshear, Charles Glover, and John Leroy climbed into Charles Dunson's station wagon for the short drive. Some of the five may have been drinking, but none was intoxicated.

To the north of the high school, they were halted at a National Guard roadblock, and told they would have to detour around the school and a fire station at Mack and St. Jean Streets because of the firing that had been occurring. Following orders, they took a circuitous route and approached Powell's home from the south.

On Lycaste Street, between Charlevoix and Goethe, they saw a jeep sitting at the curb. Believing it to be another roadblock, they slowed down. Simultaneously a shot rang out. A National Guardsman fell, hit in the ankle.

Other National Guardsmen at the scene thought the shot had come from the station wagon. Shot after shot was directed against the vehicle, at least 17 of them finding their mark. All five occupants were injured, John Leroy fatally.

At approximately the same time, firemen, police, and National Guardsmen at the corner of Mack and St. Jean Streets, 2½ blocks away, again came under fire from what they believed were rooftop snipers to the southeast, the direction of Charlevoix and Lycaste. The police and guardsmen responded with a hail of fire.

When the shooting ceased, Carl Smith, a young firefighter, lay dead. An autopsy determined that the shot had been fired at street level, and, according to police, probably had come from the southeast.

At 4 a.m., when paratroopers, under the command of Col. A. R. Bolling, arrived at the high school, the area was so dark and still that the colonel thought, at first, that he had come to the wrong place. Investigating, he discovered National Guard troops, claiming they were pinned down by sniper fire, crouched behind the walls of the darkened building.

The colonel immediately ordered all of the lights in the building turned on and his troops to show themselves as conspicuously as possible. In the apartment house across the street, nearly every window had been shot out, and the walls were pockmarked with bullet holes. The colonel went into the building and began talking to the residents, many of whom had spent the night huddled on the floor. He reassured them no more shots would be fired.

According to Lieutenant General Throckmorton and Colonel Bolling, the city, at this time, was saturated with fear. The National Guardsmen were afraid, the residents were afraid, and the police were afraid. Numerous persons, the majority of them Negroes, were being injured by gunshots of undetermined origin. The general and his staff felt that the major task of the troops was to reduce the fear and restore an air of normalcy.

In order to accomplish this, every effort was made to establish contact and rapport between the troops and the residents. Troopers—20 percent of whom were Negro—began helping to clean up the streets, collect garbage, and trace persons who had disappeared in the confusion. Residents in the neighborhoods responded with soup and sandwiches for the troops. In areas where the National Guard tried to establish rapport with the citizens, there was a similar response.

Within hours after the arrival of the paratroops, the area occupied by them was the quietest in the city, bearing out General Throckmorton's view that the key to quelling a disorder is to saturate an area with "calm, determined, and hardened professional soldiers." Loaded weapons, he believes, are unnecessary. Troopers had strict orders not to fire unless they could see the specific person at whom they were aiming. Mass fire was forbidden.

During five days in the city, 2,700 Army troops expended only 201 rounds of ammunition, almost all during the first few hours, after which even stricter fire discipline was enforced. (In contrast, New Jersey National Guardsmen and state police expended 13,326 rounds of ammunition in three days in Newark.) Hundreds of reports of sniper fire—most of them false—continued to pour into police headquarters; the Army logged only 10. No paratrooper was injured by a gunshot. Only one person was hit by a shot fired by a trooper. He was a young Negro who was killed when he ran into the line of fire as a trooper, aiding police in a raid on an apartment, aimed at a person believed to be a sniper.

General Throckmorton ordered the weapons of all military personnel unloaded, but either the order failed to reach many National Guardsmen, or else it was disobeyed.

Even as the general was requesting the city to relight the streets,

Guardsmen continued shooting out the lights, and there were reports of dozens of shots being fired to dispatch one light. At one such location as Guardsmen were shooting out the street lights, a radio newscaster reported himself to be pinned down by "sniper fire."

On the same day that the general was attempting to restore normalcy by ordering street barricades taken down, Guardsmen on one street were not only, in broad daylight, ordering people off the street, but off their porches and away from the windows. Two persons who failed to respond to the order quickly enough were shot, one of them fatally.

The general himself reported an incident of a Guardsman "firing across the bow" of an automobile that was approaching a roadblock.

As in Los Angeles 2 years earlier, roadblocks that were ill-lighted and ill-defined—often consisting of no more than a trash barrel or similar object with Guardsmen standing nearby—proved a continuous hazard to motorists. At one such roadblock, National Guard Sgt. Larry Post, standing in the street, was caught in a sudden crossfire as his fellow Guardsmen opened up on a vehicle. He was the only soldier killed in the riot.

With persons of every description arming themselves, and guns being fired accidentally or on the vaguest pretext all over the city, it became more and more impossible to tell who was shooting at whom. Some firemen began carrying guns. One accidentally shot and wounded a fellow fireman. Another injured himself.

The chaos of a riot, and the difficulties faced by police officers, are demonstrated by an incident that occurred at 2 a.m., Tuesday.

A unit of 12 officers received a call to guard firemen from snipers. When they arrived at the corner of Vicksburg and Linwood in the 12th Street area, the intersection was well-lighted by the flames completely enveloping one building. Sniper fire was directed at the officers from an alley to the north, and gun flashes were observed in two buildings.

As the officers advanced on the two buildings, Patrolman Johnie Hamilton fired several rounds from his machinegun. Thereupon, the officers were suddenly subjected to fire from a new direction, the east. Hamilton, struck by four bullets, fell, critically injured, in the intersection. As two officers ran to his aid, they too were hit.

By this time other units of the Detroit Police Department, state police, and National Guard had arrived on the scene, and the area was covered with a hail of gunfire.

In the confusion the snipers who had initiated the shooting escaped.

At 9:15 p.m., Tuesday, July 25, 38-year-old Jack Sydnor, a Negro, came home drunk. Taking out his pistol, he fired one shot into an alley. A few minutes later, the police arrived. As his common-law wife took refuge in a closet, Sydnor waited, gun in hand, while the police forced open the door. Patrolman Roger Poike, the first to enter, was shot by Sydnor. Although critically injured, the officer managed to get off six shots in return. Police within the building and on the street then poured a hail of fire into the apartment. When the shooting ceased, Sydnor's body, riddled by the gunfire, was found lying on the ground outside a window.

Nearby, a state police officer and a Negro youth were struck and seriously injured by stray bullets. As in other cases where the origin of the shots was not immediately determinable, police reported them as "shot by sniper."

Reports of "heavy sniper fire" poured into police headquarters from the two blocks surrounding the apartment house where the battle with Jack Sydnor had taken place. National Guard troops with two tanks were dispatched to help flush out the snipers.

Shots continued to be heard throughout the neighborhood. At approximately midnight—there are discrepancies as to the precise time—a machinegunner on a tank, startled by several shots, asked the assistant gunner where the shots were coming from. The assistant gunner pointed toward a flash in the window of an apartment house from which there had been earlier reports of sniping.

The machinegunner opened fire. As the slugs ripped through the window and walls of the apartment, they nearly severed the arm of 21-year-old Valerie Hood. Her 4-year-old niece, Tonya Blanding, toppled dead, a .50-caliber bullet hole in her chest.

A few seconds earlier, 19-year-old Bill Hood, standing in the window, had lighted a cigarette.

Down the street, a bystander was critically injured by a stray bullet. Simultaneously, the John C. Lodge Freeway, two blocks away, was reported to be under sniper fire. Tanks and National Guard troops were sent to investigate. At the Harlan House Motel, 10 blocks from where Tonya Blanding had died a short time earlier, Mrs. Helen Hall, a 51-year-old white businesswoman, opened the drapes of the fourth floor hall window. Calling out to other guests, she exclaimed: "Look at the tanks!"

She died seconds later as bullets began to slam into the building. As the firing ceased, a 19-year-old Marine, carrying a Springfield rifle, burst into the building. When, accidentally, he pushed the rifle barrel through a window, firing commenced anew. A police investigation showed that the Marine, who had just decided to "help out" the law enforcement personnel, was not involved in the death of Mrs. Hall.

R. R., a white 27-year-old coin dealer, was the owner of an expensive, three-story house on L Street, an integrated middle-class neighborhood. In May of 1966, he and his wife and child had moved to New York and had rented the house to two young men. After several months, he had begun to have problems with his tenants. On one occasion, he reported to his attorney that he had been threatened by them.

In March of 1967, R. R. instituted eviction proceedings. These were still pending when the riot broke out. Concerned about the house, R. R. decided to fly to Detroit. When he arrived at the house on Wednesday, July 26, he discovered the tenants were not at home.

He then called his attorney, who advised him to take physical possession of the house and, for legal purposes, to take witnesses along.

Together with his 17-year-old brother and another white youth, R. R. went to the house, entered, and began changing the locks on the doors. For protection they brought a .22 caliber rifle, which R. R.'s brother took into the cellar and fired into a pillow in order to test it.

Shortly after 8 p.m., R. R. called his attorney to advise him that the tenants had returned, and he had refused to admit them. Thereupon, R. R. alleged, the tenants had threatened to obtain the help of the National Guard. The attorney relates that he was not particularly concerned. He told R. R. that if the National Guard did appear he should have the officer in charge call him (the attorney).

At approximately the same time, the National Guard claims it received information to the effect that several men had evicted the legal occupants of the house, and intended to start sniping after dark.

A National Guard column was dispatched to the scene. Shortly after 9 p.m., in the half-light of dusk, the column of approximately 30 men surrounded the house. A tank took position on a lawn across the street. The captain commanding the column placed in front of the house an explosive device similar to a firecracker. After setting this off in order to draw the attention of the occupants to the presence of the column, he called for them to come out of the house. No attempt was made to verify the truth or falsehood of the allegations regarding snipers.

When the captain received no reply from the house, he began counting to 10. As he was counting, he said, he heard a shot, the origin of which he could not determine. A few seconds later, he heard another shot and saw a "fire streak" coming from an upstairs window. He thereupon gave the order to fire.

According to the three young men, they were on the second floor of the house and completely bewildered by the barrage of fire that was unleashed against it. As hundreds of bullets crashed through the first- and second-story windows and richocheted off the walls, they dashed to the third floor. Protected by a large chimney, they huddled in a closet until, during a lull in the firing, they were able to wave an item of clothing out of the window as a sign of surrender. They were arrested as snipers.

The firing from rifles and machine guns had been so intense that in a period of a few minutes it inflicted an estimated $10,000 worth of damage. One of a pair of stone columns was shot nearly in half.

Jailed at the 10th precinct station sometime Wednesday night, R. R. and his two companions were taken from their cell to an "alley court," police slang for an unlawful attempt to make prisoners confess. A police officer, who has resigned from the force, allegedly administered such a severe beating to R. R. that the bruises still were visible 2 weeks later.

R. R.'s 17-year-old brother had his skull cracked open, and was thrown back into the cell. He was taken to a hospital only when other arrestees complained that he was bleeding to death.

At the preliminary hearing 12 days later, the prosecution presented only one witness, the National Guard captain who had given the order to fire. The police officer who had signed the original complaint was not asked to take the stand. The charges against all three of the young men were dismissed.

Nevertheless, the morning after the original incident, a major metropolitan newspaper in another section of the country composed the following banner story from wire service reports:

> DETROIT, *July 27 (Thursday)*.—Two National Guard tanks ripped a sniper's haven with machine guns Wednesday night and flushed out three shaggy-haired white youths. Snipers attacked a guard command post and Detroit's racial riot set a modern record for bloodshed. The death toll soared to 36, topping the Watts bloodbath of 1966 in which 35 died and making Detroit's insurrection the most deadly racial riot in modern U.S. history. . . .
>
> In the attack on the sniper's nest, the Guardsmen poured hundreds of rounds of .50 caliber machine gun fire into the home, which authorities said housed arms and ammunition used by West Side sniper squads.
>
> Guardsmen recovered guns and ammunition. A reporter with the troopers said the house, a neat brick home in a neighborhood of $20,000 to $50,000 homes, was torn apart by the machine gun and rifle fire.
>
> Sniper fire crackled from the home as the Guard unit approached. It was one of the first verified reports of sniping by whites. . . .
>
> A pile of loot taken from riot-ruined stores was recovered from the sniper's haven, located ten blocks from the heart of the 200-square block riot zone.
>
> Guardsmen said the house had been identified as a storehouse of arms and ammunition for snipers. Its arsenal was regarded as an indication that the sniping—or at least some of it—was organized.

As hundreds of arrestees were brought into the 10th precinct station, officers took it upon themselves to carry on investigations and to attempt to extract confessions. Dozens of charges of police brutality emanated from the station as prisoners were brought in uninjured, but later had to be taken to the hospital.

In the absence of the precinct commander, who had transferred his headquarters to the riot command post at a nearby hospital, discipline vanished. Prisoners who requested that they be permitted to notify someone of their arrest were almost invariably told that: "The telephones are out of order." Congressman Conyers and State Representative Del Rio, who went to the station hoping to coordinate with the police the establishing of a community patrol, were so upset by what they saw that they changed their minds and gave up on the project.

A young woman, brought into the station, was told to strip. After she had done so, and while an officer took pictures with a Polaroid camera, another officer came up to her and began fondling her. The negative of one of the pictures, fished out of a wastebasket, subsequently was turned over to the mayor's office.

Citing the sniper danger, officers throughout the department had taken off their bright metal badges. They also had taped over the license plates and the numbers of the police cars. Identification of individual officers became virtually impossible.

On a number of occasions officers fired at fleeing looters, then made little attempt to determine whether their shots had hit anyone. Later some of the persons were discovered dead or injured in the street.

In one such case police and National Guardsmen were interrogating a youth suspected of arson when, according to officers, he attempted to escape. As he vaulted over the hood of an automobile, an officer fired his shotgun. The youth disappeared on the other side of the car. Without making an investigation, the officers and Guardsmen returned to their car and drove off.

When nearby residents called police, another squad car arrived to pick up the body. Despite the fact that an autopsy disclosed the youth had been killed by five shotgun pellets, only a cursory investigation was made, and the death was attributed to "sniper fire." No police officer at the scene during the shooting filed a report.

Not until a Detroit newspaper editor presented to the police the statements of several witnesses claiming that the youth had been shot by police after he had been told to run did the department launch an investigation. Not until 3 weeks after the shooting did an officer come forward to identify himself as the one who had fired the fatal shot.

Citing conflicts in the testimony of the score of witnesses, the Detroit Prosecutor's office declined to press charges.

Prosecution is proceeding in the case of three youths in whose shotgun deaths law enforcement personnel were implicated following a report that snipers were firing from the Algiers Motel. In fact, there is little evidence that anyone fired from inside the building. Two witnesses say that they had seen a man, standing outside of the motel, fire two shots from a rifle. The interrogation of other persons revealed that law enforcement personnel then shot out one or more street lights. Police patrols responded to the shots. An attack was launched on the motel.

The picture is further complicated by the fact that this incident occurred at roughly the same time that the National Guard was directing fire at the apartment house in which Tonya Blanding was killed. The apartment house was only six blocks distant from and in a direct line with the motel.

The killings occurred when officers began on-the-spot questioning of the occupants of the motel in an effort to discover weapons used in the "sniping." Several of those questioned reportedly were beaten. One was a Negro ex-paratrooper who had only recently been honorably discharged, and had gone to Detroit to look for a job.

Although by late Tuesday looting and fire-bombing had virtually ceased, between 7 and 11 p.m. that night there were 444 reports of incidents. Most were reports of sniper fire.

During the daylight hours of July 26, there were 534 such reports. Between 8:30 and 11 p.m., there were 255. As they proliferated, the pressure on law enforcement officers to uncover the snipers became intense. Homes were broken into. Searches were made on the flimsiest of tips. A Detroit newspaper headline aptly proclaimed: "Everyone's Suspect in No Man's Land."

Before the arrest of a young woman IBM operator in the city assessor's office brought attention to the situation on Friday, July 28, any person with a gun in his home was liable to be picked up as a suspect.

Of the 27 persons charged with sniping, 22 had charges against them dismissed at preliminary hearings, and the charges against two others were dismissed later. One pleaded guilty to possession of an unregistered gun and was given a suspended sentence. Trials of two are pending.

In all, more than 7,200 persons were arrested. Almost 3,000 of these were picked up on the second day of the riot, and by midnight Monday 4,000 were incarcerated in makeshift jails. Some were kept as long as 30 hours on buses. Others spent days in an underground garage without toilet facilities. An uncounted number were people who had merely been unfortunate enough to be on the wrong street at the wrong time. Included were members of the press whose attempts to show their credentials had been ignored. Released later, they were chided for not having exhibited their identification at the time of their arrests.

The booking system proved incapable of adequately handling the large number of arrestees. People became lost for days in the maze of different detention facilities. Until the later stages, bail was set deliberately high, often at $10,000 or more. When it became apparent that this policy was unrealistic and unworkable, the prosecutor's office began releasing on low bail or on their own recognizance hundreds of those who had been picked up. Nevertheless, this fact was not publicized for fear of antagonizing those who had demanded a high-bail policy.

Of the 43 persons who were killed during the riot, 33 were Negro and 10 were white. Seventeen were looters, of whom two were white. Fifteen citizens (of whom four were white), one white National Guardsman, one white fireman, and one Negro private guard died as the result of gunshot wounds. Most of these deaths appear to have been accidental, but criminal homicide is suspected in some.

Two persons, including one fireman, died as a result of fallen powerlines. Two were burned to death. One was a drunken gunman; one an arson suspect. One white man was killed by a rioter. One police officer was felled by a shotgun blast when a gun, in the hands of another officer, accidentally discharged during a scuffle with a looter.

Action by police officers accounted for 20 and, very likely, 21 of the deaths; action by the National Guard for seven, and, very likely, nine; action by the Army for one. Two deaths were the result of action by storeowners. Four persons died accidentally. Rioters were responsible for two, and perhaps three of the deaths; a private guard for one. A white man is suspected of murdering a Negro youth. The perpetrator of one of the killings in the Algiers Motel remains unknown.

Damage estimates, originally set as high as $500 million, were quickly scaled down. The city assessor's office placed the loss—excluding business stock, private furnishings, and the buildings of churches and charitable institutions—at approximately $22 million. Insurance payments, according to the State Insurance Bureau, will come to about $32 million, representing an estimated 65 to 75 percent of the total loss.

By Thursday, July 27, most riot activity had ended. The paratroopers were removed from the city on Saturday. On Tuesday, August 1, the curfew was lifted and the National Guard moved out.

WALKER REPORT

Rights in Conflict

During the week of the Democratic National Convention, the Chicago police were the targets of mounting provocation by both word and act. It took the form of obscene epithets, and of rocks, sticks, bathroom tiles and even human feces hurled at police by demonstrators. Some of these acts had been planned; others were spontaneous or were themselves provoked by police action. Furthermore, the police had been put on edge by widely published threats of attempts to disrupt both the city and the Convention.

That was the nature of the provocation. The nature of the response was unrestrained and indiscriminate police violence on many occasions, particularly at night.

That violence was made all the more shocking by the fact that it was often inflicted upon persons who had broken no law, disobeyed no order, made no threat. These included peaceful demonstrators, onlookers, and large numbers of residents who were simply passing through, or happened to live in, the areas where confrontations were occurring.

Newsmen and photographers were singled out for assault, and their equipment deliberately damaged. Fundamental police training was ignored; and officers, when on the scene, were often unable to control their men. As one police officer put it: "What happened didn't have anything to do with police work."

The violence reached its culmination on Wednesday night.

A report prepared by an inspector from the Los Angeles Police Department, present as an official observer, while generally praising the police restraint he had observed in the parks during the week, said this about the events that night:

> There is no question but that many officers acted without restraint and exerted force beyond that necessary under the circumstances. The leadership at the point of conflict did little to prevent such conduct and the direct control of officers by first line supervisors was virtually non-existent.

From **Rights in Conflict** *(New York: Bantam, 1968), pp. 1–10.*

He is referring to the police-crowd confrontation in front of the Conrad Hilton Hotel. Most Americans know about it, having seen the 17-minute sequence played and replayed on their television screens.

But most Americans do not know that the confrontation was followed by even more brutal incidents in the Loop side streets. Or that it had been preceded by comparable instances of indiscriminate police attacks on the North Side a few nights earlier when demonstrators were cleared from Lincoln Park and pushed into the streets and alleys of Old Town.

How did it start? With the emergence long before convention week of three factors which figured significantly in the outbreak of violence. These were: threats to the city; the city's response; and the conditioning of Chicago police to expect that violence against demonstrators, as against rioters, would be condoned by city officials.

The threats to the City were varied. Provocative and inflammatory statements, made in connection with activities planned for convention week, were published and widely disseminated. There were also intelligence reports from informants.

Some of this information was absurd, like the reported plan to contaminate the city's water supply with LSD. But some were serious; and both were strengthened by the authorities' lack of any mechanism for distinguishing one from the other.

The second factor—the city's response—matched, in numbers and logistics at least, the demonstrators' threats.

The city, fearful that the "leaders" would not be able to control their followers, attempted to discourage an inundation of demonstrators by not granting permits for marches and rallies and by making it quite clear that the "law" would be enforced.

Government—federal, state and local—moved to defend itself from the threats, both imaginary and real. The preparations were detailed and far ranging: from stationing firemen at each alarm box within a six block radius of the Amphitheatre to staging U.S. Army armored personnel carriers in Soldier Field under Secret Service control. Six thousand Regular Army troops in full field gear, equipped with rifles, flame throwers, and bazookas were airlifted to Chicago on Monday, August 26. About 6,000 Illinois National Guard troops had already been activated to assist the 12,000 member Chicago Police Force.

Of course, the Secret Service could never afford to ignore threats of assassination of Presidential candidates. Neither could the city, against the background of riots in 1967 and 1968, ignore the ever-present threat of ghetto riots, possibly sparked by large numbers of demonstrators, during convention week.

The third factor emerged in the city's position regarding the riots following the death of Dr. Martin Luther King and the April 27th peace march to the Civic Center in Chicago.

The police were generally credited with restraint in handling the first riots—but Mayor Daley rebuked the Superintendent of Police. While it was later modified, his widely disseminated "shoot to kill arsonists and shoot to maim looters" order undoubtedly had an effect.

The effect on police became apparent several weeks later, when they attacked demonstrators, bystanders and media representatives at a Civic Center peace march. There were published criticisms—but the city's response was to ignore the police violence.

That was the background. On August 18, 1968, the advance contingent of demonstrators arrived in Chicago and established their base, as planned, in Lincoln Park on the city's Near North Side. Throughout the week, they were joined by others—some from the Chicago area, some from states as far away as New York and California. On the weekend before the convention began, there were about 2,000 demonstrators in Lincoln Park; the crowd grew to about 10,000 by Wednesday.

There were, of course, the hippies—the long hair and love beads, the calculated unwashedness, the flagrant banners, the open lovemaking and disdain for the constraints of conventional society. In dramatic effect, both visual and vocal, these dominated a crowd whose members actually differed widely in physical appearance, in motivation, in political affiliation, in philosophy. The crowd included Yippies come to "do their thing," youngsters working for a political candidate, professional people with dissenting political views, anarchists and determined revolutionaries, motorcycle gangs, black activists, young thugs, police and Secret Service undercover agents. There were demonstrators waving the Viet Cong flag and the red flag of revolution and there were the simply curious who came to watch and, in many cases, became willing or unwilling participants.

To characterize the crowd, then, as entirely hippy-Yippie, entirely "New Left," entirely anarchist, or entirely youthful political dissenters is both wrong and dangerous. The stereotyping that did occur helps to explain the emotional reaction of both police and public during and after the violence that occurred.

Despite the presence of some revolutionaries, the vast majority of the demonstrators were intent on expressing by peaceful means their dissent either from society generally or from the Administration's polices in Vietnam.

Most of those intending to join the major protest demonstrations scheduled during convention week did not plan to enter the Amphitheatre and disrupt the proceedings of the Democratic convention, did not plan aggressive acts of physical provocation against the authorities, and did not plan to use rallies of demonstrators to stage an assault against any person, institution, or place of business. But while it is clear that most of the protesters in Chicago had no intention of initiating violence, this is not to say that they did not expect it to develop.

It was the clearing of the demonstrators from Lincoln Park that led directly to the violence: symbolically, it expressed the city's opposition to the protesters; literally, it forced the protesters into confrontation with police in Old Town and the adjacent residential neighborhoods.

The Old Town area near Lincoln Park was a scene of police ferocity exceeding that shown on television on Wednesday night. From Sunday night through Tuesday night, incidents of intense and indiscriminate violence occurred in the streets after police had swept the park clear of demonstrators.

Demonstrators attacked too. And they posed difficult problems for police as they persisted in marching through the streets, blocking traffic and intersections. But it was the police who forced them out of the park and into the neighborhood. And on the part of the police there was enough wild club swinging, enough cries of hatred, enough gratuitous beating to make the conclusion inescapable that individual policemen, and lots of them, committed violent acts far in excess of the requisite force for crowd dispersal or arrest. To read dispassionately the hundreds of statements describing at firsthand the events of Sunday and Monday nights is to become convinced of the presence of what can only be called a police riot.

Here is an eyewitness talking about Monday night:

> The demonstrators were forced out onto Clark Street and once again a traffic jam developed. Cars were stopped, the horns began to honk, people couldn't move, people got gassed inside their cars, people got stoned inside their cars, police were the objects of stones, and taunts, mostly taunts. As you must understand, most of the taunting of the police was verbal. There were stones thrown of course, but for the most part it was verbal. But there were stones being thrown and of course the police were responding with tear gas and clubs and everytime they could get near enough to a demonstrator they hit him.
>
> But again you had this police problem within—this really turned into a police problem. They pushed everybody out of the park, but this night there were a lot more people in the park than there had been during the previous night and Clark Street was just full of people and in addition now was full of gas because the police were using gas on a much larger scale this night. So the police were faced with the task, which took them about an hour or so, of hitting people over the head and gassing them enough to get them out of Clark Street, which they did.

But police action was not confined to the necessary force, even in clearing the park:

A young man and his girl friend were both grabbed by officers. He screamed, "We're going, we're going," but they threw him into the pond. The officers grabbed the girl, knocked her to the ground, dragged her along the embankment and hit her with their batons on her head, arms, back and legs. The boy tried to scramble up the embankment to her, but police shoved him back in the water at least twice. He finally got to her and tried to pull her in the water, away from the police. He was clubbed on the head five or six times. An officer shouted, "Let's get the fucking bastards!" but the boy pulled her in the water and the police left.

Like the incident described above, much of the violence witnessed in Old Town that night seems malicious or mindless:

> There were pedestrians. People who were not part of the demonstration were coming out of a tavern to see what the demonstration was . . . and the officers indiscriminately started beating everybody on the street who was not a policeman.

Another scene:

> There was a group of about six police officers that moved in and started beating two youths. When one of the officers pulled back his nightstick to swing, one of the youths grabbed it from behind and started beating on the officer. At this point about ten officers left everybody else and ran after this youth, who turned down Wells and ran to the left.
>
> But the officers went to the right, picked up another youth, assuming he was the one they were chasing, and took him into an empty lot and beat him. And when they got him to the ground, they just kicked him ten times—the wrong youth, the innocent youth who had been standing there.

A federal legal official relates an experience of Tuesday evening.

> I then walked one block north where I met a group of 12–15 policemen. I showed them my identification and they permitted me to walk with them. The police walked one block west. Numerous people were watching us from their windows and balconies. The police yelled profanities at them, taunting them to come down where the police would beat them up. The police stopped a number of people on the street demanding identification. They verbally abused each pedestrian and pushed one or two without hurting them. We walked back to Clark Street and began to walk north where the police stopped a number of people who appeared to be protesters, and ordered them out of the area in a very abusive way. One protester who was walking in the opposite direction was kneed in the groin by a policeman who was walking towards him. The boy fell to the ground and swore at the policeman who picked him up and threw him to the ground. We continued to walk toward the command post. A derelict who appeared to be very intoxicated walked up to the policeman and mumbled something that was incoherent. The policeman pulled from his belt a tin container and sprayed its contents into the eyes of the derelict, who stumbled around and fell on his face.

It was on these nights that the police violence against media representatives reached its peak. Much of it was plainly deliberate. A newsman was pulled aside on Monday by a detective acquaintance of his who said: "The word is being passed to get newsmen." Individual newsmen were warned, "You take my picture tonight and I'm going to get you." Cries of "get the camera" preceded individual attacks on photographers.

A newspaper photographer describes Old Town on Monday at about 9:00 P.M.:

> When the people arrived at the intersection of Wells and Division, they were not standing in the streets. Suddenly a column of policemen ran out from the alley. They were reinforcements. They were under control but there seemed to be no direction. One man was yelling, "Get them up on the sidewalks, turn them around." Very suddenly the police charged the people on the sidewalks and began beating their heads. A line of cameramen was "trapped" along with the crowd along the sidewalks, and the police went down the line chopping away at the cameras.

A network cameraman reports that on the same night:

> I just saw this guy coming at me with his nightstick and I had the camera up. The tip of his stick hit me right in the mouth, then I put my tongue up there and I noticed that my tooth was gone. I turned around then to try to leave and then this cop came up behind me with his stick and he jabbed me in the back.
>
> All of a sudden these cops jumped out of the police cars and started just beating the hell out of people. And before anything else happened to me, I saw a man holding a Bell & Howell camera with big wide letters on it, saying "CBS." He apparently had been hit by a cop. And cops were standing around and there was blood streaming down his face. Another policeman was running after me and saying, "Get the fuck out of here." And I heard another guy scream, "Get their fucking cameras." And the next thing I know I was being hit on the head, and I think on the back, and I was just forced down on the ground at the corner of Division and Wells.

If the intent was to discourage coverage, it was successful in at least one case. A photographer from a news magazine says that finally, "I just stopped shooting, because every time you push the flash, they look at you and they are screaming about, 'Get the fucking photographers and get the film.' "

There is some explanation for the media-directed violence. Camera crews on at least two occasions did stage violence and fake injuries. Demonstrators did sometimes step up their activities for the benefit of TV cameras. Newsmen and photographers' blinding lights did get in the way of police clearing streets, sweeping the park and dispersing demonstrators. Newsmen did, on occasion, disobey legitimate police orders to "move" or "clear the streets." News reporting of events did seem to the police to be anti-Chicago and anti-police.

But was the response appropriate to the provocation?

Out of 300 newsmen assigned to cover the parks and streets of Chicago during convention week, more than 60 (about 20%) were involved in incidents resulting in injury to themselves, damage to their equipment, or their arrest. Sixty-three newsmen were physically attacked by police; in

13 of these instances, photographic or recording equipment was intentionally damaged.

The violence did not end with either demonstrators or newsmen on the North Side on Sunday, Monday and Tuesday. It continued in Grant Park on Wednesday. It occurred on Michigan Avenue in front of the Conrad Hilton Hotel, as already described. A high-ranking Chicago police commander admits that on that occasion the police "got out of control." This same commander appears in one of the most vivid scenes of the entire week, trying desperately to keep individual policemen from beating demonstrators as he screams, "For Christ's sake, stop it!"

Thereafter, the violence continued on Michigan Avenue and on the side streets running into Chicago's Loop. A federal official describes how it began:

> I heard a 10-1 call [policeman in trouble] on either my radio or one of the other hand sets carried by men with me and then heard "Car 100—sweep." With a roar of motors, squads, vans and three-wheelers came from east, west and north into the block north of Jackson. The crowd scattered. A big group ran west on Jackson, with a group of blue shirted policemen in pursuit, beating at them with clubs. Some of the crowd would jump into doorways and the police would rout them out. The action was very tough. In my judgment, unnecessarily so. The police were hitting with a vengeance and quite obviously with relish. . . .

What followed was a club-swinging melee. Police ranged the streets striking anyone they could catch. To be sure, demonstrators threw things at policemen and at police cars; but the weight of violence was overwhelmingly on the side of the police. A few examples will give the flavor of that night in Chicago:

"At the corner of Congress Plaza and Michigan," states a doctor, "was gathered a group of people, numbering between thirty and forty. They were trapped against a railing [along a ramp leading down from Michigan Avenue to an underground parking garage] by several policemen on motorcycles. The police charged the people on motorcycles and struck about a dozen of them, knocking several of them down. About twenty standing there jumped over the railing. On the other side of the railing was a three-to-four-foot drop. None of the people who were struck by the motorcycles appeared to be seriously injured. However, several of them were limping as if they had been run over on their feet."

A UPI reporter witnessed these attacks, too. He relates in his statement that one officer, "with a smile on his face and a fanatical look in his eyes, was standing on a three-wheel cycle, shouting, 'Wahoo, wahoo,' and trying to run down people on the sidewalk." The reporter says he was chased thirty feet by the cycle.

A priest who was in the crowd says he saw a "boy, about fourteen or fifteen, white, standing on top of an automobile yelling something which was unidentifiable. Suddenly a policeman pulled him down from the car and beat him to the ground by striking him three or four times with a nightstick. Other police joined in . . . and they eventually shoved him to a police van.

"A well-dressed woman saw this incident and spoke angrily to a nearby police captain. As she spoke, another policeman came up from behind her and sprayed something in her face with an aerosol can. He then clubbed her to the ground. He and two other policemen then dragged her along the ground to the same paddy wagon and threw her in."

"I ran west on Jackson," a witness states. "West of Wabash, a line of police stretching across both sidewalks and the street charged after a small group I was in. Many people were clubbed and maced as they ran. Some weren't demonstrators at all, but were just pedestrians who didn't know how to react to the charging officers yelling 'Police!' "

"A wave of police charged down Jackson," another witness relates. "Fleeing demonstrators were beaten indiscriminately and a temporary, makeshift first aid station was set up on the corner of State and Jackson. Two men lay in pools of blood, their heads severely cut by clubs. A minister moved amongst the crowd, quieting them, brushing aside curious onlookers, and finally asked a policeman to call an ambulance, which he agreed to do. . . ."

An Assistant U.S. Attorney later reported that "the demonstrators were running as fast as they could but were unable to get out of the way because of the crowds in front of them. I observed the police striking numerous individuals, perhaps 20 to 30. I saw three fall down and then overrun by the police. I observed two demonstrators who had multiple cuts on their heads. We assisted one who was in shock into a passer-by's car."

JEROME H. SKOLNICK

The Police View of Protest and Protesters

Faced with the mounting pressures inherent in their job, the police have naturally sought to understand why things are as they are. Explanations which the police, with a few exceptions, have adopted constitute a relatively coherent view of current protests and their causes. The various propositions making up this view have nowhere been set out and made explicit, but they do permeate the police literature. We have tried to set them out as explicitly as possible.

As will be seen, this view functions to justify—indeed, it suggests—a strategy for dealing with protest and protesters. Like any coherent view of events, it helps the police plan what they should do and understand what they have done. But it must also be said that the police view makes it more difficult to keep the peace and increases the potential for violence. Furthermore, police attitudes toward protest and protesters often lead to conduct at odds with democratic ideals of freedom of speech and political expression. Thus the police often view protest as an intrusion rather than as a contribution to our political processes. In its extreme case, this may result in treating the fundamental political right of dissent as merely an unnecessary inconvenience to traffic, as subversive activity, or both.

The "Rotten Apple" View of Man

What is the foundation of the police view? On the basis of our interviews with police and a systematic study of police publications,[1] we have found that a significant underpinning is what can best be described as a "rotten apple" theory of human nature. Such a theory of human nature is hardly confined to the police, of course. It is widely shared in our soci-

From The Politics of Protest *(New York: Simon & Schuster, 1969), pp. 258–68.*

1 Among numerous other publications *Law and Order* and *The Police Chief* magazines for the past eighteen months were reviewed. We read them both for an understanding of the police perspective of their world and for their theories of appropriate response to social problems. Interviews and other reports augmented this study.

ety. Many of those to whom the police are responsible hold the "rotten apple" theory, and this complicates the problem in many ways.

Under this doctrine, crime and disorder are attributable mainly to the intentions of evil individuals; human behavior transcends past experience, culture, society, and other external forces and should be understood in terms of wrong choices, deliberately made. Significantly—and contrary to the teachings of all the behavioral sciences—social factors such as poverty, discrimination, inadequate housing, and the like are excluded from the analysis. As one policeman put it simply, "Poverty doesn't cause crime; people do."

The "rotten apple" view of human nature puts the policeman at odds with the goals and aspirations of many of the groups he is called upon to police. For example, police often relegate social reforms to the category of "coddling criminals" or, in the case of recent ghetto programs, to "selling out" to troublemakers. Moreover, while denying that social factors may contribute to the causes of criminal behavior, police and police publications, somewhat inconsistently, denounce welfare programs not as irrelevant *but as harmful* because they destroy human initiative. This negative view of the goals of policed communities can only make the situation of both police and policed more difficult and explosive. Thus, the black community sees the police not only as representing an alien white society but also as advocating positions fundamentally at odds with its own aspirations. A recent report by the Group for Research on Social Policy at Johns Hopkins University (commissioned by the National Advisory Commission on Civil Disorders) summarizes the police view of the black community:

> The police have wound up face to face with the social consequences of the problems in the ghetto created by the failure of other white institutions—though, as has been observed, they themselves have contributed to those problems in no small degree. The distant and gentlemanly white racism of employers, the discrimination of white parents who object to having their children go to school with Negroes, the disgruntlement of white taxpayers who deride the present welfare system as a sinkhole of public funds but are unwilling to see it replaced by anything more effective—the consequences of these and other forms of white racism have confronted the police with a massive control problem of the kind most evident in the riots.
>
> In our survey, we found that the police were inclined to see the riots as the long range result of faults in the Negro community—disrespect for law, crime, broken families, etc.—rather than as responses to the stance of the white community. Indeed, nearly one-third of the white police saw the riots as the result of what they considered the basic violence and disrespect of Negroes in general, while only one-fourth attributed the riots to the failure of white institutions. More than three-fourths also regarded the riots as the immediate result of agitators and criminals—a suggestion contradicted by all the evidence accumulated by the riot commission. The police, then, share with the other groups—excepting the black politicians—a tendency to emphasize perceived

defects in the black community as an explanation for the difficulties that they encounter in the ghetto.[2]

A similar tension sometimes exists between the police and both higher civic officials and representatives of the media. To the extent that such persons recognize the role of social factors in crime and approve of social reforms, they are viewed by the police as "selling out" and not "supporting the police."

Several less central theories often accompany the "rotten apple" view. These theories, too, are widely shared in our society. First, the police widely blame the current rise in crime on a turn away from traditional religiousness, and they fear an impending moral breakdown.[3] Yet the best recent evidence shows that people's religious beliefs and attendance neither reduce nor increase their propensity toward crime.[4]

But perhaps the main target of current police thinking is permissive child-rearing, which many policemen interviewed by our task force view as having led to a generation "that thinks it can get what it yells for." Indeed, one officer interviewed justified the use of physical force on offenders as a corrective for lack of childhood discipline. "If their folks had beat 'em when they were kids, they'd be straight now. As it is, we have to shape 'em up." While much recent evidence, discussed elsewhere in this report, has shown that students most concerned with social issues and most active in protest movements have been reared in homes more "permissive," according to police standards, than those who are uninvolved in these matters, it does not follow that such "permissiveness" leads to criminality. In fact the evidence strongly suggests that persons who receive heavy corporal punishment as children are more likely to act aggressively in ensuing years.[5]

The police also tend to view perfectly legal social deviance, such as long hair worn by men, not only with extreme distaste but as a ladder to potential criminality. At a luncheon meeting of the International Conference of Police Associations, for example, Los Angeles patrolman George Suber said:

2 David Boesel, Richard Berk, W. Eugene Groves, Bettye Eidson, Peter H. Rossi, "White Institutions and Black Rage," *Trans-action* (March, 1969), p. 31.

3 See, e.g., J. Edgar Hoover, quoted in John Edward Coogan, "Religion, a Preventive of Delinquency," *Federal Probation,* XVIII (December, 1954), p. 29.

4 Travis Hirschi and Rodney Stark, "Hellfire and Delinquency," publication A-96, Survey Research Center, University of California at Berkeley.

5 See, e.g., R. R. Sears, et al., "Some Child-rearing Antecedents of Aggression and Dependency in Young Children," *Genetic Psychology Monograph* (1953), pp. 135–234; E. Hollenberg and M. Sperry, "Some Antecedents of Aggression and Effects of Frustration in Doll Play," *Personality* (1951), pp. 32–43; W. C. Becker, et al., "Relations of Factors Derived from Parent Interview Ratings to Behavior Problems of Five Year Olds," *Child Development,* XXXIII (1962), pp. 509–35; and M. L. Hoffman, "Power Assertion by the Parent and Its Impact on the Child," *Child Development,* XXXI (1960), pp. 129–43.

You know, the way it is today, women will be women—and so will men! I got in trouble with one of them. I stopped him on a freeway after a chase—95, 100 miles an hour. . . . He had that hair down to the shoulders.

I said to him, "I have a son about your age, and if you were my son, I'd do two things." "Oh," he said, "what?" "I'd knock him on his ass, and I'd tell him to get a haircut."

"Oh, you don't like my hair?" "No," I said, "you look like a fruit." At that he got very angry. I had to fight him to get him under control.[6]

Nonconformity comes to be viewed with nearly as much suspicion as actual law violation; correspondingly, the police value the familiar, the ordinary, the status quo, rather than social change. These views both put the police at odds with the dissident communities with whom they have frequent contact and detract from their capacity to appreciate the reasons for dissent, change, or any form of innovative social behavior.

Explaining Mass Protest

It is difficult to find police literature which recognizes that the imperfection of social institutions provides some basis for the discontent of large segments of American society. In addition, organized protest tends to be viewed as the conspiratorial product of authoritarian agitators—usually "Communists"—who mislead otherwise contented people. From a systematic sampling of police literature and statements by law enforcement authorities—ranging from the Director of the Federal Bureau of Investigation to the patrolman on the beat—a common theme emerges in police analyses of mass protest: the search for such "leaders." Again, this is a view, and a search, that is widespread in our society.

Such an approach has serious consequences. The police are led to view protest as illegitimate misbehavior, rather than as legitimate dissent against policies and practices that might be wrong. The police are bound to be hostile to illegitimate misbehavior, and the reduction of protest tends to be seen as their principal goal. Such an attitude leads to more rather than less violence; and a cycle of greater and greater hostility continues.

The "agitational" theory of protest leads to certain characteristic consequences. The police are prone to underestimate both the protesters' numbers and depth of feeling. Again, this increases the likelihood of violence. Yet it is not only the police who believe in the "agitational" theory. Many authorities do when challenged. For example, the Cox Commission found that one reason for the amount of violence when police cleared the buildings at Columbia was the inaccurate estimate of the number of demonstrators in the buildings:

6 *Washington Post,* December 15, 1969, p. B3.

> It seems to us, however, that the Administration's low estimate largely resulted from its inability to see that the seizure of the building was not simply the work of a few radicals but, by the end of the week, involved a significant portion of the student body who had become disenchanted with the operation of the university.[7]

In line with the "agitational" theory of protest, particular significance is attached by police intelligence estimates to the detection of leftists or outsiders of various sorts, as well as to indications of organization and prior planning and preparation. Moreover, similarities in tactics and expressed grievances in a number of scattered places and situations are seen as indicative of common leadership.

Thus Mr. J. Edgar Hoover, in testimony before this commission on September 18, 1968, stated:

> Communists are in the forefront of civil rights, anti-war, and student demonstrations, many of which ultimately become disorderly and erupt into violence. As an example, Bettina Aptheker Kurzweil, twenty-four year old member of the Communist National Committee, was a leading organizer of the "Free Speech" demonstrations on the campus of the University of California at Berkeley in the fall of 1964.
>
> These protests, culminating in the arrest of more than 800 demonstrators during a massive sit-in, on December 3, 1964, were the forerunner of the current campus upheaval.
>
> In a press conference on July 4, 1968, the opening day of the Communist Party's Special National Convention, Gus Hall, the Party's General Secretary, stated that there were communists on most of the major college campuses in the country and that they had been involved in the student protests.[8]

Mr. Hoover's statement is significant not only because he is our nation's highest and most renowned law enforcement official, but also because his views are reflected and disseminated throughout the nation—by publicity in the news media and by FBI seminars, briefings, and training for local policemen.

Not surprisingly, then, views similar to Mr. Hoover's dominate the most influential police literature. For instance, a lengthy article in the April, 1965, issue of *The Police Chief,* the official publication of the International Association of Chiefs of Police, concludes, referring to the Berkeley "Free Speech Movement":

> One of the more alarming aspects of these student demonstrations is the ever-present evidence that the guiding hand of communists and extreme leftists was involved.[9]

[7] The Cox Commission, *Crisis at Columbia* (New York: Vintage, 1968), p. 164.

[8] National Commission on Causes and Prevention of Violence, *Transcript of Proceedings* (Washington, D.C.: U.S. Government Printing Office, 1969), p. 56.

[9] *The Police Chief,* April, 1965, p. 10.

By contrast, a "blue-ribbon" investigating committee appointed by the Regents of the University of California concluded:

> We found no evidence that the FSM was organized by the Communist Party, the Progressive Labor Movement, or any other outside group. Despite a number of suggestive coincidences, the evidence which we accumulated left us with no doubt that the Free Speech Movement was a response to the September 14th change in rules regarding political activity at Bancroft and Telegraph, not a pre-planned effort to embarrass or destroy the University on whatever pretext arose.[10]

And more recently, the prestigious Cox Commission, which was headed by the former Solicitor General of the United States and investigated last spring's Columbia disturbances, reported:

> We reject the view that describes the April and May disturbances primarily to a conspiracy of student revolutionaries. That demonology is no less false than the naive radical doctrine that attributes all wars, racial injustices, and poverty to the machinations of a capitalist and militarist "Establishment."[11]

One reason why police analysis so often finds "leftists" is that its criteria for characterizing persons as "leftists" is so broad as to be misleading. In practice, the police may not distinguish "dissent" from "subversion." For example, listed in *The Police Chief* article as a "Communist-linked" person is a "former U.S. government employee who, while so employed, participated in picketing the House Committee on Un-American Activities in 1960."[12] Guilt by association is a central analytical tool, and information is culled from such ultraright publications as *Tocsin* and *Washington Report*. Hostility and suspicion toward the civil rights movement also serve as a major impetus for seeing Communist involvement and leadership. *The Police Chief* found it significant that black civil rights leaders such as James Farmer, Bayard Rustin, John Lewis, James Baldwin, and William McAdoo were among "the swarm of sympathizers" who sent messages of support to the FSM.[13]

Some indication of how wide the "communist" net stretches is given by a December, 1968, story in the *Chicago Tribune*. The reporter asked police to comment on the Report of this commission's Chicago Study Team:

> While most district commanders spoke freely, many policemen declined to comment unless their names were withheld. The majority of these said the Walker report appeared to have been written by members of the United States Supreme Court or Communists.[14]

[10] The Byrne Commission Report submitted to the Special Committee of the Regents of the University of California on May 7, 1965; most easily available in *Los Angeles Times*, May 12, 1965, Part IV, pp. 1–6. Quoted section, p. 5.

[11] Cox Commission, p. 189.

[12] *The Police Chief*, April, 1965, p. 36.

[13] *Ibid.*, pp. 42–44.

[14] Donald Yabush, *Chicago Tribune*, December 3, 1968, p. 1.

Supplementing the problem of police definition and identification of leftists is a special vision of the role that such persons play. Just as the presence of police and newsmen at the scene of a protest does not mean they are leaders, so the presence of a handful of radicals should not necessarily lead one to conclude that they are leading the protest movement. Moreover, studies of student protest—including the Byrne Report on the Free Speech Movement and the Cox Report on the Columbia disturbances —indicate that "the leadership," leaving aside for the moment whether it is radical leadership, is able to lead only when events such as administration responses unite significant numbers of students or faculty. For example, the FSM extended over a number of months, and the leaders conducted a long conflict with the university administration and proposed many mass meetings and protests, but their appeals to "sit-in" were heeded by students only intermittently. Sometimes the students rallied by the thousands; at other times the leadership found its base shrunken to no more than several hundred. At these nadir points the leaders were unable to accomplish anything significant; on their own they were powerless. Renewal of mass support for the FSM after each of these pauses was not the work of the leadership, but only occurred when the school administration took actions that aroused mass student feelings of betrayal or inequity. The "leadership" remained relatively constant in its calls for support—and even then had serious internal disputes—but the students gave, withdrew, and renewed their support independently, based on events. Clearly, the leaders did not foment student protest on their own; and whatever the intentions or political designs of many FSM leaders, they never had the power to manufacture the protest movement.

One special reason for this kind of police analysis of student protest may derive from police unfamiliarity with the student culture in which such protests occur. When this culture is taken into account, one need not fall back upon theories of sinister outside organizers to explain the ability of students to organize, plan, and produce sophisticated leaders and techniques. Even at the time of the Free Speech Movement in 1964, many of the students, including campus leaders, had spent at least one summer in the South taking part in the civil rights struggles. Moreover, everyone had read about or seen on television the "sit-ins" and other nonviolent tactics of the civil rights movement. Also, while the police in Berkeley saw the use of loudspeakers and walkie-talkies as evidence of outside leadership, the former had long been standard equipment at student rallies and meetings, and the latter were available in nearby children's toy stores (and were largely a "put-on" anyway). Finally, with the intellectual and human resources of thousands of undergraduates, graduate students, and faculty at one of the most honored universities in the world, one would hardly expect less competent organization and planning.

A similar analysis may be made of conspiracy arguments relying on similarities in issues and tactics in student protests throughout the nation;

explanations more simple than an external organizing force can be found. There is no question that there has been considerable contact among student protesters from many campuses. For example, students who are undergraduates at one university often do graduate work at another. And television news coverage of protest, student newspapers, and books popular in the student culture have long articulated the grievances and tactics around which much unrest revolves. Thus, when it is also considered that students throughout the country do face similar circumstances, it is hardly surprising for similar events to occur widely and to follow a recognizable pattern. Interestingly, collective actions, such as panty raids, have spread through the student subculture in the past without producing sinister conspiracy theories.

A related problem for police is sorting among certain types of claims from and statements about radical movements. Chicago prior to and during the Democratic National Convention is a case in point. To quote from the report of the commission's Chicago Study Team:

> The threats to the City were varied. Provocative and inflammatory statements, made in connection with activities planned for convention week, were published and widely disseminated. There were also intelligence reports from informants.
>
> Some of this information was *absurd,* like the reported plan to contaminate the city's water supply with LSD. But some were *serious;* and both were strengthened by the authorities' *lack of any mechanism for distinguishing one from the other.*
>
> The second factor—*the city's response—matched in numbers and logistics, at least, the demonstrators' threats.*[15]

Surely it is unsatisfactory not to distinguish the absurd from the serious. And just as surely, the incapacity to distinguish can only result in inadequate protection against real dangers, as well as an increased likelihood of unnecessary suppression and violence. Again, this illustrates some of the problems of the police view when confronted with modern mass protest. The police are more likely to believe that "anarchist" leaders are going to contaminate a city's water supply with LSD than they are to believe that a student anti-war or black protest is an expression of genuine, widespread dissatisfaction.

An interesting footnote to this discussion of police ideas about protest may be added by noting that, if the standards used by leading police spokesmen to identify a conspiracy were applied to the police themselves, one would conclude that police in the United States constitute an ultra-right wing conspiracy. For example, one would note the growing police militancy with its similar rhetoric and tactics throughout the nation, and the presence of such outside "agitators" as John Harrington, president

[15] Chicago Study Team, *Rights in Conflict* (New York: Bantam, 1968), pp. vii–viii, emphasis added.

of the Fraternal Order of Police, at the scene of particular outbursts of militancy. We hasten to add that we do not feel that this is an adequate analysis of the situation. Police, like students, share a common culture and are subject to similar pressures, problems, and inequities; the police across the country respond similarly to similar situations because they share common interests, not because they are a "fascist"-led conspiracy.

VI

CRIMES BY THE POLICE

The police, as the "guardians of law" and "protectors of order," are legally granted the right to use force and violence in their daily work.[1] Their "crime-fighting" activities are generally classified around seven major categories of crime as defined by the FBI.[2] These "index crimes" are: murder, rape, robbery, aggravated assault, burglary, larceny over fifty dollars and auto theft.[3]

The crimes that are not categorized, not studied, and ignored by the FBI, and state and local law enforcement agencies are the crimes committed by the police against the very public they are responsible for protecting. Similar to the FBI "index crimes," police crimes include murder, robbery, assault, extortion, drug traffic, and other forms of corruption.

The extent of corruption and crime by the police is not a newly discovered phenomenon. In 1894 the Lexow Commission investigated reported corruption of the New York City police. The findings of the commission, detailed in eighteen volumes, described a "systematic and pervasive pattern of police corruption, brutality, election fraud, payoffs for appointments and promotions, political interference in transfers and assignments, police involvement in confidence frauds, and the police conception that they were above the law." [4]

The Wickersham Commission, a National Commission on Law Observance and Enforcement, appointed by Herbert Hoover in 1930, conducted a nation-wide investigation of the police. The commission, concentrating its research on police misconduct within police stations and not

1 Egon Bittner, *The Functions of the Police in Modern Society* (Washington, D.C.: United States Government Printing Office, 1970); see also Ralph Miliband, *The State in Capitalist Society* (New York: Basic Books, 1969), pp. 51–52.

2 David Gordon, "Class and the Economics of Crime," *Review of Radical Political Economics* 3, no. 3 (Summer, 1971), pp. 52–54.

3 Federal Bureau of Investigation, *Crime in the United States: Uniform Crime Reports—1971* (Washington, D.C.: Government Printing Office, 1972), p. 1.

4 James F. Richardson, *The New York Police: Colonial Times to 1901* (New York: Oxford University Press, 1970), p. 240.

in the streets, stressed the "lawlessness of law enforcement authority." [5]

The report cited numerous incidents of police brutality and crime, including "street brutality by policemen, loose kidnapping or false arrests, unlawful imprisonment and 'incommunicado' imprisonment in police jails, the use of unfair pressure to get evidence and confessions, and perjury indulged in by policemen to gain convictions." [6]

Investigations of the police since 1931 continue to document their illegal and criminal behavior. The most recent, the *President's Commission on Law Enforcement and the Administration of Justice,* also reported the problem of excessive brutality by the police.[7] The 1972 report of the Knapp Commission on Police Corruption spent two and one-half years investigating the problem of corruption in the New York City Police Department. The findings of the commission were extensive. Numerous cases of police accepting bribes and demanding pay-offs in gambling, prostitution, and narcotics rackets were uncovered.[8]

While the Knapp Commission was set up to investigate only corruption, two other major areas of criminal police behavior, brutality and murder, were not studied, even though these practices are a part of illegal police behavior. Other investigations have documented these practices of the police. A 1935 New York City Report, made after the uprisings in Harlem, cited instances of police brutality, including "the detention of innocent men in jail, and even the mutilation and killing of persons upon slight provocation." [9]

In a sociological study of the police, made in 1951, William Westley found that seven out of ten, or sixty-nine percent of the police officers interviewed, justified the use of violence on illegal grounds, such as disrespect and gaining information to solve a crime.[10]

Researchers in a recent study of the police in three American cities, Boston, Chicago, and Washington, D.C. (all cities noted for well-trained, highly paid, professional police departments) accompanied police in their daily rounds. They observed the excessive use of force in fifty percent of the police-citizen encounters. In 40 percent of these incidents, defiance of the officer's authority was the factor precipitating the police violence.[11]

5 Ernest J. Hopkins, *Our Lawless Police* (New York: Viking Press, 1931), p. 3.

6 Ibid., p. 7.

7 President's Commission on Law Enforcement and the Administration of Justice, *Task Force Report: The Police* (Washington, D.C.: Government Printing Office, 1967), pp. 181–82.

8 *Knapp Commission Report on Police Corruption* (New York: George Braziller, 1972), pp. 61–195.

9 The Mayor's Commission on Conditions in Harlem, *The Negro in New York* (New York: Municipal Archives, 1936), p. 69.

10 William Westley, "Violence and the Police," *The American Journal of Sociology,* July, 1953, pp. 34–41.

11 Albert J. Reiss, Jr., "Police Brutality—Answers to Key Questions," *Trans-Action,* (July–August, 1968), pp. 10–19.

After reporting these findings, one high police official demanded to know which officers had been observed. He commented, "Any officer who is stupid enough to behave that way in the presence of outsiders deserves to be fired." [12]

Women receive a special kind of treatment from the police. Third World and poor women, who often have no alternative except prostituting for survival, are arrested, harassed, and frequently beaten by the police. One study of prostitutes described the three major sources of violence against the prostitute: the customer, the police, and the pimp, in that order.[13] Wealthier white prostitutes or call girls, who are rarely the victims of police harassment or brutality, can afford the high priced payoffs needed for police protection.[14]

The victims of rape are also frequently the victims of police harassment. The police typically respond in a callous, cynical manner. One victim described her encounter with the police:

> The rape was probably the least traumatic incident of the whole evening. If I'm ever raped again, which I will never be because I've armed myself, I wouldn't report it to the police because of all the degradation and questioning.[15]

The police try to protect themselves against charges of brutality through a network of camaraderie, with strong demands for secrecy and solidarity.[16] Arbitrary arrests and summary punishments are protected by using false arrests, cover charges, pyramiding charges, lying, throwaways, and alibis.[17] When the police respond violently to a citizen, they are almost compelled to arrest that person, giving them a justifiable excuse for their brutality. After the arrest, which may or may not be legitimate, the officer has to insure the validity of his actions. Obtaining a conviction may mean altering the charge to a more serious offense, or giving false testimony. Lying is used to cover up a mistake and criminal charges buttress the lie.[18]

Falsification of evidence and lying is not limited to local police officers. I. F. Stone details the extensive lying, manipulation of facts, and

12 Ibid., p. 15.

13 "Prostitution," *Off Our Backs,* January, 1973, p. 4. The study gave a breakdown of injuries to the prostitute: sixty-four percent by the customer, twenty percent by the police, and sixteen percent by the pimps.

14 See, for example, *The Knapp Commission Report on Police Corruption,* op. cit., pp. 116–22.

15 Susan Griffin, "Rape: The All-American Crime," *Ramparts,* September, 1971, p. 32.

16 William Westley, "Secrecy and the Police," *Social Forces* 34, no. 3 (March, 1956): 254–57 and Jerome H. Skolnick, *Justice Without Trial* (New York: John Wiley & Sons, 1966), pp. 49–53.

17 Paul Chevigny, *Police Power: Police Abuses in New York City* (New York: Pantheon Books, 1969), p. 136.

18 Ibid., p. 143.

cover-ups that were used by the National Guard, as well as the FBI, in their defense of the cold-blooded murders of four college students at Kent State. There was a similar fabrication of evidence uncovered in the investigation of the killings at Jackson State University, in Mississippi.[19] A variety of lies and cover-ups have been found in investigations of civil rights murders in the South.[20]

Throwaways, usually knives and guns, are often carried by policemen to place on their victims of fatal brutality. The throwaway provides a ready made excuse of self-defense for an officer or officers involved in a homicide. New patrolmen are usually advised of the importance of "carrying a hidden tossaway knife or gun that can be planted on a suspect to corroborate an excuse of self-defense." [21]

Police homicides are hidden statistics, not generally considered when crimes by the police are discussed. However, recent studies have begun to examine the extent and victims of this crime. A study of the Chicago police and their fatal use of force concluded that "a black in Chicago was over six times as likely as a white to be killed by the police." [22] In a similar, although not as detailed study of police homicides in California, the rate for black men being killed by the police was nine to ten times higher than for white men.[23]

The Chicago investigation reported that twenty-seven percent of the studied cases of civilian deaths by the police had strong evidence suggesting police misconduct. Of these seventy-six police homicide cases, the police pressed charges against the officers involved in only two cases; the State's Attorney presented evidence to a grand jury for four cases; the grand jury indicted one officer; and for the one case that went to trial, the policeman was acquitted.[24]

Arthur Kobler, a psychology professor, in a study of more than 1150 cases of police homicides, concluded that:

> Police officers, black or white, firing weapons at citizens of all skin colors and ages can be confident that there will be few consequences . . . I know of only three successful criminal prosecutions. These cases included one where the killer's partner testified that a gun had been planted, another in

[19] The President's Commission on Campus Unrest, *The Killings at Jackson State* (Washington, D.C.: U.S. Government Printing Office, 1970).

[20] See, for example, Leon Friedman, *Southern Justice* (New York: Pantheon, 1966).

[21] William W. Turner, *The Police Establishment* (New York: G. P. Putnam's Sons, 1968), p. 46. See also Rodney Stark, *Police Riots* (Belmont, Calif.: Wadsworth Publishing Co., 1972), pp. 55–84, and Albert J. Reiss, Jr., *The Police and the Public* (New Haven: Yale University Press, 1970).

[22] Ralph Knoohuizen, Richard P. Fahey, and Deborah J. Palmer, *The Police and Their Use of Fatal Force in Chicago* (Chicago: Chicago Law Enforcement Study Group, 1972), p. 74.

[23] Paul Buell and Paul Takagi, "Code 984: Death by Police Intervention," (unpublished article, School of Criminology, University of California at Berkeley, 1971).

[24] Knoohuizen, Fahey, Palmer, *op. cit.*, p. 32.

which the killer had been having an affair with the wife of the deceased, and a third in which the penalty was one day in jail.[25]

The extent of police corruption, brutality, and violence is massive and must be examined within the context of two major factors: the organizational demands of policing, and American society as a whole. Police departments demand police effectiveness, reduced crime rates, and increased police efficiency; quotas may even be a routine part or "working norm" of departmental policy. In a study of the Oakland, California Police Department, it was reported that motorcycle police were responsible for writing at least two moving violation tickets per hour.[26] The occupational duties, "production demands," and conflicts between maintaining order within the boundaries of the law create what has been described as a "working personality" for the police.[27] The police are socially and professionally isolated into a type of subculture, with norms of secrecy, solidarity, and machismo. These norms foster the isolation of the police from the community that they are supposed to serve. Their machismo behavior, which stresses "toughness" and male superiority, allows the police to behave aggressively and frequently violently, without the threat of being reprimanded.

Police behavior is a microcosm of political life. In a society that emphasizes profit and the accumulation of wealth, it should not be surprising that these goals have become an integral part of police practice. The evidence presented in this section suggests that police violations are not isolated incidents of individual "bad" policemen, but are a systematic part of the police role, just as corruption and violence are a systematic part of American government. These practices, supported, justified, and legitimized by the police, are reinforced by the society, and by the kind of work that the police are responsible for doing.

The police are functionaries doing the dirty work of society. This dirty work takes various forms. The police must work with the victims of murders, fires, accidents, and suicides. They frequently have to deal with drunks and derelicts. At the same time, they may be putting their lives in danger while attempting to enforce unenforceable laws (e.g., gambling, alcohol, and drugs). A part of dirty work is controlling and confining populations and individuals who are defined as dangerous or subversive.[28] When more subtle methods of social control such as schooling and the media fail, the police are called upon to act repressively in order to insure ruling class domination.

25 Quoted in John Fleischman, "Police Blast Citizens 33–1: The Score on the Killing Ground," *Coast* 14, no. 5 (May, 1973): 33.

26 Jerome H. Skolnick, op. cit., p. 55.

27 Ibid., pp. 42–70.

28 Lee Rainwater, "The Revolt of the Dirty Workers," *Trans-Action,* November, 1967, pp. 2, 64.

Police violence and corruption are a microcosm of the more general forms of exploitation within the United States. The recent exposés of Watergate document the extent of this corruption, reaching into even the highest office of the government, the Presidency. Price-fixing, the sale of unsafe products (e.g., automobiles, drugs, paints), consumer fraud, advertising and other forms of financial deception; inadequate and poor health care; war crimes committed in Southeast Asia; brutality in prisons; and the absence of justice in the courts, all document the pervasiveness of this brutality and corruption.

The victims of price-fixing and corruption, brutality, and violence by the police, government, and industry, are most often poor, young, and Third World. Proportionally, more black people are brutalized or murdered, arrested, and imprisoned than whites. Young, poor, and Third World people are clubbed, beaten, and murdered for protesting against and struggling to survive within a society that has institutionalized inequality, poverty, and racism.

Police malpractice can neither be reformed nor eliminated as long as brutality and corruption in America are considered as isolated exceptions. Nor can they be eliminated as long as the police are used to protect established economic and political arrangements.

Suggested Reading

American Friends Service Committee, *Struggle for Justice.* Hill and Wang, 1971.

BITTNER, EGON. *The Functions of the Police in Modern Society.* Washington, D.C.: U.S. Government Printing Office, 1970.

CHEVIGNY, PAUL. *Police Power and Police Abuses in New York City.* New York: Pantheon Books, 1969.

CRAY, ED. *The Enemy in the Streets: Police Malpractice in America.* New York: Anchor Books, 1972.

GORDON, DAVID. "Class and the Economics of Crime." *Review of Radical Political Economics* 3, no. 3 (Summer, 1971).

Knapp Commission Report on Police Corruption. New York: George Braziller, 1972.

KNOOHUIZEN, RALPH; FAHEY, RICHARD P.; and PALMER, DEBORAH J. *The Police and Their Fatal Use of Force in Chicago.* Chicago: Chicago Law Enforcement Study Group, 1972.

LA FAVE, WAYNE. *Arrest: The Decision to Take A Suspect Into Custody.* Boston: Little, Brown & Co., 1964.

The Mayor's Commission on Conditions in Harlem. *The Negro in New York.* New York: Municipal Archives, 1936.

The President's Commission on Campus Unrest. *The Killings at Jackson State.* Washington, D.C.: U.S. Government Printing Office, 1970.

RAINWATER, LEE. "The Revolt of the Dirty Workers." *Trans-Action* 5, no. 1 (November, 1967): 2, 64.

REISS, ALBERT J. JR. *The Police and the Public.* New Haven: Yale University Press, 1971.

SKOLNICK, JEROME H. *Justice Without Trial: Law Enforcement in Democratic Society.* New York: John Wiley & Sons, 1967.

STARK, RODNEY. *Police Riots.* (Belmont, Calif.: Wadsworth Publishing Co., 1972).

WESTLEY, WILLIAM. *Violence and the Police: A Sociological Study of Law, Custom and Morality.* Boston, Mass.: MIT Press, 1971.

WILSON, JAMES Q. *Varieties of Police Behavior: The Management of Law and Order in Eight Communities.* Cambridge, Mass.: Harvard University Press, 1968.

Report on Police Corruption

The Extent of Police Corruption

We found corruption to be widespread. It took various forms depending upon the activity involved, appearing at its most sophisticated among plainclothesmen assigned to enforcing gambling laws. In the five plainclothes divisions where our investigations were concentrated we found a strikingly standardized pattern of corruption. Plainclothesmen, participating in what is known in police parlance as a "pad," collected regular bi-weekly or monthly payments amounting to as much as $3,500 from each of the gambling establishments in the area under their jurisdiction, and divided the take in equal shares. The monthly share per man (called the "nut") ranged from $300 and $400 in midtown Manhattan to $1,500 in Harlem. When supervisors were involved they received a share and a half. A newly assigned plainclothesman was not entitled to his share for about two months, while he was checked out for reliability, but the earnings lost by the delay were made up to him in the form of two months' severance pay when he left the division.

Evidence before us led us to the conclusion that the same pattern existed in the remaining divisions which we did not investigate in depth. This conclusion was confirmed by events occurring before and after the period of our investigation. Prior to the Commission's existence, exposures by former plainclothesman Frank Serpico had led to indictments or departmental charges against nineteen plainclothesmen in a Bronx division for involvement in a pad where the nut was $800. After our public hearings had been completed, an investigation conducted by the King's County District Attorney and the Department's Internal Affairs Division —which investigation neither the Commission nor its staff had even known about—resulted in indictments and charges against thirty-seven Brooklyn plainclothesmen who had participated in a pad with a nut of $1,200. The manner of operation of the pad involved in each of these

From the Knapp Commission Report on Police Corruption (*New York: George Braziller, 1973*), *pp. 1–7.*

situations was in every detail identical to that described at the Commission hearings, and in each almost every plainclothesman in the division, including supervisory lieutenants, was implicated.

Corruption in narcotics enforcement lacked the organization of the gambling pads, but individual payments—known as "scores"—were commonly received and could be staggering in amount. Our investigation, a concurrent probe by the State Investigation Commission and prosecutions by Federal and local authorities all revealed a pattern whereby corrupt officers customarily collected scores in substantial amounts from narcotics violators. These scores were either kept by the individual officer or shared with a partner and, perhaps, a superior officer. They ranged from minor shakedowns to payments of many thousands of dollars, the largest narcotics payoff uncovered in our investigation having been $80,000. According to information developed by the S.I.C. and in recent Federal investigations, the size of this score was by no means unique.

Corruption among detectives assigned to general investigative duties also took the form of shakedowns of individual targets of opportunity. Although these scores were not in the huge amounts found in narcotics, they not infrequently came to several thousand dollars.

Uniformed patrolmen assigned to street duties were not found to receive money on nearly so grand or organized a scale, but the large number of small payments they received present an equally serious if less dramatic problem. Uniformed patrolmen, particularly those assigned to radio patrol cars, participated in gambling pads more modest in size than those received by plainclothes units and received regular payments from construction sites, bars, grocery stores and other business establishments. These payments were usually made on a regular basis to sector car patrolmen and on a haphazard basis to others. While individual payments to uniformed men were small, mostly under $20, they were often so numerous as to add substantially to a patrolman's income. Other less regular payments to uniformed patrolmen included those made by after-hours bars, bottle clubs, tow trucks, motorists, cab drivers, parking lots, prostitutes and defendants wanting to fix their cases in court. Another practice found to be widespread was the payment of gratuities by policemen to other policemen to expedite normal police procedures or to gain favorable assignments.

Sergeants and lieutenants who were so inclined participated in the same kind of corruption as the men they supervised. In addition, some sergeants had their own pads from which patrolmen were excluded.

Although the Commission was unable to develop hard evidence establishing that officers above the rank of lieutenant received payoffs, considerable circumstantial evidence and some testimony so indicated. Most often when a superior officer is corrupt, he uses a patrolman as his "bagman" who collects for him and keeps a percentage of the take. Because the bagman may keep the money for himself, although he claims to be collecting for his superior, it is extremely difficult to determine with any accuracy when the superior actually is involved.

Of course, not all policemen are corrupt. If we are to exclude such petty infractions as free meals, an appreciable number do not engage in any corrupt activities. Yet, with extremely rare exceptions, even those who themselves engage in no corrupt activities are involved in corruption in the sense that they take no steps to prevent what they know or suspect to be going on about them.

It must be made clear that—in a little over a year with a staff having as few as two and never more than twelve field investigators—we did not examine every precinct in the Department. Our conclusion that corruption is widespread throughout the Department is based on the fact that information supplied to us by hundreds of sources within and without the Department was consistently borne out by specific observations made in areas we were able to investigate in detail.

The Nature and Significance of Police Corruption

Corruption, although widespread, is by no means uniform in degree. Corrupt policemen have been described as falling into two basic categories: "meat-eaters" and "grass-eaters." As the names might suggest, the meat-eaters are those policemen who, like Patrolman William Phillips who testified at our hearings, aggressively misuse their police powers for personal gain. The grass-eaters simply accept the payoffs that the happenstances of police work throw their way. Although the meat-eaters get the huge payoffs that make the headlines, they represent a small percentage of all corrupt policemen. The truth is, the vast majority of policemen on the take don't deal in huge amounts of graft.

And yet, grass-eaters are the heart of the problem. Their great numbers tend to make corruption "respectable." They also tend to encourage the code of silence that brands anyone who exposes corruption a traitor. At the time our investigation began, any policeman violating the code did so at his peril. The result was described in our interim report: "The rookie who comes into the Department is faced with the situation where it is easier for him to become corrupt than to remain honest."

More importantly, although meat-eaters can and have been individually induced to make their peace with society, the grass-eaters may be more easily reformed. We believe that, given proper leadership and support, many police who have slipped into corruption would exchange their illicit income for the satisfaction of belonging to a corruption-free Department in which they could take genuine pride.

The problem of corruption is neither new, nor confined to the police. Reports of prior investigations into police corruption, testimony taken by the Commission, and opinions of informed persons both within and without the Department make it abundantly clear that police corruption has been a problem for many years. Investigations have occurred on the average of once in twenty years since before the turn of the century, and yet conditions exposed by one investigation seem substantially unchanged when the next one makes its report. This doesn't mean that the police have a monopoly on corruption. On the contrary, in every area where police corruption exists it is paralleled by corruption in other agencies of government, in industry and labor, and in the professions.

Our own mandate was limited solely to the police. There are sound reasons for such a special concern with police corruption. The police have a unique place in our society. The policeman is expected to "uphold the law" and "keep the peace." He is charged with everything from traffic control to riot control. He is expected to protect our lives and our property. As a result, society gives him special powers and prerogatives, which include the right and obligation to bear arms, along with the authority to take away our liberty by arresting us.

Symbolically, his role is even greater. For most people, the policeman is the law. To them, the law is administered by the patrolman on the beat and the captain in the station house. Little wonder that the public becomes aroused and alarmed when the police are charged with corruption or are shown to be corrupt.

Departmental Attitudes Towards Police Corruption

Although this special concern is justified, public preoccupation with police corruption as opposed to corruption in other agencies of government inevitably seems unfair to the policeman. He believes that he is unjustly blamed for the results of corruption in other parts of the criminal justice system. This sense of unfairness intensifies the sense of isolation and hostility to which the nature of police work inevitably gives rise.

Feelings of isolation and hostility are experienced by policemen not just in New York, but everywhere. To understand these feelings one must appreciate an important characteristic of any metropolitan police department, namely an extremely intense group loyalty. When properly understood, this group loyalty can be used in the fight against corruption. If misunderstood or ignored, it can undermine anti-corruption activities.

Pressures that give rise to this group loyalty include the danger to which policemen are constantly exposed and the hostility they encounter from society at large. Everyone agrees that a policeman's life is a dangerous one, and that his safety, not to mention his life, can depend on his ability to rely on a fellow officer in a moment of crisis. It is less generally realized that the policeman works in a sea of hostility. This is true, not only in high crime areas, but throughout the City. Nobody, whether a burglar or a Sunday motorist, likes to have his activities interfered with. As a result, most citizens, at one time or another, regard the police with varying degrees of hostility. The policeman feels, and naturally often returns, this hostility.

Two principal characteristics emerge from this group loyalty: suspicion and hostility directed at any outside interference with the Department, and an intense desire to be proud of the Department. This mixture of hostility and pride has created what the Commission has found to be the most serious roadblock to a rational attack upon police corruption: a stubborn refusal at all levels of the Department to acknowledge that a serious problem exists.

The interaction of stubbornness, hostility and pride has given rise to the so-called "rotten-apple" theory. According to this theory, which bordered on official Department doctrine, any policeman found to be corrupt must promply be denounced as a rotten apple in an otherwise clean barrel. It must never be admitted that his individual corruption may be symptomatic of underlying disease.

This doctrine was bottomed on two basic premises: First, the morale of the Department requires that there be no official recognition of corruption, even though practically all members of the Department know it is in truth extensive; second, the Department's public image and effectiveness require official denial of this truth.

The rotten-apple doctrine has in many ways been a basic obstacle to meaningful reform. To begin with, it reinforced and gave respectability to the code of silence. The official view that the Department's image and morale forbade public disclosure of the extent of corruption inhibited any officer who wished to disclose corruption and justified any who preferred to remain silent. The doctrine also made difficult, if not impossible, any meaningful attempt at managerial reform. A high command unwilling to acknowledge that the problem of corruption is extensive cannot very well argue that drastic changes are necessary to deal with that problem. Thus neither the Mayor's Office nor the Police Department took adequate steps to see that such changes were made when the need for them was indicated by the changes made by Officers Frank Serpico and David Durk in 1968. This was demonstrated in the Commission's second set of public hearings in December 1971.

Finally, the doctrine made impossible the use of one of the most effective techniques for dealing with any entrenched criminal activity, namely persuading a participant to help provide evidence against his partners in crime. If a corrupt policeman is merely an isolated rotten apple, no reason can be given for not exposing him the minute he is discovered. If, on the other hand, it is acknowledged that a corrupt officer is only one part of an apparatus of corruption, common sense dictates that every effort should be made to enlist the offender's aid in providing the evidence to destroy the apparatus.

*I. F. STONE**

Fabricated Evidence in the Kent State Killings

I

In a country so passionate about law and order it should not be necessary to remark that falsification of evidence is a crime, and agreement to do so in concert with others is conspiracy to obstruct justice. Were students to shoot down National Guardsmen or other law officers, and were the FBI then to turn up evidence that those who did the shooting agreed among themselves to tell investigators a fabricated story, it is hard to believe the news would be relegated to the back pages and met with indifference.

This—albeit in reverse—is what happened in the Jackson State and Kent State killings. In both cases, the FBI and other government agencies have turned up evidence that the Guardsmen and law officers who did the shootings also agreed among themselves to tell FBI investigators a false story. But it would take a very delicate seismograph to locate the resultant outcry. Apparently it does make a difference when the victims are only black and/or students.

In an age of instant communication, some news still seems to travel by ox cart. The fabrication of evidence in the Jackson and Kent State killings is an example. It is important because it offers another avenue of prosecution by federal grand juries, now that both the Ohio and Mississippi grand juries have refused to indict any of the Guardsmen or law officers for murder, which is a state crime.

To those who think murder is too strong a word one may recall that even Agnew three days after the Kent State shootings used the word in an interview on the David Frost show in Los Angeles. Agnew admitted in response to a question that what happened at Kent State was murder, "but

---

From The New York Review of Books, *December 3, 1970, pp. 28–31. Reprinted with permission from* The New York Review of Books. *Copyright © 1970 Nyrev, Inc.*

* As of August 1973, the U.S. Department of Justice has reopened its investigation of the Kent State killings, suggesting the accuracy and insight of Stone's analysis.

not first degree" since there was—as Agnew explained from his own training as a lawyer—"no premeditation but simply an over-response in the heat of anger that results in a killing; it's a murder. It's not premeditated and it certainly can't be condoned."

Now that murder on the two campuses *has* been condoned by the two state guard juries, what is the federal government going to do about it? One possibility is prosecution under the civil rights statutes—and it is a commentary on the position to which students have been relegated that they, like Negroes, must look to civil rights statutes as their last resort for justice.

Another possibility is prosecution for conspiracy to obstruct justice and for making false statements to the FBI. That Jackson city police and Mississippi highway patrolmen lied to the FBI and destroyed evidence was plain enough in the Scranton Commission report on Jackson State when it was released October 1. Little attention was paid to this aspect of it, however, perhaps because the report failed explicitly to emphasize these deceptions as an area for federal grand jury action.

That there was similar evidence of fabrication at Kent State was not mentioned in the Scranton Commission report on those killings when it was released October 4. The fabrication angle of the Kent State shootings was revealed for the first time nine days later by Senator Stephen Young, Democrat of Ohio. But the news and its significance have barely begun to percolate into public consciousness.

The speech and its reception, or non-reception, by the media would itself make a useful investigation by a school of journalism. The forum Young chose for breaking the story was hardly obscure. He broke it in a speech on the Senate floor on October 13. The way he broke it was sensational, or at least it would seem so by any normal standard of news. He read to the Senate hitherto unrevealed passages from a secret report prepared in the Justice Department last July summarizing the FBI's findings at Kent State. *"We have reason to believe,"* the senator quoted from this document to the Senate, *"that the claim by the National Guard that their lives were endangered by the students was fabricated subsequent to the events."*

He might as well have been carrying on a soliloquy in the Capitol basement. Though advance copies of the speech were made available in the press galleries, the speech was a non-event. It went unreported by the small army of wire-service, newspaper, radio, and TV correspondents who cover the Senate.

It took ten days for the story to reach Ohio, or about the time it would take to send it by bicycle. On October 23, the Akron *Beacon-Journal* splashed news of the speech across the top of page one: "Young: Guards Fabricated Peril." I was at Kent State at the time and had with me both the Young speech and a copy of the Justice Department summary on which it was based. I assumed that either the wire services or the *Beacon-*

Journal had caught up with the *Congressional Record.* Not until I began to work on this account for *The New York Review* did I finally uncover the real story on how the news was broken.

It began with a young New York insurance broker, Peter Davies, who was so upset by the Kent State shootings that he wrote a letter of protest to President Nixon and sent a copy to Arthur Krause, father of Allison Krause, one of the students killed. They struck up a friendship and have been working together on the case. Davies read Young's speech in the *Congressional Record* on the night of October 22 and he and Krause at once began telephoning newspapers all over the country.

They called *The New York Times,* the New York *Post,* the Akron *Beacon-Journal,* the Boston *Globe,* the Chicago *Sun-Times,* the St. Louis *Post-Dispatch,* the Washington *Post,* and in Pittsburg, where Krause lives, the *Post-Gazette* and the *Press.* They also telephoned CBS, NBC, and WOR in New York.

Once the *Beacon-Journal* broke the story, it was picked up by the AP, but only on its Ohio state service. The UPI sent out a few paragraphs on its national wire under a Kent, Ohio, dateline. But it buried Young's speech under an account of a minor explosion at a black student headquarters on the Kent State campus.

The New York Times, after a phone call from Davies the night of October 22 and a personal visit with a copy of the Young speech on the morning of October 23, finally ran the UPI story from Kent on page 72 of its Sunday paper, October 25, but with all references to Young's speech omitted!

The AP's reaction was curious. The Boston *Globe* queried the New York office of the AP after Davies phoned the *Globe* with the tip the night of October 23. The *Globe* asked if the AP would be moving the *Beacon-Journal* story. The AP phoned back in an hour and said it was an old story and to ignore it. The *Globe* then phoned Davies who in turn phoned the AP and protested that every newsman whom he and Krause telephoned said this was the first they had heard of it.

Thereupon the AP man said that the FBI had refused to confirm the story and that the Justice Department had said Young did not have access to its files. But, as Davies pointed out to the AP man, neither the FBI nor the Justice Department had denied the authenticity of Young's account. The AP nevertheless declined to put the story on its national wire. The Boston *Globe* later published the UPI account in its Sunday paper of October 25.

There was no response on TV to the phone calls. The reaction of the newspapers varied. The New York *Post* ran the fullest account in its weekend issue of October 24–25 but buried it so far back in the paper (page 48) that many readers, including Davies, missed it. Krause reached Ben Bradlee of the Washington *Post,* which ran a top story on page 4, October 25: " 'Fabrication' Laid to Guard At Kent." This pointed out that not until Young's October 13 speech "had the question been raised of the Guard's consciously inventing an excuse for its conduct."

On October 27 I showed the thirty-five-page Justice Department summary of the FBI findings on national television during the Dick Cavett show and read the passage about fabrication. The next day James Wechsler of the New York *Post* was the first and (so far as I know) the only columnist to analyze the Young speech and its implications. A day later a *New York Times* reporter called to ask me where I had obtained a copy of the Justice Department summary. (I refused to disclose the source.) On Saturday, October 31, *The New York Times* published excerpts from the hitherto unpublished summary with a story of its own, which did a first-rate job of comparing the FBI findings with the report of the special Ohio grand jury. But, inexplicably, it buried the fabrication reference on an inside page; and it failed to publish an important part of the Justice Department's summary concerning fabrication (of which more later). In an editorial November 7, *The New York Times* called for a federal grand jury to investigate the Kent State shootings but did not mention the FBI's findings that evidence had been fabricated.

II

"A significant cause of the deaths and injuries at Jackson State College," said the Scranton Commission report on the killings there, "is the confidence of white officers that if they fire weapons during a black campus disturbance they will face neither stern departmental discipline nor criminal prosecution or conviction." This view, it added, "received confirmation by the Mississippi Highway Safety Patrol investigation and by the report of the Hinds County Grand Jury." After the report on the Kent State killings by the Ohio special Portage County grand jury, law officers may feel as free to shoot white students as they do black.

Federal grand jury action in both cases would demonstrate that the nation will not allow a double standard of law and order, that official lawlessness and overreaction will be punished, too, as a deterrent for the future. The alternative is to leave a rankling sense of injustice on the nation's campuses. This has already deepened the gulf between the generations, as police brutality has long deepened it between the races.

In Mississippi, the local police lied to the mayor and the FBI when they denied that they fired at Jackson State, as the Hinds County grand jury itself recognized. The police replaced their ammunition after the shootings to fool the mayor when he inspected their guns. They and the highway patrol disposed of the shell casings after the shooting to prevent their use as ballistic evidence. But the state highway patrol, while it got rid of its own shells, saved some of those fired by city police so that they could, if necessary, disprove the earlier story that the highway patrolmen alone had fired.

Neither the city police nor the highway patrol told the FBI they had disposed of this critical evidence. Not until a special federal grand jury was convened last June and issued subpoenas did the highway patrol admit that it held any shell casings and hand them over to the FBI. The Scranton report said the FBI then traced these shells back to city policemen and "when confronted with this fact at least three city policemen admitted shooting."

This cries out for further investigation. A federal false claims statute makes it a felony punishable by a fine of $10,000 or imprisonment of up to ten years or both to make a willfully false statement to any agency of the US government. The facts as known raise the possibility of a conspiracy to destroy evidence and obstruct justice. But the special federal grand jury in Mississippi recessed last June after one week of activity during which it heard only a few witnesses and turned over the few remaining shell casings to the FBI. There should be a nationwide demand for its reactivation and for convening another special federal grand jury in Ohio to make a similar investigation of what happened at Kent State.

What has come to light so far is but a meager portion of the information gathered. So far two FBI summaries concerning Kent State have surfaced. These were prepared by the civil rights division of the Justice Department for possible federal prosecution, and copies were sent to the Ohio authorities for their use. The first was a ten-page memorandum, the main contents of which leaked last July to the Akron *Beacon-Journal*. The story was then picked up by other papers when the civil rights division confirmed the existence of this summary.

That earlier summary, unlike the single-spaced thirty-five-page summary from which Senator Young read to the Senate, does not seem to have contained any reference to the possibility that some Guardsmen got together and fabricated their story of the shootings. I am told that the FBI was asked by the Scranton Commission to look further into this angle; a federal grand jury could learn what further report, if any, was made by the FBI. One passage of the thirty-five-page FBI summary that *The New York Times* did not publish says, after explaining why there was some reason to believe Guardsmen had fabricated their story of being in danger:

> Additionally, an unknown Guardsman, age 23, married, and a machinist by trade, was interviewed by members of the Knight newspaper chain. He admitted that his life was not in danger and that he fired indiscriminately into the crowd. He further stated that the Guardsmen had gotten together after the shooting and decided to fabricate the story that they were in danger of serious bodily harm or death from the students.
>
> The published newspaper article quoted the Guardsman as saying: "The guys have been saying that we got to get together and stick to the same story,

> that it was either our lives or them, a matter of survival. I told them I would tell the truth and couldn't get in trouble that way."

This interview was included in an eight-page special issue on the Kent State shootings published by the Akron *Beacon-Journal* last May 24. It was the work of a team of Knight newspaper reporters, one of the finest and most courageous examples of American journalism I have encountered. Its conclusions were confirmed by the first ten-page summary of the FBI findings, the main contents of which were published by the Akron *Beacon-Journal* last July 23.

"FBI: No Reason For Guard To Shoot At Kent State" was the two-column headline across its page one that day. It quoted the ten-page FBI summary as finding that the shootings "were not necessary and not in order." Though publication of this story drew an angry letter to the *Beacon-Journal* from J. Edgar Hoover, he did not challenge the content of the story but only the use of the word "conclusions" in reporting what the FBI had found. Hoover said the FBI never makes conclusions but only reports the facts as found to the Justice Department.

Apparently Hoover was upset because the facts turned up on the wrong side of the political fence. One top Washington source told me that the FBI men assigned to investigate started out with a strong bias against the students and ended up pretty much on the other side.

The same section of the Knight newspaper report, from which the newly disclosed FBI summary quotes the passage above, also gives examples of the kind of fears and rumors to which the Guardsmen were subjected. "Some," the Knight newspaper reported, "said they feared they would be activated and sent to Vietnam if they talked about what happened."

The question which immediately comes to mind after reading the passage I have quoted from the FBI summary is why the FBI, with one hundred or so investigators on campus, was content to quote the Knight newspaper story without investigating on its own. When I inquired, I was told by one Scranton Commission source that the Commission asked the FBI to locate the anonymous machinist Guardsman and to try to verify his story. Obviously he would be a key person in any investigation of the fabrication angle. I have been unable to learn whether and what the FBI reported in response to this directive.

From another Scranton Commission source I also learned that the raw FBI depositions from Guardsmen excited suspicion because about thirty of them used virtually identical phrases in describing their danger from the students. "It sounded like that movie *Z* all over again," this source told me.

The Ohio grand jury doesn't sound at all like the movie *Z*. Though no less than three special prosecutors were appointed to direct it, not one showed the movie prosecutor's passion for sniffing out fabrication. On the contrary the most prominent of the three has since revealed a ferocious bias. This was Seabury Ford, sixty-eight-year-old chairman of the Portage County Republican Party. He told the Akron *Beacon-Journal,* October 24, that the National Guard "should have shot all the troublemakers."

It was hardly surprising after that to learn how slackly the grand jury proceedings were run by these prosecutors. The chief prosecutor, Robert Balyeat, has now admitted that the Justice Department summary containing the reference to fabrications by the Guardsmen had not been submitted to the grand jury. His excuse—that it was not normal practice "to present to the grand jury conclusions that have been prepared by another investigative body. The Scranton Commission report was not presented either" (Anthony Prisendorf, New York *Post,* November 3).

This sounded reasonable until the Akron *Beacon-Journal* a week later discovered that the prosecutors had held back not only the Justice Department summary but a key witness mentioned in it. The *Beacon-Journal* (November 10) learned that National Guard Captain Raymond Srp (not a misprint, that's how he spells his name) was never called before the grand jury. The *Beacon-Journal* said his lawyer confirmed this fact.

This is important because Captain Srp was the highest ranking Guard officer cited by the FBI investigators in explaining why they came to believe that the other Guardsmen were lying when they said that they shot because their lives were in danger. The Justice Department's thirty-five-page summary, just before it gets to this revelation, says,

> Six Guardsmen, including two sergeants and Captain Srp of Troop G, stated pointedly that the lives of the members of the Guard were not in danger and that it was not a shooting situation.

Apparently the prosecutors, in failing to call this Guard captain as a witness, were not too anxious to get the full story before the grand jury. Had it heard Captain Srp it might not have been so ready to absolve the Guardsmen who did the killing.

These newest revelations strengthen the case for impaneling a new grand jury in Ohio or a special federal grand jury or both. In either case the public should demand the appointment of a special prosecutor of such stature and independence that he can be trusted to insist on a free hand and to pursue the investigation with a zeal the special prosecutors on the Portage County grand jury never showed, except perhaps in an eagerness to whitewash the National Guard.

Ideally the newly elected Democratic governor and the newly elected Democratic attorney general of Ohio ought to empanel a new state grand jury. The Kent State affair has been deeply entangled in state and national politics. Retiring Governor Rhodes and his attorney general had hoped to ride an inflammatory campaign against the students to victory in their party primary. They failed, and the Republican Party then failed to defeat the Democrats by exploiting anti-student feelings as Nixon did nationally.

The special Portage County grand jury was a pawn in this dirty partisan game. *Not to absolve the National Guard would have been to condemn Governor Rhodes who made the decision to put them on the campus.* Now that this game has failed at the polls, it is the duty of the victorious Ohio Democrats—and a test of their courage—to start the investigation afresh and see that justice is done. Otherwise the only alternative is a national campaign for a federal grand jury.

A federal grand jury would have the power to subpoena not just civil rights division summaries of FBI reports but the raw reports themselves. The Scranton Commission said it had the benefit of 8,000 pages of reports by the FBI. A federal grand jury could also obtain the record of the investigation the Ohio National Guard made, the results of which were submitted to the Ohio grand jury. It might prove fruitful to compare the stories told by the Guardsmen to the FBI and the stories they told the National Guard investigators. Governor Scranton and members of his Commission have a duty now to speak out more plainly for a federal grand jury. In making their own report, they were inhibited by the fact that at the time the Ohio grand jury had not yet reported. The Scranton Commission said its task was "especially sensitive" because:

> At the outset of the investigation, the Kent incidents had not been placed before any grand jury, either county, state or federal. During our investigation, the Attorney General of Ohio announced the convening of a state grand jury. The grand jury began proceedings in September as this report was being written. We deem it of paramount importance that the Commission do nothing to interfere with the criminal process. We therefore have not sought to establish and report the names of persons who might be guilty of city, state or federal offenses. . . .

But now that the Ohio grand jury has turned in a report absolving the Guardsmen, blaming the college administration, and indicting only students and one faculty member, the Scranton Commission should be free to get at the full story. The Ohio grand jury flatly contradicts the Scranton report and the FBI findings as summarized by the Department of Justice. Where the Commission found the shootings "unnecessary, unwarranted and inexcusable," the grand jury report declares that the Guardsmen "fired their weapons in the honest and sincere belief and under circumstances which would have logically caused them to believe that they would suffer serious bodily injury had they not done so. They are not, therefore, subject to criminal prosecution under the laws of this state for any death or injury resulting therefrom." This amounts to an invitation to shoot again in the future.

III

In its main report the Scranton Commission last September concluded that "only the President can offer the compassionate, reconciling moral leadership that can bring the country together again," and that he alone had "the platform and the prestige to urge all Americans, at once, to step back from the battlelines into which they are forming." *The New York Times* in an editorial November 7, "Unjustified Gunfire," on Kent State, said, "Now that the political campaign is over . . . this action is more than ever in order."

But the campaign itself showed how hollow is this hope. Nixon used the platform of the campaign for leadership in the opposite direction. Four days before the Kent State killings he assailed the radicals as "campus bums" and at Phoenix in the final hours of the campaign he had escalated the rhetoric to the point where he was assailing them as "the same thugs and hoodlums that have always plagued a good people."

One has to be far gone in self-deception to hope that a man who talks such blind nonsense will now turn around and become compassionate and reconciling. Campus radicals tend to include the best and most sensitive students, not the "bums"; the desperate white and black radicals who have turned to violence would be much easier to deal with if they were simply "the thugs and hoodlums that have always plagued a good people." Student violence is mindlessly self-destructive but ending it will require an effort to understand the sources of the desperation that underlies it. Nixon campaigned not only against the extremists but against those who seek reconciliation by understanding, by social reform, and by reducing to a minimum the official violence that American society takes for granted.

As Nixon said at Phoenix, "Everyone denounces violence." The choice, he said, is between those like himself who believe in tough law enforcement and those who hold "that violence will end as we end the war . . . that violence will end as we end hunger and poverty in America." This dangerously oversimplifies the real issue and points a course toward greater division and deeper unrest. It spells more trouble on campus. It is the duty of Governor Scranton and his fellow commissioners themselves to take up the task of moral leadership they had urged on the President, awake the country to the injustices at Jackson and Kent State, and fight for federal grand jury action under independent prosecutors lest "law and order" continue to seem only a synonym for repression.

VII

CONTROLLING THE POLICE

The selections and analysis presented so far suggest that the police are an important part of the state apparatus, involved in counterinsurgency in other countries as well as at home, armed with increasingly sophisticated weaponry, encouraged by a growing police-industrial complex, and an instrument of policy that they generally support but do not initiate. Although it is important to understand that during the last 100 years the police have become a formidable and dangerous power, it should not be concluded that they are monolithic and invincible or incapable of being controlled. This century alone is filled with efforts, some successful and some unsuccessful, to resist, reform, and control the police. This section includes an analysis of the failure of liberal reforms and a proposal for community control of the police (Riley), and an account of a successful effort by a southern Black community to organize a counterpolice force for purposes of self-defense (Nelson).

Police reform, as we know it today, can be traced to the Progressive Era at the turn of the century, to liberal police theorists such as August Vollmer and Raymond Fosdick, to official commissions such as Wickersham, and to various criminologists and criminological journals. These earlier ideas are continued and reproduced in the President's Crime Commission (1967) and the Kerner Commission (1968), as well as in the work of contemporary established theorists such as James Q. Wilson, Jerome Skolnick, and Arthur Niederhoffer.

Liberal reforms of the police assume not only that it is possible to create a well-regulated and humanitarian criminal justice system without transforming class and racial relations, but also that the police can play an important role in harmonizing conflicts and shaping new adjustments to existing economic and political conditions.[1]

Under the banner of "professionalism,"[2] various reforms have been

[1] Elliott Currie, "Emergence of Liberal Police Ideology and Strategy in the Progressive Era and Beyond" (unpublished note, School of Criminology, University of California at Berkeley, June 1973).

[2] The central aspects of professionalism are summarized in the following recommenda-

tried: psychological screening of recruits, human-relations training, hiring Third World officers, community-relations programs, and even civilian review boards. Where these approaches have been tried, they have either completely failed or helped to reinforce existing paramilitary patterns of police organization. As Arthur Waskow points out, "among the most 'professional' big city forces has been that of Los Angeles; among those most carefully screened to exclude sadists has been that of Chicago; among those with a 'strong civilian review board has been that of Philadelphia." [3]

Police unions and leaders have generally resisted any reforms, no matter how moderate, which interfere with their apparent autonomy. In San Francisco, police officials harassed and eventually undermined their own community-relations division because it had become "too sympathetic to the citizens' viewpoints" and was called the "Commie Relations Department" by more conservative officers.[4] In New York, the Policemen's Benevolent Association waged a successful referendum campaign to defeat a civilian review board established by Mayor Lindsay's liberal police commissioner, Howard Leary.[5] And the recruitment of Third World officers into white-controlled, centralized police departments has created enormous identity problems for black and brown officers, who find themselves in a position of "double marginality"—treated as outcasts or traitors by their own community and victimized by racism within the department.[6]

Liberal police reforms attempt to rationalize the existing system and delegate new responsibilities to the state while leaving intact the distribution of power.[7] This approach must be distinguished from more radical or structural reforms that recognize, as David Riley points out, that "the issue is not whether political control is exercised over the police,

---

tion: "Better training, supervision, and recognition, together with more effective minority group recruitment, are needed if our hopes of producing police excellence are to materialize." James Campbell, Joseph Sahid and David Stang, *Law and Order Reconsidered* (New York: Praeger, 1970), p. 307. For variations on the theme of professionalism, see Jerome Skolnick, *Professional Police in a Free Society* (New York: National Conference of Christians and Jews, 1967); The President's Commission on Law Enforcement and Administration of Justice, *The Police* (Washington, D.C.: U.S. Government Printing Office, 1967); Rodney Stark, *Police Riots* (Belmont, Calif.: Wadsworth, 1972), chap. 8; and Egon Bittner, *The Functions of the Police in Modern Society* (Washington, D.C.: U.S. Government Printing Office, 1970).

3 Arthur I. Waskow, "Community Control of the Police," *Trans-Action,* December, 1969, p. 4.

4 Alvin Rosenfeld, "The Friendly Fuzz," *The Nation,* April 21, 1969, pp. 503–7.

5 Ed Cray, "The Politics of Blue Power," *The Nation,* April 21, 1969, pp. 493–96; see, also, William Turner, *The Police Establishment* (New York: G. P. Putnam, 1968).

6 Alex, Nicholas, *Black in Blue: A Study of the Negro Policeman* (New York: Appleton, 1969).

7 On the more general issue of reformism, see André Gorz, *Strategy for Labor* (Boston: Beacon, 1964).

but who exercises it." [8] In recent years, there have been several efforts, notably by Black communities, to politically restructure the police either through creating counterpolice organizations or legislating neighborhood police under civilian control.

Harold Nelson's essay documents how a southern Black community, faced with continual attacks from Klansmen and their sympathizers, aggravated by a negligent and often hostile, white police department, created an organization to defend themselves. At about the same time, the Black Panther Party for Self-Defense was being organized in Oakland, California, where they established a system of armed patrols who followed the police, instructing suspects of their legal rights, and preventing brutality.[9] Point number seven of the Party's ten-point program, created in 1966, stated:

> We want an immediate end to POLICE BRUTALITY and MURDER of black people.
>
> We believe we can end police brutality in our black community by organizing black self-defense groups that are dedicated to defending our black community from racist police oppression and brutality.[10]

The Panthers' program of self-defense was part of a more general resurgence of political militancy by Blacks in the 1960s, which emphasized the colonized status of people of color in the United States through demands for self-determination and political-cultural autonomy.[11] "When the law fails to protect Negroes from white attack," wrote Malcolm X, "then those Negroes should use arms, if necessary, to defend themselves." [12] The idea of self-defense was basic to the Panthers. "The Panther never attacks first," said Huey Newton, "but when he is backed into a corner, he will strike back viciously." [13]

The main thrust of Black demands in the 1960s was the idea of community control and the creation of parallel community institutions.[14] In the areas of education and policing, especially, this demand was expressed in propaganda, political programs, and community struggles.[15] From reactive strategies of self-defense, the Panthers and other organiza-

[8] David Riley, "Should Communities Control Their Police?," *Civil Rights Digest*, Fall, 1969, p. 34.

[9] Philip S. Foner, ed., *The Black Panthers Speak* (New York: Lippincott, 1970).

[10] Ibid., p. 3.

[11] See, for example, Eldridge Cleaver, *Revolution in the White Mother Country and National Liberation in the Black Colony* (Oakland, Calif.: Black Panther Party, 1968); see, also, Jerome Skolnick, director, *The Politics of Protest* (New York: Simon & Schuster, 1969), chap. 4.

[12] Malcolm X, *The Autobiography of Malcolm X* (New York: Grove, 1966), p. 366.

[13] Quoted in Skolnick, *The Politics of Protest,* op. cit., p. 152.

[14] Ibid., pp. 149–62.

[15] See, for example, Annette T. Rubinstein, ed., *Schools Against Children: The Case for Community Control* (New York: Monthly Review, 1970); and Alan A. Altschuler, *Community Control* (New York: Pegasus, 1970).

tions pushed more positive programs of self-determination. "Community control of police is the key," wrote Bobby Seale in 1968.

> We will have neighborhood divisions with neighborhood councils, who are duly elected in the particular neighborhoods . . . The point of community control of the police is that those people living in those neighborhoods will actually do the hiring and firing of the policemen who patrol that area, and those policemen will be people from those neighborhoods . . . Community control of police is one of the most functional and most necessary programs to make all the other basic community programs work.[16]

At the same time that the Panthers were organizing in Black communities, many student communities were experiencing considerable conflict with the police as a result of antiwar demonstrations, college protests, and drug arrests. In student and youth communities such as Berkeley, Madison, Isla Vista, Ann Arbor, the East Village and Haight-Ashbury, political organizations began to develop neighborhood structures and, what Tom Hayden called, "free territories." [17]

These parallel developments in Black and student communities culminated in a working proposal for community control of the police, developed by the Black Panther Party in 1969 [18] and put into practice through a referendum campaign in Berkeley in 1970–71. The Berkeley proposal called for direct control of the police by locally elected councils in three neighborhood districts and required officers to live in the neighborhood in which they worked. Despite a well-financed and often deceptive campaign against the proposal by the local political and economic establishment, over 16,000 persons or about one third of the electorate (*before* the eighteen-year-old vote was passed) voted for community control of the police in a city where the police had generally enjoyed a relatively progressive reputation. Berkeley, however, is by no means a representative American city. The struggle for community control in cities with large Third World populations like the campaign presently under way in Chicago—will provide a more concrete test of this kind of political organizing.

The movement for community control of the police must be clearly distinguished from basically liberal proposals such as psychological testing of recruits or even civilian review boards. It involves the creation of new centers of popular power, the decentralization of decision-making, and a restriction on the powers of the state apparatus.[19] As Arthur Waskow points out, such a program can not be established "without intense political conflict," for it challenges not only the professional insulation of the police but the roots of their power.[20] Such a project should not be under-

16 Bobby Seale, *Seize the Time* (New York: Vintage, 1968), pp. 419–22.
17 Tom Hayden, *Trial* (New York: Holt, Rinehart & Winston, 1970).
18 Foner, op. cit., p. 179.
19 Gorz, op. cit., p. 8.
20 Waskow, op. cit., p. 7.

taken lightly or without proper planning because those who benefit from the police—corporations, political elites, banks, real estate and construction companies, universities, etc.—will not give up their control without a fierce fight.[21]

Suggested Reading

ALEX, NICHOLAS. *Black in Blue: A Study of the Negro Policeman.* New York: Appleton, 1969.

ALTSCHULER, ALAN. *Community Control: The Black Demand for Participation In Large American Cities.* New York: Pegasus, 1970.

ARONOWITZ, STANLEY. "The Dialectics of Community Control." *Social Policy,* May–June, 1970, pp. 47–51.

CRAY, ED. "The Politics of Blue Power." *The Nation,* April 21, 1969, pp. 493–96.

FONER, PHILIP S., ed. *The Black Panther Speaks.* New York: Lippincott, 1970.

FREUND, JEFFREY R. "Neighborhood Police Districts: A Constitutional Analysis." *California Law Review* 57, no. 4, (October, 1969): 907–47.

GORZ, ANDRÉ, *Strategy for Labor: A Radical Proposal.* Boston: Beacon, 1964.

HAYDEN, TOM. *Trial.* New York: Holt, Rinehart & Winston, 1970.

RED FAMILY. *To Stop A Police State: The Case for Community Control.* Berkeley, California: Pamphlet, 1971.

ROSENFELD, ALVIN. "The Friendly Fuzz." *The Nation,* April 21, 1969, pp. 503–7.

RUBINSTEIN, ANNETTE T., ed. *Schools Against the Children: The Case for Community Control.* New York: Monthly Review, 1970.

SEALE, BOBBY. *Seize the Time.* New York: Vintage, 1968.

SKOLNICK, JEROME H. *The Politics of Protest,* chaps. 4 and 7. New York: Simon & Schuster, 1969.

TURNER, WILLIAM. *The Police Establishment.* New York: G. P. Putnam, 1968.

WASKOW, ARTHUR I. "Community Control of the Police." *Trans-Action,* December, 1969: pp. 4–7.

21 Paul M. Sweezy, "The Implications of Community Control," in Rubinstein, op. cit., p. 293.

DAVID P. RILEY

Should Communities Control Their Police?

Attempted Solutions

Police officials in a number of cities are aware of their police-ghetto problem, and some are trying to do something about it. But they are finding it more and more difficult to break through the increasingly polarized atmosphere. The main attempts to do so have been police-run community relations programs and recruitment drives to hire more black and brown officers. Both attempted solutions have been met by very grave and probably by now insurmountable obstacles.

The most revealing report on such efforts by police departments is a survey of 13 major cities across the country conducted by the *New York Times* in the spring of 1969. The survey found that "virtually every department" has increased its efforts to hire black policemen and to institute community relations programs. But the *Times* survey concluded that despite these widespread efforts, "the hostility between the police and the Negro communities has worsened in some cities and in others remains the most explosive issue in race relations."

The report on the survey tells the same story that the National Crime Commission, the Kerner Commission, and other studies have told. Isolated within the police department, community relations programs have little effect on officers not in the program, and they have little impact in the community which generally feels that they are not community relations but public relations programs designed to improve the police department's image. In addition, hiring more black officers is very slow going, because of the stigma of the police in the black community as being the enemy. Besides, the survey reports, black people are frequently more hostile toward black officers than white, because they are considered traitors who have gone over to the enemy.

The main effort in terms of community relations programs has been the establishment of community relations units or divisions within police

From Civil Rights Digest, *Fall, 1969, pp. 27–35. Reprinted in edited form.*

departments, composed of officers who concentrate on community relations work in some precincts. Though the 13 major cities in the *Times* survey are expanding their programs, establishing community relations units has been a slow process in many cities. A 1966 Michigan State study found that only 38 percent of the cities with a population over 100,000 had community relations units at all. An earlier survey of such cities and smaller ones with more than 5 percent nonwhite population found that such community relations units as did exist consisted of from one to ten officers, with an average of three officers in a unit; the survey was conducted by the International Association of Chiefs of Police (IACP).

Many major cities now have much larger community relations units, but according to the Michigan State study, all the units surveyed face problems of being isolated from and downgraded by the rest of the police department. Sometimes the belittling comes from beat patrolmen, and sometimes from top police officials; usually, as in the case of San Francisco and Washington, D.C., it comes from both.

For most policemen, community relations is still viewed as the unmanly, unimportant part of police work; it is unfavorably regarded as "dabbling in social work and negotiating with persons hostile to the police," says the National Crime Commission. Sensitivity to community relations "hasn't filtered down" to the man on the beat, according to an assistant to the mayor in Detroit. It has met outright resistance or indifference at both top and bottom levels in Washington, D.C., according to the former head of the community relations unit. In San Francisco, regular officers reportedly call it the "Commie Relations" unit; they call community relations officers "Nigger lovers," or don't speak to them at all; and according to one report, "There are precinct stations in San Francisco which community relations men never enter."

Chief Thomas Cahill in San Francisco, who was a member of the National Crime Commission and has the image of being a very enlightened chief, lost faith in his community relations unit after the 1966 Hunter's Point disturbance. "I was the only police chief in America without a riot. They spoiled my record," Cahill told Dante Andreotti who established the community relations unit and described his experience in a *Fortune* magazine article. When Andreotti asked that the community relations officers' general rank be raised, thus increasing pay and status, Cahill refused. "He told me the men weren't qualified. They didn't investigate and they didn't arrest people," Andreotti reported.

It is not surprising that with such an attitude toward community relations on the part of police, there has been little or no progress toward lessening police-ghetto tensions, as the *New York Times* discovered. The Crime Commission reports the findings of extensive studies that "most departments believed the primary purpose of community relations was to sell the police image to the public." With all the lip service to community relations and devotion to public relations of police departments, it is very clear, as such studies have concluded, that community relations units "have not generally won the confidence of minority groups."

In today's polarized atmosphere, even the most imaginative community relations program to come out of a police department appears to be doomed to failure. In Washington, D.C., a psychologist from the National Institute of Health got a $1.4 million grant from OEO for a "Pilot Precinct Project," which would give special "sensitivity training" to officers, establish unarmed youth patrols, hire 125 civilians to do clerical work, coordinate social services, and help run neighborhood store-front centers in the precinct out of which police officers would work in teams with the civilians.

The project was officially funded in August, 1968. Today, more than a year later, it has yet to get underway; its story illustrates the suspicious, hostile reception which police-run community relations programs receive in the ghetto today. The local poverty program got evasive, deceptive responses from the police department when it asked for more citizen participation in the project. Meetings to discuss the project were disrupted by militant citizens who claimed that the project would simply set up a spy network for the police and that the community would be bribed by the 125 jobs into participating in the project. Several young community leaders formed an ad hoc steering committee to demand community control of the project and of precinct police policies as well. After a number of more moderate organizations called for the dismissal of the project director for being unreponsive to the community, the mayor suspended operation of the project this spring.

Extended negotiations between the city's public safety director and the community steering committee followed; the two sides were apparently working out an agreement providing for full community control of the project and some community voice in deciding police policies. But with the consolidation of precincts into larger districts, the city broke off the negotiations and said the project would be instituted on a district-wide basis.

Thus the city is now apparently going to try to impose on the community a project dreamt up, designed, and directed by a white psychologist who is resented in the community and who now claims that his project really has nothing to do with citizen control but is simply an attempt to "improve police services." Leaders of the ad hoc committee have promised to disrupt any meetings the project tries to hold in the community. Even if that doesn't happen and the project actually does get underway, it is difficult to see how the project can have any real impact on police-ghetto tensions, having been so severely criticized and discredited in the community. Recently, members of the community steering committee sat in at the project's office and held a "people's court" session; the court found the hapless project director and the city's public safety director guilty of "conspiracy to defraud the black people."

With the escalation of police-ghetto tensions, it is now clear that police-run community relations programs have little real impact on the community. Washington's experience with the Pilot Precinct Project suggests further that it is perhaps now becoming impossible even to establish such programs at all, so polarized is the atmosphere in which they operate.

Aside from such projects, other attempts to improve police-community relations have included establishing citizens advisory committees and improving the mechanism for hearing citizen complaints against officers. Such attempts have been even less serious and have generally made even less of a dent than the meager impact community relations unit may have had.

The 1964 IACP survey found that only eight cities out of 165 had established precinct advisory committees and only 19 had citywide committees. Today, 5 years later, other cities have presumably established such committees. But, like the advisory committees of the past, they are "essentially self-defeating," in the words of the Crime Commission, because "generally membership includes only those persons who agree with the police or otherwise do not cause trouble." That means businessmen, civic organization leaders, and others whose stake in the community is obvious; it does not mean the very people who should be advising and talking to the police, namely the youth and the poor with whom the police have the most contact on the beat.

As for mechanisms for hearing citizen complaints against officers, they are generally secretive, intimidating, and almost completely lacking of due process. A *Harvard Law Review* study in 1963 found that 70 percent of the police departments surveyed had no formal hearings at all for complaints, even serious ones; almost half of those that did had secret hearings. A detailed report of the Washington American Civil Liberties Union in 1968 described the many ways the police discourage the filing of complaints and intimidate complainants in the process of themselves "investigating" citizen complaints against them. The Crime Commission cites examples of many cities where the same situation exists. As the Michigan State study concluded, "there exists widespread distrust of the internal police trial procedures by the major minority groups around the country." External review procedures are not much better. One *Harvard Law Review* article criticized the ineffective Civilian Complaint Review Board in Washington, D.C. (which is now virtually dormant) as "a mere illusion of civilian control over police proceedings."

Another attempt to deal with police-ghetto tensions has been recruitment drives for more black and brown officers. This attempt also is foundering on the pervasive atmosphere of police-ghetto hostility. Black policemen are caught in the middle between the prejudice from black people because they are policemen and the prejudice from white policemen because they are black. Prejudice by the white policemen against Negroes and Negro policemen is rampant, as evidenced by the Crime

Commission survey cited above and other studies; discrimination against black policemen in terms of promotion, assignment, and police socializing is also widespread, according to the Crime Commission and others.

One result is that black officers in many cities are forming their own separate policemen's organizations to fight such discrimination; a National Society of Afro-American Policemen has also been formed. Another result is the resignation of some black officers, such as the *Wall Street Journal's* story on Sgt. Joe Johnson, a veteran of 22 years on the Los Angeles force, who resigned because of the tension of being a black cop today. The final event which led to his resignation was a meeting of policemen at which some white officers apparently questioned the loyalty of Negro officers to the police department in certain situations. Sgt. Johnson emphatically saw himself as a policeman first and a Negro second; even the suspicion of disloyalty upset him: "I felt like ripping my badge off right there," he said.

Sgt. Johnson's predicament is a very real one for many other black officers, and one that becomes more acute as the atmosphere becomes more polarized. The psychological strain of being at the same time a member of two distinct groups who are at war with each other is a heavy emotional burden. For some it is too heavy; in Washington, D.C., a number of black officers are regularly retired from the force by a board of medical examiners when they come before the board physically shaking from the psychological strain and emotional conflict. Some manage to resolve the conflict and turn out to be good officers who understand the lives of the ghetto people they deal with and thus can begin to break down some of the hostility. Others resolve or try to resolve the conflict in a different way: they become more oppressive and brutal than many white policemen in an effort to prove to their white colleagues that they are policemen first and Negroes second. It is a futile effort finally, given the widespread, continuing prejudice among white officers; and the futility of it often leads to more brutality against citizens since frustration must find an outlet somewhere. Such officers only worsen the problem of police-ghetto tensions.

Thus simply recruiting more black policemen is not a solution. To help at all, you need the right kind of black policemen, those who will resolve the conflict with responsiveness and sensitivity, not with brutality. Such policemen are most likely to be those coming out of the ghettos themselves, but recruitment of them is extremely difficult, given the view of many ghetto youths that the police are a kind of occupying army for the white power structure. It is like asking Indians to join the cavalry. In Washington, D.C.—where the city is 70 percent black and the police department 70 percent white—a well-advertised local campaign to recruit men from the city resulted in only a single applicant. At the same time, the department's nationwide tour of military bases resulted in 197 applicants; although other D.C. recruitment programs have increased the percentage of Negro recruits, generally four out of five of the men recruited from the military are white. So it is these mostly white, former military men who are supposed to help show a black city that the police are not really an occupying army for the white society.

The ambiguous role of black policemen points up the dilemma of the police's middle position. On the one hand, black officers are useful because they are better crowd appeasers and can find out more information in black communities for the police; that is why black militants tend to hate black police of any kind because, as police officers, they have become agents for the power structure. On the other hand, black policemen generally know and understand the problems of the black community better and, given a chance, could help solve them. The role of the black policeman depends upon the role of the police in our divided society; it depends upon the degree to which the police emphasize carrying out the law enforcement wishes of the power structure rather than helping the poor. . . .

The Solution of Community Control

Despite all the disagreement that exists on issues of law enforcement, two facts are virtually universally accepted: first, that no laws can be enforced or order kept successfully unless the police and the community cooperate with each other; and secondly, that today in our urban ghettos there is very little of that necessary mutual cooperation and support. The police are quite right to plead and beg for community support as essential for successful law enforcement. The trouble is that given the history and the present climate of police-ghetto relations, the police cannot expect to get and will not get the ghetto community support they need without also themselves changing in fundamental ways. . . .

An approach to law enforcement which sees this fundamental police role as unalterable and at the same time asks for fundamental alterations in the community's role is unfair and unrealistic and cannot succeed. But it is the approach most law enforcement officials take today. *You will not get community support of the police until you get police support of the community,* and (it is very clear from present police attitudes and positions) you will not get that until you have some community control of the police.

In better-off, white communities, the police do support the community—they do what the people in power who dominate the community want them to do—and the community, naturally, supports the police. It is not quite as simple as that today with the increasingly unconventional behavior of middle class white youth who are also in their own way challenging the power structure, and who are harassed by the socially isolated policeman whose conventional lower middle class mentality is threatened by such behavior. But, though there may be a political struggle between different philosophies, basically it is true that white communities control their police; black communities simply want to do the same thing. To the extent that the police are becoming autonomous, and even some white communities are losing civilian control over them, then it is even more important to establish community control.

Eminent psychologists such as Erik Erikson, Bruno Bettleheim, and Erich Fromm have all stressed the importance for the individual's psychological health of being able, in Bettleheim's words, "to act in one's own behalf" and have some effect on one's environment. Social psychologists make the same point about a group or community of people: having some effect on events affecting them, some control over their destiny, is important for a group's social health. It is particularly important, of course, for a group of people so long denied that control and political power while others all around them have had it.

Because of isolation and increasing cultural awareness of their distinctiveness, the ghettos have become communities of their own; they therefore have a psychological need and a political right to control the affairs of their community. Once we grant that fact of social reality, then we can no more deprive the ghettos of community control of their police than we can deprive Greenwich or Chevy Chase or Winnetka of community control of theirs. It may present more complex problems to grant the ghettos that control than for towns somewhat separated from the metropolis, but those problems do not remove the social realities which justify that control.

Proposals for community control differ; but those developed in Washington, D.C., generally call for some community control (or "major community involvement," depending upon one's semantic preference) in two areas of police work: setting law enforcement policies at the precinct level, and handling citizen complaints against officers. For setting precinct policies, the proposals recommend elected *citizen precinct boards* in each precinct. The boards would have at least the powers to select top precinct police officials, to review citizen complaints against officers and require transfer out of the precinct of the most ineffective officers, and to work with police officials in determining law enforcement and personnel policies for the precinct. In the area of citizen complaints, the proposals call for an elected *citywide citizens board* (possibly the chairmen of the respective precinct boards) which would have an independent investigative and legal staff, would hear all cases of citizen complaints against officers, and would determine what action should be taken, reviewable by the mayor and where appropriate by the Civil Service Commission and the courts.

Such proposals have raised many objections, the most immediate one being a fear of a police revolt or mass resignation in response. The precinct board element could be tried in one or two precincts on an experimental basis, which would diminish police objections. But it certainly would not eliminate them; the threat of a police revolt is a real one. But such a confrontation might not be a bad idea, especially in a city with a large black voting population that may be able to influence the confrontation to come out in their favor. Large numbers of resignations may be the only way to rid the police department of the backward, prejudiced white officers who impede progress and add to the frustrations of liberal mayors who may try to institute reforms. If community control would cause the worse policemen to leave, it might also attract inner-city people to join the force. Community control could change police work in the ghetto from an impossibly hellish assignment to a constructive, positive job in which the police and the people work together to make the community more livable, and fight together against its oppressors to make the society more just. . . .

*HAROLD A. NELSON**

The Defenders: A Case Study of an Informal Police Organization

Introduction

In many Southern communities, the concept of "law and order" has one meaning for whites and another for Negroes. In oversimplified terms, whites tend to equate it with adherence to traditional Southern mores. These mores *are* the law regardless of what judges, federal officials or Congress may have said to the contrary. Order exists when community behavior patterns are in strict compliance with the dictates of the mores. Primary responsibility for maintaining this order rests with local law enforcement agencies. It is their responsibility to protect the "Southern way of life" by crushing any challenge to it which may arise in the community.

Negroes equate this definition of law and order with the determination of whites to maintain a system which operates solely for their own benefit and which is rooted in illegality and brute force. They see themselves confined to a world governed not by law and order but by a vicious white populace which maintains its dominant position because it holds a monopoly of power. Law enforcement agencies are nothing more than the "white man's army" committed to protecting the "white man's society" by any means they choose to employ. These agencies function not for the protection and welfare of all citizens but for that of whites alone. No agency exists for the protection of Negroes from the dominant group and no mechanism is provided within the mores whereby they may challenge the monopoly of power held by whites.

At issue is whether a group which perceives itself thus victimized can

From Social Problems *15 (Fall, 1967): 127–47. Reprinted in edited form (footnotes omitted) with permission of the author and publisher.*

* I wish to acknowledge the many contributions of "William Smith" to my understanding of the Defenders. Not only did he spend long hours educating me in the general area of racial problems in the South, but he gave extended assistance in the preparation of this paper. I am deeply indebted to him, for without his aid, this paper could not have been written.

alter this situation. If it is denied services normally provided by law enforcement agencies, can it provide at least some of them for itself? More generally, can such a group develop a mechanism by which it can successfully confront the monopoly of power arrayed against it and effectively challenge the mores which govern the community?

This paper is concerned with the efforts of Negroes in a Southern community to accomplish these goals. It describes the development of an informal police organization which not only provided certain services to Negroes, but also acted as the vehicle whereby traditional mores were challenged and a redistribution of power in the community was effected.

Origin of the Defenders

Southville is located in a Deep Southern state. Its population of 50,000 persons includes 18,000 Negroes. It is the largest city in a county of 100,000 persons, approximately one-third of whom are Negroes. While the county is heavily agricultural, Southville is sufficiently industrialized to rank as one of the important industrial areas of the state. Prior to 1964, the city maintained the traditional patterns of segregation characteristic of most Southern communities. Local law enforcement agencies employed only white persons and were disliked and distrusted by the city's Negro population. A long-time and widespread dissatisfaction with racial conditions was shared by the community's Negroes, but prior to 1964 no organized attempt was made to change this situation. In that year, a Negro minister was installed in one of the largest Negro churches in Southville with the understanding that he would also act as a civil rights leader. With the aid of several ministers and laymen, he organized the Southville Action Organization, which initiated a series of mass meetings and freedom schools. After several months, S.A.O. drew up a list of demands for changes in the city's segregation practices and presented them to the city commission. The commission rejected the demands, and S.A.O. countered by holding Southville's first protest march. Law officers and S.A.O. leaders agreed in advance on procedures to be followed during the demonstration. Although the marchers adhered to these procedures, police used electric cattle prods and night sticks to harass the protesters.

Response to S.A.O. and the demonstrations by white public officials was predictable. Communist influence was suspected and "outside agitators" were seen as stirring up "a few dissidents" who in no way reflected the dominant mood in the Negro community. Calls were issued for the restoration of "harmony between the races." This could best be accomplished, it was held, by disbanding S.A.O. and removing its minister-leader from his pulpit and from the city. These expressions faithfully reflected the mood of most of Southville's white citizens. While the great majority was passive in its response, the Ku Klux Klan applauded the public pronouncements and publicly dedicated itself to firm opposition to the activities and demands of S.A.O. Civil rights activists interpreted this as confirmation of their belief that there was no important difference between the belief-system and objectives of public officials and those of the Klan. Law officers were especially distrusted. Many were believed to be Klansmen and the rest were seen as Klan sympathizers. Almost all were believed to be prepared to carry out any orders issued by the Klan. Negro activists were certain that the officers were eagerly awaiting an opportunity to conduct Klan inspired violence against them.

During the next three months, S.A.O. activity increased. New and stronger demands were made, stores were boycotted, marches were held with increasing frequency, violence against the activists accelerated and tensions in the community increased. Finally, city officials announced a ban on further demonstrations and charged the police with enforcing it. To S.A.O. leaders, this was the same as announcing a ban on change in favor of tradition and charging the Ku Klux Klan with enforcing it. They announced that they would defy the ban, and a date was set for the proposed march.

More than a thousand persons appeared for the demonstration. As the leaders led the marchers out of the church they were confronted by police, sheriff's deputies, firemen and "special deputies," some of whom were suspected of being Klansmen. The leaders were promptly arrested. Immediately thereafter, law officers charged the demonstrators, forcing them back into the church with nightsticks, cattle prods, fists and water hoses. Tear gas was shot into the building, and the officers continued their attack as the demonstrators fled from the gas-filled church. As the protesters dispersed, they were chased into neighboring areas. Homes of those living nearby were invaded, and persons not involved in the demonstration came under indiscriminate attack. Numerous arrests were made, and several of the demonstrators were hospitalized as a result of beatings and gassing. Word of the incident spread rapidly. Stories of police brutality against men, women and children circulated throughout the Negro sections of the city. The police had, in the eyes of the Negroes, confirmed that if they were not Klansmen, they might as well be, and that they would use any measures of force and violence they wished against those who dared defy white Southern racial mores.

When Southville's evening newspaper carried a distorted account of the events together with a justification of the actions of the law officers, Negroes interpreted as proof that the officers had been carrying out the orders of the "white power structure." This seemed to be the opening shot in an all out war to kill the civil rights movement in the city. Faith in the effectiveness of the nonviolent posture of S.A.O. was seriously undermined, and most of its leading spokesmen were in jail. That evening, Negroes armed themselves, some waiting for an expected night-ride of Klansmen through their neighborhoods, others hoping to ambush police cars, and still others planning to go to the business district of the city and burn it to the ground. In the early evening hours, an unstructured, unorganized violent retaliation seemed certain. While the total number of Negroes planning to take part in offensive violence was not large, it would have been sufficient to destroy much of the downtown area of Southville and to cause widespread injury and death to whites.

At this same time, one of the S.A.O. members began taking steps to thwart the impending riot. He did this not because he feared violence or was opposed to it in principle, nor because he believed massive retaliation was not merited, but because he felt it was futile. He opposed it because it was unstructured, disorganized, lacking in plan or lasting value and because it would result in death and injury to a great many innocent persons. It was his desire to translate the prevailing mood into something which could permanently restrict the activities of police and Klan, and which would provide a forceful mechanism for changing the community's power distribution. He called together several close friends, convinced them that a disorganized riot would serve no useful purpose, and together they set out to find the rioters-in-waiting to convince them also. One by one they were found and the case was argued. The message was simple: "If we're going to do this thing, let's do it right"; and "right" meant organization and planning. One by one, the potential rioters were persuaded to surrender their arms on the promise that the weapons would be returned at a meeting which would be held that night. So great was the respect commanded by this small group, and especially by its leader, that the riot was averted.

The meeting held that night centered on proposed retaliation for the day's events. A major source of bitterness was the abject failure of law officers to perform their duties in even a minimally acceptable manner. Under prodding by the meeting's chairman, immediate retaliation became less important in the minds of those in attendance than a basic alteration in the power distribution in Southville. The chairman argued that if the police failed to perform their duties, either they would have to be forced to do so, or someone else would have to perform them. If the Klan was determined to run rampant, someone would have to control it. If men, women and children were to be beaten, someone would have to prevent it. The meeting ended with the agreement that that "someone" would have to be a new organization dedicated to bringing about a basic redistribution of power in the city. A meeting was called for the following night to establish such an organization.

The second meeting was attended by some 300 persons. They included gang leaders and members, white collar and blue collar workers, the highly educated and the uneducated. Chairing this meeting, as he had the first, was William Smith, who had led the effort to thwart the riot. Almost immediately, the question arose as to who should be the leader of the new organization. Smith's name was suggested and there was no dissent.

At this point, Smith advised the meeting that he would accept only on condition that he be allowed to choose a small executive board which would devise a series of qualifications for membership and evaluate the candidacy of each applicant. His and the board's decisions would be final. Further, he stated that all decisions regarding policy would be set by the board and would be binding on all members. Finally, he said that all members would be required to pledge their lives to him and the organization. He asked for a formal vote on whether those in attendance still wished him to head the organization. He was unanimously elected. He then announced that the organization would be called the Defenders.

Organizational Structure

Smith patterned the organization along the lines of a military combat unit. Four levels were established: the leader, his executive board, a cadre of lieutenants, and the rank and file membership. The leader and his executive board were designated as policy makers, strategists and final authority for tasks to be undertaken by the organization. The lieutenants were assigned some limited authority, primarily in conducting investigations, and the rank and file were to carry out assignments handed down from the executive board.

From the 300 persons attending the organizational meeting, 100 were selected for membership, and the organization has remained approximately at that number since then. Roughly one-half the membership may be described as "hard-core" and is distributed throughout all four levels. The remaining 50 members are utilized for special assignments, usually when large numbers of persons are needed for some task. At any time, the leader can mobilize 50 members and have them prepared for a task in less than two hours.

Membership in the Defenders is conferred only after a thorough investigation. Final authority for acceptance or rejection of a candidate rests with the executive board. Individual board members may veto any potential member and are not hesitant to do so. (In one instance, a board member vetoed his brother's candidacy.) The board imposes various criteria for membership, some of which are clearly objective and which serve as preliminary filtering devices, and others which demand a more subjective evaluation. No one is admitted to candidacy unless he has served at least six weeks under active war combat conditions. This experience is considered of crucial importance in familiarizing the individual with extreme crisis situations and the imminent possibility of death, conditions which he must be prepared to face in the performance of his organizational duties. This is an effective device for eliminating those persons who see crisis and possible death as "romantic episodes" through lack of experience with such events. It seeks to insure that those admitted to membership realize the seriousness of the commitment they are making. A second requirement is that the potential candidate be married and, preferably, have a family. Meeting this requirement indicates to the organization a willingness to assume responsibility. It indicates, further, the belief that a married man is a more stable member of the community than a single person, and that he will have a stronger dedication to correcting community injustices because of their effects upon his family. The candidate must be judged to be "head of his household." Any person likely to place his wife's opposing wishes above organizational demands is a threat to the operations of the organization. Any wife who would constantly raise counter demands is a threat to the commitment all members must give to the Defenders. Such threats are not tolerated, and persons likely to come under them are disqualified.

The organization believes its work may be carried out most effectively without general publicity or public attention. Therefore, the candidate is expected to be discreet and "close-mouthed." He must be judged capable of keeping classified information secret and must be able to restrict knowledge of his activities to those persons deemed appropriate by his organization. This may include restricting knowledge of his membership to the organization executive board and hard-core members alone. Any person who is known to drink immoderately is automatically excluded. The heavy drinker is seen as "a talker" and therefore not trustworthy. In addition, his drinking may cause him to be unavailable at some time when the organization needs him. In this regard, Smith has set the standard. He drinks very rarely, and never has more than one drink at any social gathering.

The candidate's personal conduct must be above reproach. A rigid code of personal morality is applied as a standard, and any deviation from it effectively eliminates him from consideration. Of necessity, the candidate's background is submitted to searching scrutiny. If he is found acceptable to this point, he is submitted to final tests. Various persons, both men and women, are assigned to interact with him socially and to observe his conduct, under as many conditions as possible. For example, he may be told "confidential" information and asked not to reveal it, and then deliberately encouraged to do so by persons working secretly for the organization. He is, in effect, given an extensive final opportunity to disqualify himself by some act deemed unacceptable to the organization. If he passes this test he is then accepted into membership, with the understanding that any time he violates the code of the Defenders, he is subject to its punishment up to and including expulsion. This has occurred only once in the organization's history. He is then administred an oath in which he swears to be "his brother's keeper," even at the cost of his own life.

Membership in the organization is drawn from a wide range of occupations, educational backgrounds, ages and areas of residence. By maintaining a heterogeneous membership, as representative as possible of the

Negro population, the information network nurtured and maintained by the organization is made as inclusive as possible. As a result, status within the organization is not determined by amount of formal education, occupational prestige or income level. Rather, it is allotted on the basis of performance of assigned duties and degree of responsibility conferred within the organization. Each member, because of his particular socioeconomic position in the community, is seen as being able to make a unique contribution to the organization. He is valued because he holds a particular social position regardless of whether the general community would so value that position. For example, neighborhood and route salesmen are occupationally valuable, since their work allows them a flexibility of movement and puts them in wide contact with the community, placing them in a position to gain valuable information. Historically, the Klan has used such occupations to gather information in Negro neighborhoods. Members of the Defenders, acting unofficially, were able to convince several companies that Negroes were more likely to buy from Negro salesmen than from white, and then supplied several of their own members to fill these positions. This had the effect of reducing the Klan information network at the same time it increased their own.

The organization functions in a semi-secret manner. It operates on the principle that those who need to know of its existence do know or will be informed of it. The efficiency of the Defenders' information network guarantees that anyone who may not know will be informed should the occasion arise. However, it sees no value in general publicity, and consciously avoids it. One reason for this is because of the kinds of investigations it conducts and data which it gathers. Another reason is the belief that the whites will be more amenable to pressure and compromise if they are assured that the general public is not aware they are yielding to such pressure.

Organizational Activities

The tasks which the organization has undertaken include protection, investigation, intelligence, and a form of "crime" prevention.

The immediate impetus for the creation of the Defenders was provided by the perceived failure of law officers to perform their role adequately for Negro citizens. While this failure was most obvious in conjunction with civil rights activities, it was not limited to them. A long-standing complaint against the police was that *no* Negro could be certain he would receive the same treatment, concern or respect as would a white person. The organization conceives of its duty, therefore, as more encompassing than concern with massive civil rights demonstrations alone. Rather, it holds the prerogative to choose to assume responsibility in any situation in which a person has suffered some injustice for which law officers would normally be expected to take some action but where it is not expected that they will perform their role adequately. The organization may become involved either at the request of an individual or without such request if the situation seems to have important implications for other persons in the community. (In one instance, dynamite was set off near a group of homes. Without waiting for a specific request for aid, the organization concerned itself with the situation.) Should an individual request the aid of the Defenders, it may or may not be given. Representatives of the organization must be satisfied that the party requesting aid has suffered some injustice and that he was not the instigator. It must also be satisfied that the complainant is willing to give his full cooperation to the organization, including providing all information which he possesses. Should the organization conclude that the complainant is withholding information, it may refuse to enter the case. Should it enter and then conclude that he is the offending party, it may withdraw. At this point, the Defenders must act in a supra-police function. Differing from the police, the organization has no court system to determine ultimate guilt or innocence, hence it must accept some responsibility in this area. Since it must do so, it is important that the Defenders obtain all available information. If it is convinced that some of this information is being withheld by the complainant, the most "responsible" decision it can make is that some presumption of guilt thereby exists and on this basis it withdraws. Since most of its activities center about allegation of Negroes against whites, it seeks to be absolutely certain of its "legal" [i.e. moral] position before it moves against offending whites.

At the organization's inception, it was faced with two immediate problems. To that time, segregation and its attendant patterns of white supremacy had been enforced formally by law enforcement agencies and informally by the Ku Klux Klan. When law was not sufficient to do so, extra-legal methods were employed to establish and maintain an atmosphere of fear and intimidation. No effective counterforce or neutralizing agent existed; the test of the Defenders' viability was whether it could establish itself as such a force. Smith saw the organization's first task as eliminating the Klan as a force in Negro life and the second as restricting the police to their normal duties. If the police could not be forced to fulfill their legal role, they *could* be blocked from performing an extra-legal one. Klan and police, then, had to be confronted with sufficient power to limit effectively their sphere of influence. The mere announcement to these agencies of the formation of a "protective organization" was not sufficient, nor was it expected to be. The dominant stereotype of Negroes held by these groups as docile, fearful, cowardly, and deathly afraid of police and Klan necessitated direct confrontation to disprove the stereotype.

Two incidents were of major importance in limiting Klan activities. From the inception of S.A.O., it had been the practice of the Klan leader to be near the scene of any movement activity. At any time a meeting was held he would "patrol" the area in his car. This gesture expressed his contempt for S.A.O. and his stated conviction that the Klan, not S.A.O., would be the dominant force in Negro life. One evening as he began his vigil, armed Defenders appeared in front of the meeting place. As the Klansmen began to drive by, he saw that they were prepared to fire at him and he quickly maneuvered his car so that a truck was between him and the church and immediately left the area. Not only did he "run," but he never again appeared at the site of S.A.O. activity.

By this single act, the organization had demonstrated publicly to its own members, civil rights activists, Negro townspeople, and the Klan leader and fellow Klansmen that the old order had changed, at least partially. If the organization was prepared to confront the Klan leader, it was obvious that it was equally prepared to confront lesser Klansmen. From the date of this incident, the number of Klan cars seen in Negro neighborhoods decreased considerably, and those which did appear passed through quickly. The Klan relinquished its control over these areas, but sought to limit the Defenders to these same neighborhoods. On another evening, in a peripheral area of the city, a car loaded with Klansmen opened fire on a car holding Defenders. One of the members noted later that "they shot too soon," and when the Defenders' car pulled closer, its passengers returned the fire and the Klansmen fled. These two incidents demonstrated to the Klan the determination of the Defenders to eliminate Klan influence among Negroes and to insert itself into the power structure of the community. Although other incidents did occur, for all intents and purposes, large scale organized semi-public Klan activity against Negroes ended with these incidents. Negro neighborhoods were now effectively closed to Klansmen. Neither did they attempt to intimidate the Defenders again.

While the police officially recognized the organization's formation, they opposed its existence and sought to discredit and destroy it. Official recognition came in the form of a meeting between Smith and a high ranking police officer. The official told him the organization could gain no power, would accomplish nothing, and would not be tolerated by the police. His statements, on the surface, constituted a dismissal of the organization as inconsequential, but carried the deeper message that the police would not permit their own power to be challenged or restricted. The police set out to do what the Klan had failed to do—to frighten the Defenders into submission. Individual members were subjected to various forms of harassment. When this failed, the police increased their pressure. A critical point was reached early one morning when a number of police cars appeared at Smith's home. Crouched behind their cars with weapons drawn and spotlights directed at the front door, the police ordered "the occupant" of the house to come out. When he did, they demanded his name and he pointed to a sign on the lawn which carried his name and house number. Again they demanded his name and he told them to look at the sign. The question was repeated several times, always with the same answer. The incident ended with the police finally asking him if he were a "John Greene" for whom they were allegedly looking. He replied that his name was on the sign and that, further, they knew full well who he was. At this, the police claimed a case of mistaken identity and left. Smith is convinced that the police had so acted in the hope of frightening him into running or making some other move which would have given them a "justification" for killing him. When he did not, they lost their nerve and, in some confusion, withdrew. Failing to frighten and thereby to discredit the leader, they arrested a number of his members. Smith countered by informing the Chief that unless his men were released, he would "turn loose" the remaining members of the organization. The arrested men were immediately released. Smith then met with the Chief and told him that the organization would remain in existence, that its members could not be frightened, and that if any harm came to them or their families, "blood would flow." He stated his intention to see that extra-legal activities carried out by police against Negroes were stopped by any means necessary. Subsequent to this meeting, not only did harassment of the Defenders cease, but reports of police brutality against Negroes in general declined rapidly.

The first task of the organization had been accomplished. The Klan had been defeated and its effectiveness as a social control mechanism among Negroes severely diminished. No longer could it operate openly as a public, unofficial arm of the police. Secondly, the police had been confronted and their extra-legal power to a great extent stripped from them. The organization had inserted itself into the power structure of the city and had to be considered by any group planning activity against Negroes. In effect, a "war of fear" had been waged to determine the order of power not only in the Negro sections of the city but over the lives of Negroes in general. The Defenders had clearly won.

With their failure to destroy the Defenders, the police resorted to a different strategy. Rather than actively opposing those connected with civil rights activities, they passively refused to perform any meaningful functions whatsoever regarding them. Apparently, it was assumed that by so doing, mobs of whites would control the activities of the activists. This was a miscalculation which inserted the Defenders directly into the role of policemen and thereby increased the organization's role and broadened its sphere of influence and power. Adoption of this passive role coincided with the "testing" of a restaurant to determine if it would comply with the newly passed Civil Rights Act of 1964. The owner did comply by serving the testers. However, in the process, a group of whites began to gather in front of the business. Although some police were present, they made no attempt to disperse those gathering. In a short period of time, approximately 600 whites appeared, and the crowd began defacing the business. Still the police took no action, nor did they threaten any arrests. As the crowd developed into a mob challenging the testers to come out, the police informed the testers that they could not control the mob nor guarantee the safety of those inside the building, thus washing their hands of the whole affair. Smith was notified of the situation and immediately dispatched several cars to the scene. Defenders spirited the testers to the cars and they drove off. The cars went immediately to a prearranged location which had been "staked out" by other members of the organization. Had the mob followed, which it did not, it would have been caught in a trap. The Defenders had not only provided the police function of protection but had also constructed its own form of "crowd control."

Protection quickly became a major function of the organization. A great many civil rights activists had received anonymous threats of violence and death. Law enforcement agencies were unwilling to provide protection for the persons involved, their families or their homes, therefore the Defenders assumed this responsibility.

The organization's protective role extends to whites as well as Negroes. A few white persons had acted in concert with S.A.O. and hence were no more assured of police protection than were Negro activists. Streets on which they lived were patrolled by car, they were guarded when they were in places of potential danger, and, in general, were given the same services provided Negro activists. Smith pointed out on several occasions that when a member swore to "be his brother's keeper" this meant "his brother regardless of race."

Organizational protection also extends to visitors to the city who might be in danger because of their support of the civil rights movement. On these occasions, the Defenders have supplanted the police in providing escort and protective services. On one such occasion, aides to the white person involved were put in contact with the leader. Smith shared their doubts as to the probable dedication of the police to protecting the person in question. When asked whether he would provide the protection he agreed, but only under certain conditions. Smith and the aides were to agree upon a detailed timetable of the activities of the visitor while he was in Southville. Once he arrived, he and his associates were to be subject to any orders Smith gave them. When this was agreed to, Smith took the schedule of events to an organizational staff meeting. There decisions were made as to the number of Defenders needed, which members would be used, and what the specific duties of each would be. Late one evening, a "dry run" was held to determine the adequacy of the plan. Alternate plans were worked out in the event of a crisis, and plans were made for the disposition of any persons attempting to disrupt the activities. Some three hours before the visitor arrived in the city, each member was in his assigned position and various buildings had been inspected to assure that they were secure. Occasionally, police appeared near scenes of the activities, but at no time did they attempt to assert a special prerogative to be present. The members, in turn, regarded them with the same degree of watchfulness they reserved for any suspicious white persons. At no time were weapons displayed, but in the words of one member, "A man *might* get one shot at . . . but he'd never get the second one off." Only when the visitor had been escorted out of Southville did the organization cease its alert.

At times, the organization goes beyond normal protective duties. In one case, a family in a community some twenty miles from Southville was being subjected to a serious form of harassment. Both husband and wife had been physically assaulted by whites, and the husband had been hospitalized as a result of the attack. His wife contacted members of S.A.O. who in turn contacted Smith. He met with her and it was agreed that neither she nor her children were safe in the community, therefore it was decided to bring them to Southville. The Defenders assumed responsibility for moving her and her family to the city, securing a house and assuring financial support of the family until a job was found for her eldest son. When doubts arose as to whether her husband was receiving proper medical treatment, a Southville doctor was contacted who agreed to treat the man if he were transferred to the city's hospital. Smith then contacted a local ambulance service and received assurance that it would transfer the man at any time it was deemed necessary.

A second broad task of the organization, closely related to protection, is that of investigation. The purpose is to insure as complete knowledge as possible of plans and activities of anyone or any group having any relation to Negroes, civil rights advocates or their opponents. This includes any information which could conceivably relate to potential organizational duties and tasks. The insistence of the leader that the organization have as complete and accurate data as possible regarding any incident *before* the Defenders enter a case makes investigation of great importance and places great responsibility upon the men selected to do the investigating. The men charged with this task constitute the organization's intelligence unit.

As soon as Smith is informed of an incident with which the Defenders might become involved, he dispatches investigators to interview witnesses and to gather any other pertinent information. Seldom do investigators make public their duties. Rather, interviewing and data gathering are carried on without revealing that an investigation is under way or that the organization is in any way involved in the situation. Not infrequently, Defenders are present with the police and both agencies collect information at the same time.

In addition to the mechanism for specific investigations, the organization maintains a highly efficient and effective permanent data gathering system. This system has provided sufficient information to permit quick identification of automobile ownership from license numbers and, in many cases, from description of the car when the license is not available. Dossiers are maintained on all persons with whom the organization has had dealings or with whom it is felt it might come in contact at some later date. These dossiers include not only addresses, descriptions, and information on current activities, but also rather extensive background data including past behavior and activities. The organization has demonstrated the ability to obtain data which is kept in locked files in public and private offices and which is, supposedly, unavailable to the public.

Historical records are also maintained and investigations of incidents which occurred long before the organization's creation have been carried out. In one case, a record has been compiled of a lynching which occurred in Southville 30 years ago. Included in the record are the names of persons, including many still alive, who took part in the planning and actual lynching of the victims and who went unpunished at the time. Included is information on the present whereabouts of several key figures who left Southville shortly after the murders. Only when the last of the major figures in the case has died will it be marked "closed." Records are also maintained on important public figures who have had some connection with Southville. These include information not only on current activities but on activities in which they participated as much as 30 and 40 years ago. These current and historical records are maintained because of the possibility that they may, at some time, be of value in providing information regarding some incident or event of interest to the Defenders. Hence, they might provide important data regarding the decision to enter a case and the type of action to be taken.

The "crime prevention" phase of the Defenders' duties also illustrates the high degree of organization of the group. Smith was aware from the outset that at times the organization would have "no choice" but to act, to commit its resources and the lives of its members to some task. However, he wanted to insure that this would occur only when absolutely necessary and when he could be satisfied that no other method for handling the situation was available. Investigation makes it possible for him to determine if there is just cause for action. Intelligence makes it possible for him to become aware of developing, potentially dangerous situations. With this knowledge, he may act to prevent an incident from occurring, rather than being limited to acting only after some incident has occurred which demands a form of retribution. A critical component of this prevention function is the Defenders' surveillance team which is maintained in all Negro sections of the city. This team is comprised of members, each of whom has been assigned responsibility for a particular Negro neighborhood. These persons are to keep fully informed about the activities of residents of the neighborhoods, especially those activities which might result in some kind of racial incident. Primarily, members of the team are to identify potential "trouble-makers" and observe their activities. Should these persons become a "threat to the peace," a report is made to Smith, and representatives of the organization talk to the person involved, explaining to him that his activities may cause a serious situation if continued. So great is the respect for the Defenders that this action has been sufficient to control such persons. This form of prevention seeks to assure, insofar as possible, that Negroes will not be the cause of racial incidents and that the organization will not have to become involved in situations which could have been avoided or handled in a peaceful way.

The Leader

To a major extent, the organization is the creation of William Smith and reflects both his personality and his belief system. Others in positions of authority in the organization closely mirror many of his own characteristics. Prominent among these are a dislike of emotional displays, a strong emphasis on rationality, decisiveness of action, and a controlled anger at the racial situation in the state and nation. Smith and most of the members give the impression of being introspective, intelligent, articulate, highly rational and decisive. Not only do individual members reflect his own personality system, but the organization itself reflects his beliefs and goals to the extent that a knowledge of the man contributes to a clearer picture of the organization, its self-conceived duties, and its goals.

Smith is in his middle thirties. He was born on a farm near Southville and his childhood was spent "in a house made of 1 x 12 boards" from which "you could see the stars above and the pigs below." As a child he "picked cotton at 40 cents a hundred when I could only pick 50 pounds a day," and "chopped cotton for 20 cents a day." At the end of each season, he remembers that the landlord would say to his family, "You had a good summer; you're almost out of debt." Although in some years he could attend school only three months out of the year, he completed high school and sought to continue his education informally by studying various subjects which interested him. In conversation, he gives the impression of having had considerably more than a high school education. Upon graduation, he went to work in Southville in order to finance a college education for one of his sisters. He is a Korean war veteran and was wounded in combat. Upon returning to Southville, he was employed in a local plant as a skilled worker. It was here that he built a wide reputation as a militant activist and highly effective leader. After a bitter fight with the company, he succeeded in bringing Southville's first integrated union to the plant, and was elected an officer in the local. During the next eight years the plant was constantly divided by labor-management disputes. As a union officer he was a central figure in each of the disputes and was fired by the plant manager each of the five times a strike occurred and several other times as well. On each occasion, he charged unfair labor practices and was reinstated as the result of arbitration or court order. On one occasion, it took him three years to win back his job, a period during which he was blacklisted in the city and during which "many nights there wasn't enough to eat." While never head of the local, a weak white president allowed him to assume de facto leadership. During strikes, the field representative of the international union dealt with him rather than the president, since he had assumed administrative tasks involving finances, picket lines and other responsibilities which no other official would or could undertake successfully.

On several occasions, white strikers were arrested by police. No white union official could be found who was willing to post bond or even to visit the strikers in jail due to their fear of the city's anti-union police. Smith assumed this task as well. The fact that he was not afraid to do so increased the respect he commanded among all members of the local. The fact that he was looked to for leadership by *all* union members is of some interest, since this included persons who were also members of the Ku Klux Klan. The facts of his continuing victories over the plant manager, and the Klan's official lack of sympathy for strikes and unions in general, let alone bi-racial unions, weakened its influence over its union members. This permitted Smith to gain a position of power among all members, regardless of race or private belief. . . .

Smith is conscious of the critical position he holds in the organization and the power he can exert at any time. He is also aware that this power is a highly volatile substance. In not greatly overstated terms, he has the power of peace and war in Southville, and life and death over many of its citizens. He has within his control the instruments for causing widespread death and destruction, and a well-disciplined and devoted group of men who would make use of these instruments if he gave his authorization. This is something he wants to avoid if at all possible. In conversations, he stresses the need of a person in his position to know not only everything possible about the community but about his own personnel as well. He must know the personalities and the idiosyncrasies of each of his men so that he may assign them those duties they can best perform. While he has profound respect for each of his men, he knows that their talents vary, that each must be "handled" somewhat differently from his peers and that it is his responsibility as leader to perform this duty without error. He is aware that his men are part of any situation they enter, and he must know each of them thoroughly in order to assign them correctly to these situations, for any mismatch of man and situation could have serious repercussions.

He is also aware that the power he possesses could be used in a variety of ways and probably could be expanded considerably. Smith evinces no desire to use his organization for financial gain (e.g., he has refused large sums of money to back particular political candidates), nor does he show any desire to expand the functions of his organization. At no time has he attempted to supplant police authority where the police have been willing to perform their role. On one occasion when dynamite was set off in a residential area, the organization could have exploited this situation as a vehicle for expanding its quasi-public authority. Instead, it chose to encourage police to carry out an investigation and limited its own activities to gathering data and insuring that the police investigation was a thorough one. On another occasion, during the period in which the police were attempting to harass the organization, Smith was picked up for questioning and released late at night. On various occasions Southern police have notified violent whites before late-night releases of civil rights activists. Aware of this, Smith refused to leave the station unless he were escorted home by the police. Although his own men could have done this, he preferred that the police be forced to do it. Since he was sure they feared the certain retaliation which would follow if he were harmed while in their custody, Smith continued to demand their protection. After considerable argument, they acceded to his demand and his insistence that they perform their role.

Smith's reaction to the subject of "black identity" is revealing. He is strongly opposed to any concept or organization which places emphasis on "blackness" or "Negro-ness." He downgrades racial themes, preferring to see the ultimate source of most problems as the distribution of power. He is concerned with the redistribution of power and gaining a measure of it for those who are presently powerless. Powerlessness transcends racial lines, and consequently, his interests and concerns transcend them also.

Smith's activities in his bi-racial union exemplify his beliefs. Because of his success as a union leader, he has been called upon frequently to advise other groups of workers. Often, many of the workers involved have been ardent segregationists. In one instance, he was contacted by a Klansman whose history of anti-Negro activities was in the Defenders' files. The Klansman had been fired for attempting to organize his fellow workers in protest against harsh working conditions in a local plant. He asked Smith for advice in regaining his job and in organizing the workers. Smith gave both advice and other forms of aid. Later, the Klansman learned of the file and asked Smith why he had consented to help him when almost all the workers were white and many, including himself, were Klansmen. Smith's response was characteristic. The Klansman was engaged in a struggle to gain power for heretofore powerless persons. He had asked for help, his cause was worthy, and his actions had earned him a right to it. It was the problem of powerlessness, not Klan affiliation, which was relevant to this situation.

Ironic as it may seem, Smith is a strong supporter of the nonviolent movement. At any time in which he has participated in S.A.O. demonstrations, he has accepted its canon of nonviolence. More generally, he sees it as having tactical value and as being the only plausible methodology for large scale protests and demonstrations. To be effective, the tactic of defensive violence is restricted to small, carefully selected and highly organized groups operating out of rationally constructed plans. Unplanned and disorganized violence produces few, if any, positive results since it is not directed toward the redistribution of power within a community. To Smith, civil rights leaders should espouse nonviolence and seek to utilize this method to alter power allocations. Groups such as the Defenders should employ their own methods to accomplish this same goal. Should violence of any type occur, public leaders should disown responsibility for it and deplore its use, thereby providing the proper role model for the vast majority of civil rights activists.

Smith is convinced that groups such as the Defenders lessen the chances of violence in a community. White violence abates in the face of a potentially violent counter-force which, in turn, lessens the probability of mass disorganized riots by Negroes. Smith offers Southville as a case in point. The Defenders was created in the atmosphere of an impending riot. Since its creation, the community has been free from even a rumor of a possible riot.

Conclusion

Although the Defenders does not seek publicity, it is well known among Negroes in Southville. It enjoys great respect and is a source of considerable pride, primarily because it is proof that white Southern mores can be successfully challenged and that a change in the distribution of power can be effected. Violence, so often employed by whites, is revealed as a two-edged sword. With considerable pleasure, Negroes note that "white men are not as tough as they thought they were," and that Negroes, in the person of the Defenders, have proved themselves more than a match for violent white power. They are aware that it is now much less likely that they will be the victims of arbitrarily administered white violence. They know also that they have a champion which will extract a heavy price from the perpetrators of any such violence. For Negroes in Southville, this represents a most important and valued kind of social change.

The nonviolent S.A.O. also welcomes the Defenders, whose existence has strengthened their bargaining position. Prior to the creation of the Defenders, white officials were confronted solely by the alternatives of accepting or rejecting S.A.O. demands. Subsequent to its creation, additional variables had to be considered. The alternative to S.A.O. demands no longer is the maintenance of the status quo but the possibility that the city may be transformed into a battlefield which will destroy Southville. Formerly, acquiescence to S.A.O. demands had been the less attractive alternative. The Defenders has served to make the nonviolent S.A.O. considerably more attractive to white officials than it once was.

Ridicule has replaced fear as the dominant reaction of Negroes to the Ku Klux Klan. While the Klan continues to issue pronouncements reaffirming its dedication to Southern white mores and predicting victory in the struggle to maintain them, Negroes view these statements with contempt. Occasional pronouncements by the Klan leader that the Klan is nonviolent are viewed with amusement. Considering the Defenders' existence and the Klan's unwillingness to confront that organization, there is no other choice. While the Klan still inspires hatred, its power to control the action of Negroes is rapidly vanishing. In Southville, the Klan has become little more than a social club, without the power to enforce its desires. It is now much more concerned with national politics than with local racial conditions. Its failure to control these conditions has forced it to look elsewhere if it is to *seem* an active organization.

The role played by law enforcement agencies has undergone considerable change. These agencies are much less a "white man's army" and much more in conformity with the normal police role. While individual officers may continue as Klansmen, the quasi-public relationship between the Klan and law agencies has ceased. On occasion, officers do overstep the boundaries of their role, but when this occurs, they are much more likely to be censured by their superiors. In one instance, an officer made a racial slur against Smith. Immediately, Smith registered a complaint with the officer's superiors. The issue was resolved when both the officer and the police chief apologized for the remark. In the main, white officers maintain a distant and "correct" attitude toward the Defenders. However, two newly employed Negro officers have reacted somewhat differently. They have talked with Smith and have asked for any assistance the Defenders would be willing to give in maintaining peace and order in Negro sections of the city.

The vast majority of white persons remain unaware of the Defenders' existence. They speak of the recent past as a time of "racial unrest" and are pleased that this is no longer the case. They tend to attribute this change to the "inherent good will between the races" which exists in the city. They accept the desegregation which has occurred as proof of the good will of whites, and attribute the impetus for this change to the basic decency of white persons rather than to efforts by Negroes. S.A.O. is viewed not only as unnecessary but as having introduced conflict where none should have been. Change has been accomplished more despite that organization than because of it. Whites are proud of their law enforcement agencies, reject any allegations of brutality against Negroes and credit much of the return of peace to the "professionalism" of law enforcement agencies. These agencies are praised for their impartiality, good sense, and good will toward all citizens. Neither the newspaper nor white officials have sought to advance any other expanation for the changes which have occurred in Southville.

The Defenders was organized to alter the distribution of certain types of power in the community. It removed the threat of fear, intimidation and violence from the lives of Negroes. As a result, it became a kind of referee enforcing a set of rules by which S.A.O. and white officialdom would confront each other on the subject of social change. So long as organized violence was the sole prerogative of the white population, S.A.O. was overmatched in the struggle. The presence of the Defenders removed the threat of violence and permitted S.A.O.'s nonviolent methodology to confront a Defenders-insured nonviolent white opposition. This permitted the issues of racial change to be debated and settled within the framework of peaceful coexistence. The Defenders' continued existence acts to insure that violence will remain neutralized in the struggle.

Members of the Defenders believe that Southville is a microcosm of the total society. Throughout the nation, they see the commitment to nonviolence among Negroes diminishing rapidly. No longer is it possible to rely upon a nonviolent response to white violence and police brutality. They see the issue not as whether there will be violence but the form that violence will take. Unless organizations such as their own which lend support to the more broadly based nonviolent movement become the rule, there will be an ever increasing random violence. This random, goalless and widespread violence will be the result of the abandoning of hope that a redistribution of power is possible in the American society.

It is the Defenders' belief that their organization has prevented this kind of desperate violence because it has proved to Negroes in Southville that it is possible to challenge successfully the monopoly of power held by whites. The organization is firm in its belief that it has accomplished this because it speaks the only kind of language many persons in power understand.